PA
GE
S

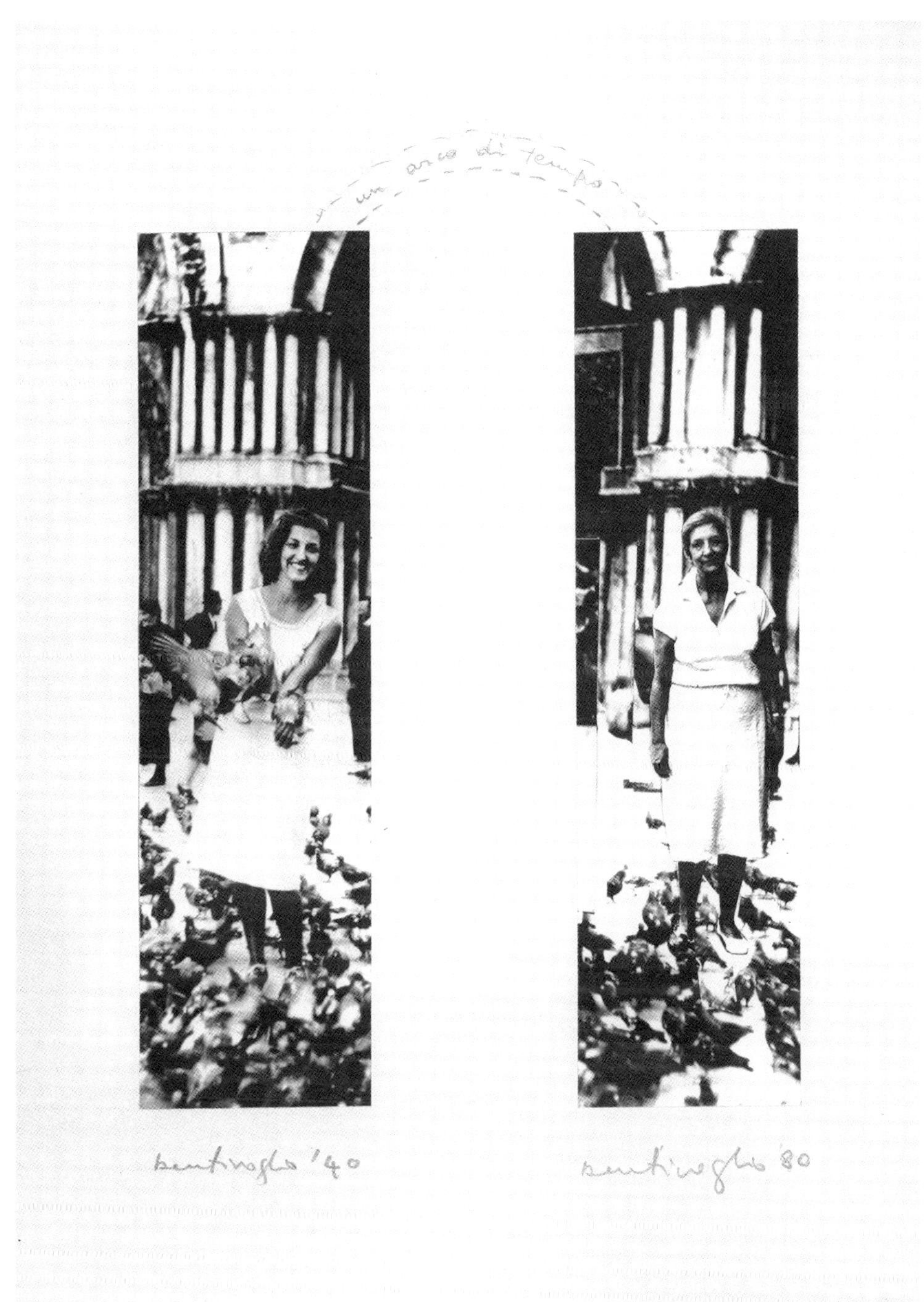

PLATE 1—
Un arco di tempo (An Arch of Time), 1980.
Xerography collage on board, 13⅞ × 9⅞ in.
(35.24 × 25.08 cm).

si   no
si   no
si   no
  nimi

PLATE 2——
Sinonimi (Synonyms), 1971.
Etching on paper, 13¼ × 9½ in.
(33.66 × 24.13 cm).

si = yes; *no* = no

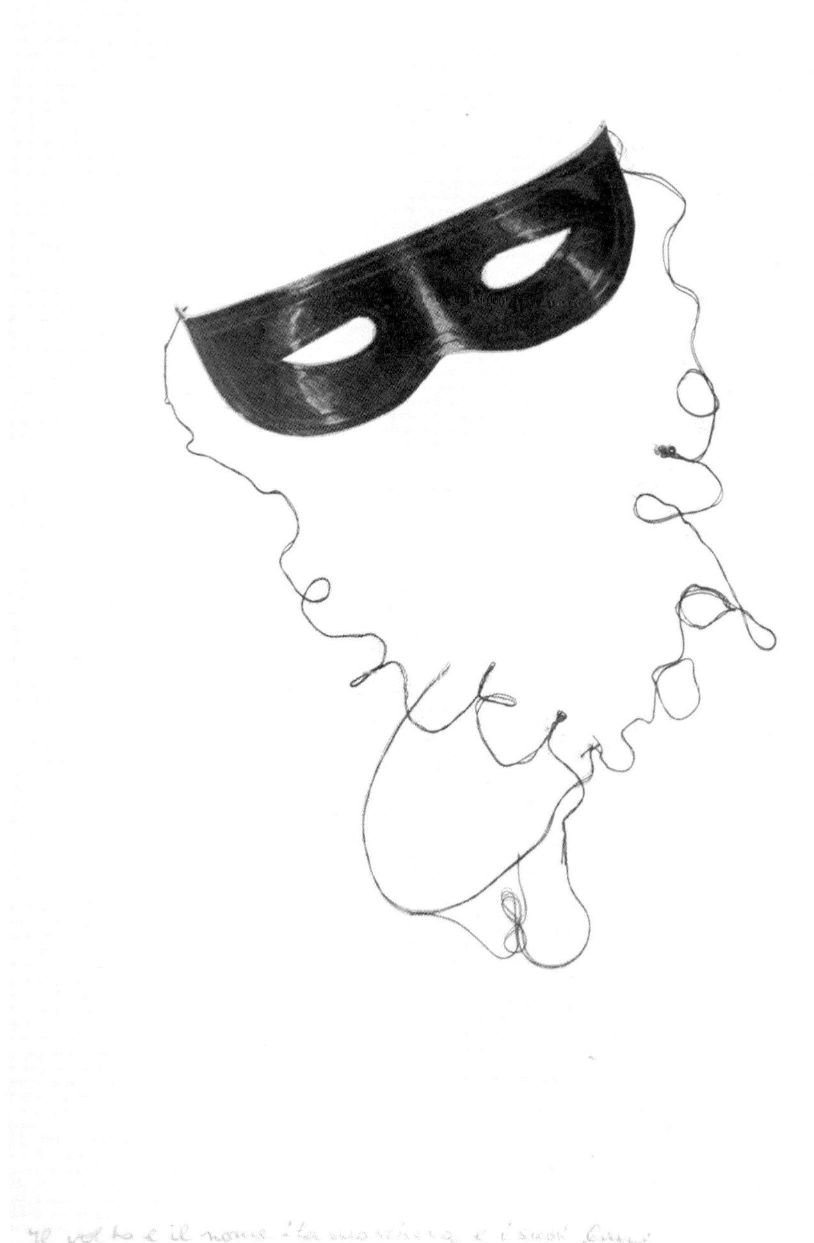

PLATE 3—
*Il volto e il nome: la maschera e i suoi lacci (The Face and
the Name: The Mask and Its Strings)*, 1995. Mixed media
on paper and board, 17¾ × 13¼ in. (45.09 × 33.66 cm).

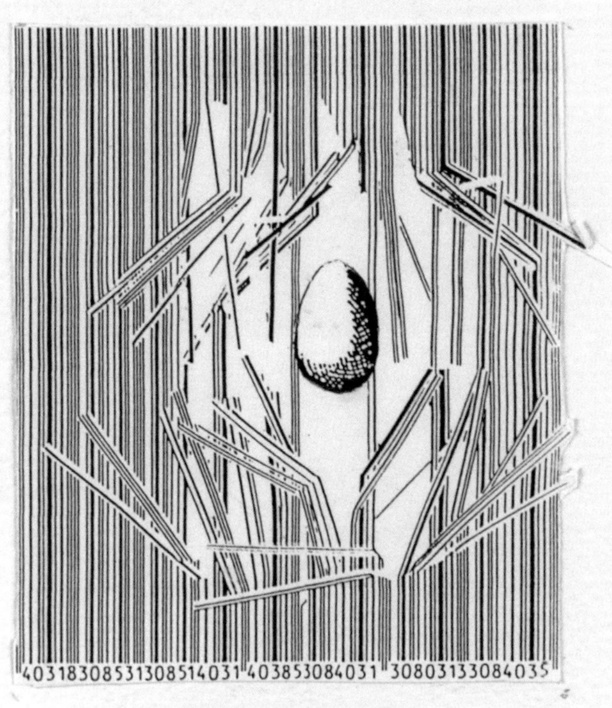

PLATE 4 —
Davide e Golia (David and Goliath), 1989.
Collage, 10¾ × 7¾ in. (27.31 × 19.69 cm).

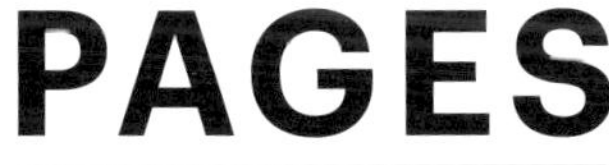

PAGES

Mirella Bentivoglio

Selected Works
1966—2012

Organized and edited by
Frances K. Pohl

With contributions by
Rosario Abate
Mirella Bentivoglio
Leslie Cozzi
Benjamin Kersten
John David O'Brien
Frances K. Pohl
Franca Zoccoli

Pomona College Museum of Art

PAGES

— 8
Director's Foreword
Kathleen Stewart-Howe

— 11
Notes on Pages
Frances K. Pohl

— 57
Interview with Mirella Bentivoglio
Benjamin Kersten

— 63
Back to the Pictogram: An Inquiry into the Nature of Communication
Franca Zoccoli

— 77
Curatorial Practice and the Language of Italian Feminism in the Work of Mirella Bentivoglio
Leslie Cozzi

— 91
Operation Orpheus
Mirella Bentivoglio

— 117
Arachne's Imprint: An Interview with John David O'Brien about Mirella Bentivoglio
Frances K. Pohl

— 129
Mirella Bentivoglio— A Biographical Note
Rosaria Abate

— 136
Selected Exhibition History

130
Selected Bibliography

— 147
Exhibition Checklist

— 150
Acknowledgments

DIRECTOR'S FOREWORD

One of the most engaging and enjoyable aspects of the Pomona College Museum of Art's program is the opportunity to work with faculty members in developing challenging original exhibitions. "Pages: Mirella Bentivoglio, Selected Works 1966–2012" is just such a project. Developed by Professor Frances K. Pohl, Dr. Mary Ann Vanderzyl Reynolds '56 Professor of Humanities and Professor of Art History at Pomona College, with the close cooperation of the artist, "Pages" is an example of what Pomona College and its museum are all about: original scholarship, interdisciplinary collaboration, hands-on learning, and innovative exhibitions.

On behalf of the college and the museum, I would like to express my deep gratitude to Mirella Bentivoglio for her generous participation in this exhibition and for providing our campus community and museum visitors with this opportunity to explore the breadth of her oeuvre, which includes works in a variety of forms and media. I owe a debt of gratitude to the best of colleagues, Professor Pohl, who has been the driving force behind this exhibition. An earlier exhibition, in 2003, also curated by Professor Pohl, united Mirella Bentivoglio and American artist Ben Shan in a consideration of the use of letter forms in their very distinct art practices. Pohl and the museum staff at the time realized that this investigation of one aspect of Bentivoglio's work left much more to be explored. Now, over a decade later, we have expanded upon that first look to explore the myriad facets of Bentivoglio's work. We are grateful for the essays and interviews by Rosaria Abate, Leslie Cozzi, Benjamin Kersten, John David O'Brien, Professor Pohl, and Franca Zoccoli, whose contributions to the catalog undertake a scholarly consideration of this important artist.

Museum exhibitions and programs develop at a nexus where artists, scholars, curators, designers, students, and funders meet around a significant project. This project is no exception and the roster of participants and supporters is long. We gratefully acknowledge the Carlton and Laura Seaver Endowment and the Rembrandt Club for support of this publication; the Matson Endowment for Exhibitions; and the Janet Inskeep Benton '79 Museum Fund. Senior Curator

Rebecca McGrew worked closely with Pohl to realize this exhibition. Under the artist's direction, Senior Preparator Gary Murphy recreated elements of one of her public interventions, *Moduli a E (E Combinations)*, within the exhibition and provided his usual standard of excellence in exhibition design and installation. With support from the Summer Undergraduate Research Program, Benjamin Kersten (PO '15) traveled to Rome with Professor Pohl and assisted in interviewing the artist and transcribing interviews, as well as preparation of the exhibition checklist. The entire staff of the museum has had a hand in this project: Associate Director and Registrar Steve Comba oversaw photography for the catalog; Academic Curator Terri Geis and Museum Outreach Coordinator Justine Bae developed programs complementing the exhibition; Administrative Assistant Barbara Coldiron provided the administrative coordination so important in a project of this scope. I am grateful to each of them for their dedication and enthusiasm in bringing this exhibition to fruition.

— Kathleen Stewart Howe
Sarah Rempel and Herbert S. Rempel '23
Director and Professor of Art History
Pomona College Museum of Art

PLATE 5 —
Pagina/finestra (Window/Page), 1971.
Serigraph on plexiglass, 14 × 7 ³⁄₁₆ × ¹⁄₁₆ in.
(35.56 × 18.29 × .21 cm).

piove = it is raining

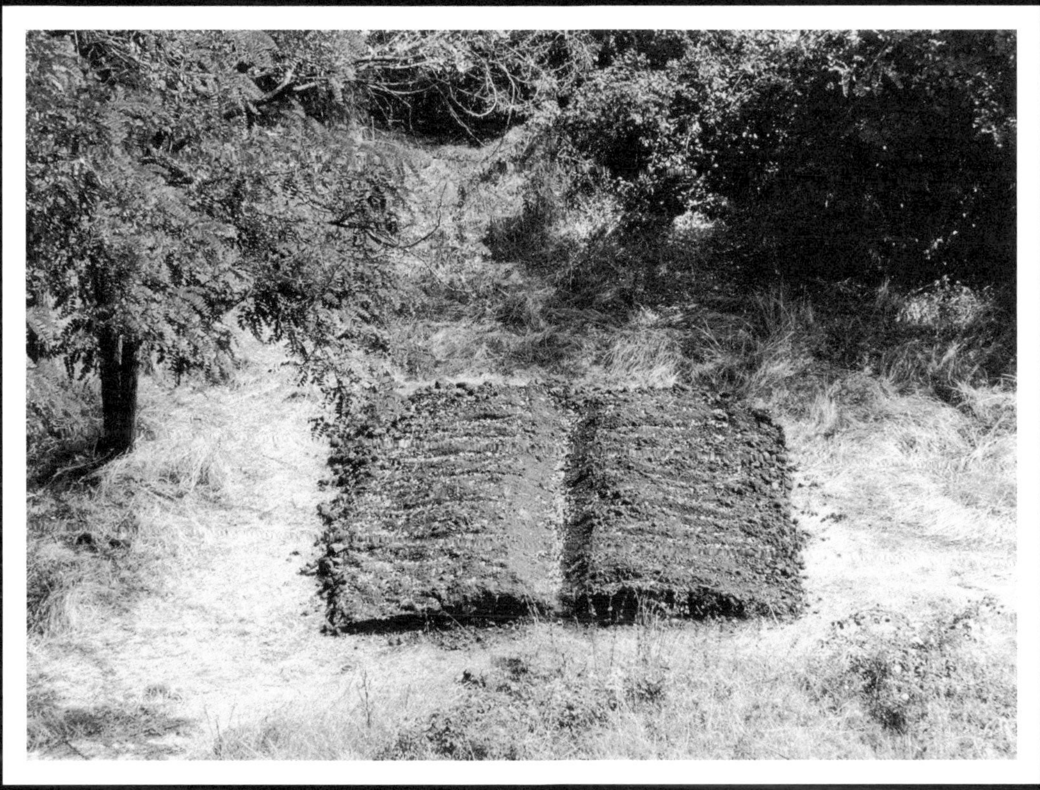

FIGURE 1—
Libro campo (Field Book), 1998. Photographic reproduction of land-poetry installation, Bassano in Teverina, Italy. Digital print, 15¾ × 21⅝ in. (40 × 54.9 cm).

NOTES
ON PAGES

Frances K. Pohl

I.

In 1998 Mirella Bentivoglio was invited to contribute a work to an exhibition organized in conjunction with the Stelle Cadenti (Falling Stars) festival in Bassano in Teverina, a small hill town north of Rome. The Los Angeles artist John David O'Brien was there, and he describes the resulting work, *Libro campo (Field Book)* (1998) (Figure 1), as he saw it on the opening night of the exhibition:

> The evening was windy and cool. It had rained the afternoon of the day before…. As I approached the terrace that led down to the medieval burgh where most of the exhibition was on view, I noticed a group of onlookers peering over the wall down into the area where *Field Book* was. Curious, I looked over myself. What an extraordinary surprise was waiting! *Field Book* was isolated in the dark, illuminated by a single powerful spotlight. It seemed beautifully complete in the garden below, as though it must have always been here. Tawny leaves, blown out of the trees by the storm, had settled in its furrows like words in lines of text on pages. The mass of upturned earth, darkened by the rain, stood out against the surrounding straw brilliantly…. [This] stunning surprise in the garden, a *Field Book* wrought by a storm, remains my strongest recollection of that evening in Bassano in Teverina. A moment of unimagined Visual Poetry brought about by the serendipitous collaboration between Mirella Bentivoglio and an afternoon cloudburst.[1]

Thus, in *Libro campo*, prepared by Bentivoglio using tons of soil, the artist expresses simultaneously the creativity of the human mind and of the earth. She achieves this double meaning through the image of the open book. Although she had given up her earlier practice as a linear verse poet, she had not left behind her fascination with the page, that space that functions as a support for poetic ideas and that refers back continually to the visualization of language that began with the invention of writing. *Pages: Mirella Bentivoglio, Selected Works 1966–2012* at the Pomona College Museum of Art provides an overview of the many manifestations of the page, as single sheets or as multiples bound into book form, within the work of Mirella Bentivoglio.

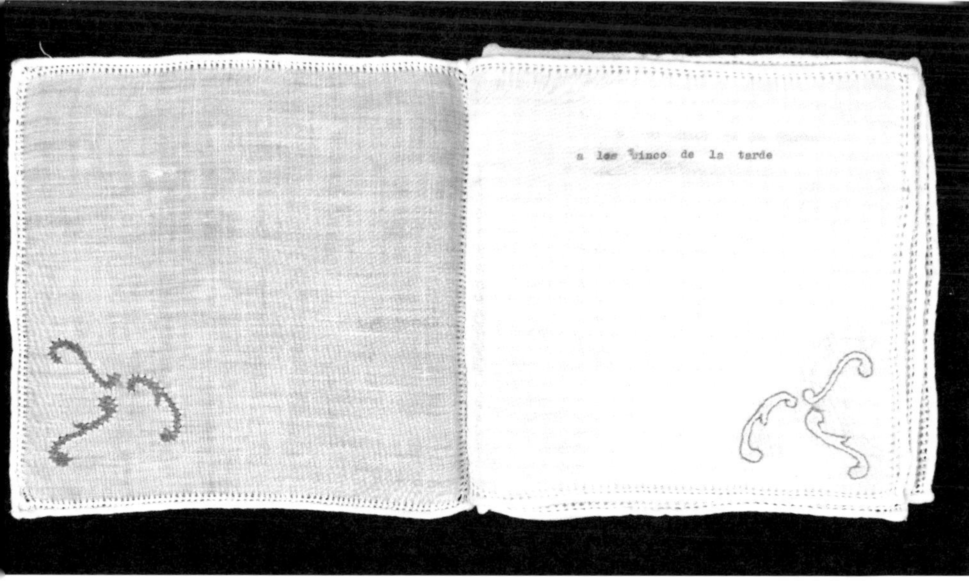

II.

The title of *A las cinco de la tarde (Ladies Afternoon Tea) (At Five in the Afternoon [Ladies Afternoon Tea])* (1973) (Figure 2), with its delicate embroidered cloth pages resembling dainty handkerchiefs, is taken from an obsessively repeated line in the first section of the Spanish poet Federico García Lorca's "Lament for Ignacio Sánchez Mejias":

> At five in the afternoon.
> It was exactly five in the afternoon.
> A boy brought the white sheet
> *at five in the afternoon.*
> A frail of lime ready prepared
> *at five in the afternoon.*
> The rest was death, and death alone
> *at five in the afternoon.*[2]

Over four long sections, each containing several verses, Lorca describes the heroic endeavors of this Spanish bullfighter and, in excruciating detail, his agonizing death—"In the distance the gangrene now comes/*at five in the afternoon./*Horn of the lily through green groins/*at five in the afternoon.*"[3] For Bentivoglio, ironically, five in the afternoon is when ladies gather not in public bullfighting arenas, but in the parlors of their homes, where they drink tea and impale their victims on their sharp gossiping tongues.

FIGURE 2—
A las cinco de la tarde (Ladies Afternoon Tea) (At Five in the Afternoon [Ladies Afternoon Tea]), 1973. Ink on stitched cloth, 6½ × 6½ in. (16.51 × 16.51 cm).

Frances K. Pohl

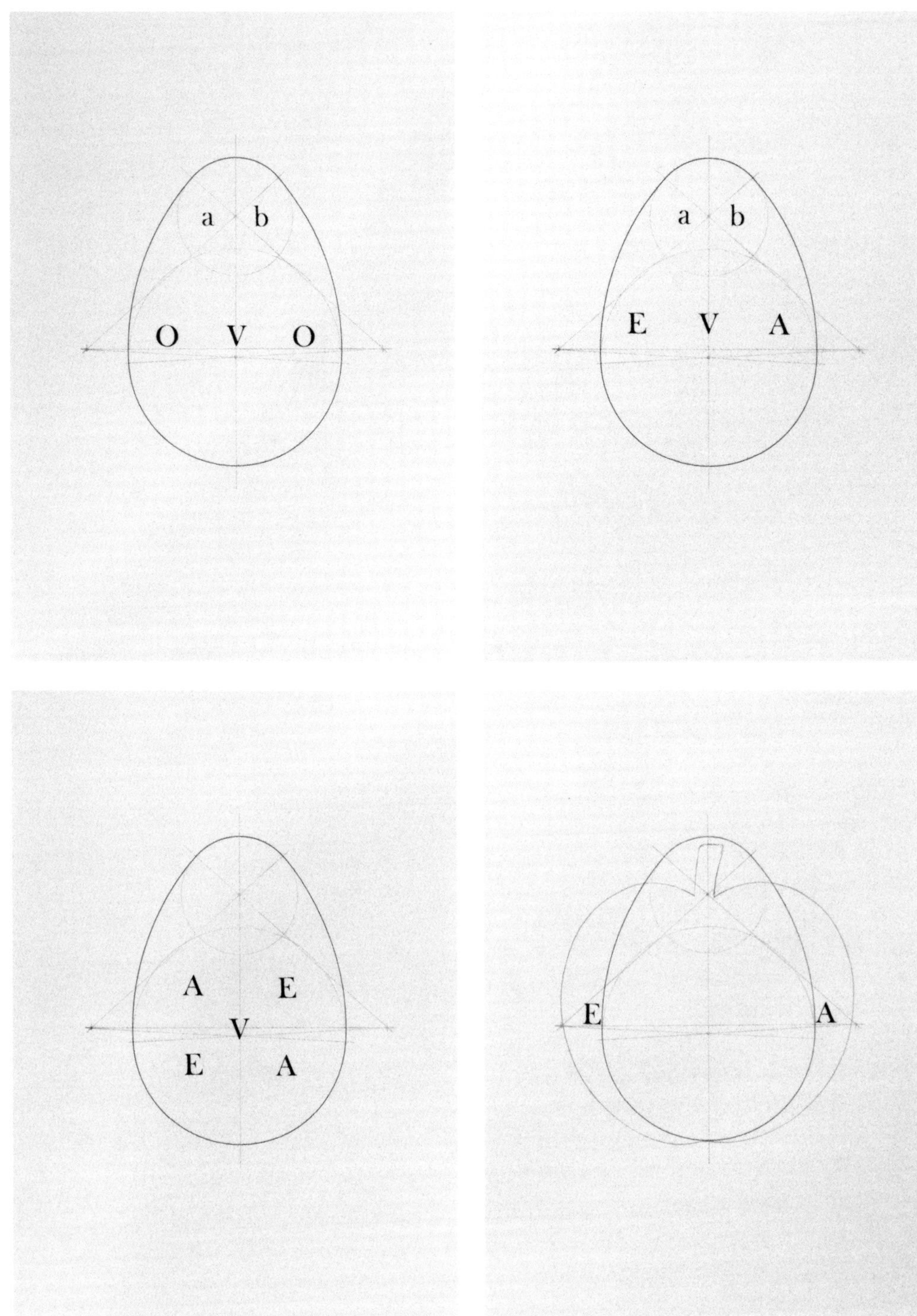

FIGURE 3 —
Ab ovo, ab Eva, Ave Eva, ea, 1979–86.
Four serigraph prints on paper, 13⅝ ×
9⅝ in. (34.61 × 24.45 cm) each.

ab ovo = from the beginning; *ab Eva* = from Eve; *Ave Eva* = Hail Eve; *ea* = she

Shortly before being hanged and quartered in 1595, the Jesuit poet Robert Southwell wrote: "Spell Eva back and Ave shall you find."[4] Embedded in this short statement is a sentiment that ultimately led to Southwell's demise, for it was his commitment to the celebration of Catholicism in Queen Elizabeth I's ardently anti-Catholic England that resulted in his torture and death.[5] The poetic aspect of this play with language, with the order of letters on a page, as well as the commitment to celebrating a persecuted community, can be found in Bentivoglio's *Ab ovo, ab Eva, Ave Eva, ea* (1979) (Figure 3). The Latin phrase *ab ovo* means literally "starting from the egg," or metaphorically "starting from the beginning." This Latin expression is still used regularly by Italians today. The phrase maintains its Latin origins in Bentivoglio's work as it moves through a series of transformations across four pages: *ab ovo* (from the beginning), *ab Eva* (from Eve), *Ave Eva* (Hail Eve), *ea* (she). For Bentivoglio, this transformation represents "the birth of self-conscious femininity, accentuated by the shape of an apple, alluding to the starting point: Eve's choice of the mystery of life."[6] Self-conscious femininity is thus constituted through the merging of the organic (the egg, the apple) and the conceptual (the geometric forms that constitute the armature of the work's composition and that follow the ideal Renaissance proportions known as the "Golden Section").

IV.

The chemist James Gimzewski has created a small computer chip that rejects the ordered circuitry of more traditional computer chips and is made up, instead, of "an ugly tangle of wires randomly crisscrossed and interwoven like hairs in a tiny dust ball."[7] For Gimzewski, "[T]he tangled design of the chip is the reason for its resilience. The synapses of the brain are, after all, similarly organic and just as untidy."[8] The tangled mass of Bentivoglio's *Soggettivismo oggettivato (Objectified Subjectivism)* (1972) (Figure 4), out of which emerges the word *groviglio,* which means "tangle" in Italian, is equally reminiscent of a tiny dust ball and similarly resonates with the untidy processes out of which consciousness emerges. The last two typographic letters of *groviglio* contrast sharply with the loose script that precedes them; while the content, *io,* means "me" or "I" in Italian, the choice of clear typographic letters to express it signifies, for Bentivoglio, the emergence of an anonymous common language that marks entrance into a broader community. This common language allows for the distance or objectivity necessary to comprehend the tangled mass that is human consciousness, yet is always connected in an essential way to that which it attempts to understand.

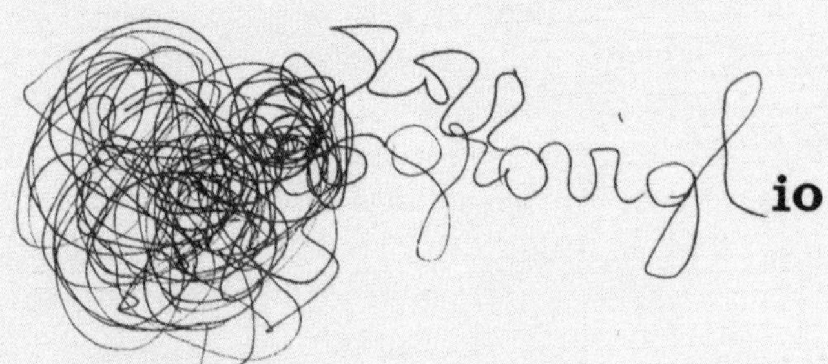

FIGURE 4 —
Soggettivismo oggettivato (Objectified Subjectivism), 1972. Lithograph on paper, 9 × 10¾ in. (22.86 × 27.31 cm).

groviglio = tangle; *io* = me

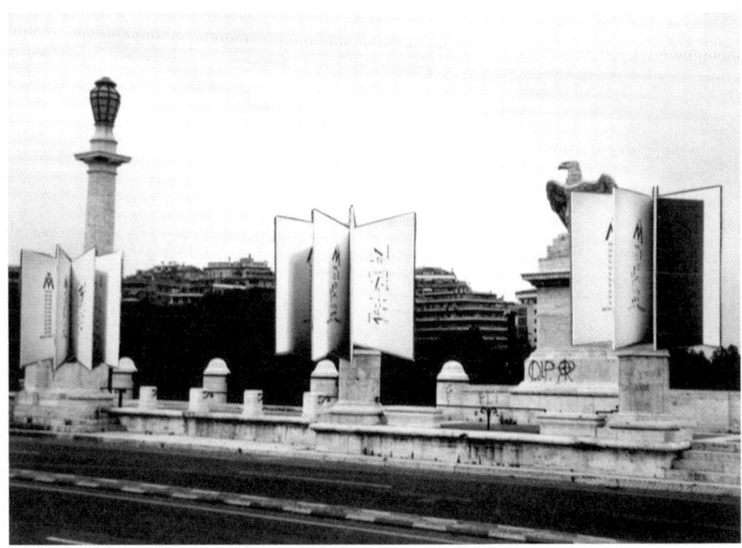

V.

In his 1972 novel *Le città invisibili (Invisible Cities)*, the Italian author Italo Calvino writes:

> The city...does not tell its past, but contains it like the lines of a hand, written in the corners of the streets, the gratings of the windows, the banisters of the steps, the antennae of the lightning rods, the poles of the flags, every segment marked in turn with scratches, indentations, scrolls.[9]

Bentivoglio set out to read the corners, gratings, scratches, indentations, and scrolls of the city and to reframe certain passages, creating her own oppositional narratives. She deconstructs the architectural and sculptural monuments to great men in works such as *Monumento (Monument)* (1968 [1966]) (Figure 6) and reveals their conceptual and linguistic underpinnings: *nume* (godlike), *me non tu* (me not you), *mento* (I am telling lies), *muto* (I am dumb; or, I am mutating), *temo* (I fear). She later reshapes the panels of *Monumento* into an open-paged book, which she then collages onto photographs of urban architectural monuments, forcing a counter-reading of the urban narrative. For example, the book appears on the truncated columns of a fascist bridge in Rome by the architect Armando Brasini (*Monumento Memento [Memento*

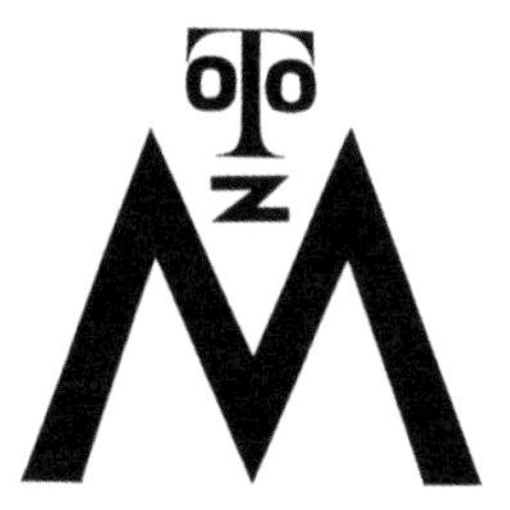

NUME
NUME
NUME
NUME
NUME
NUME
NUME
NUME
NUME
NUME
MONUMENTO

nume = godlike

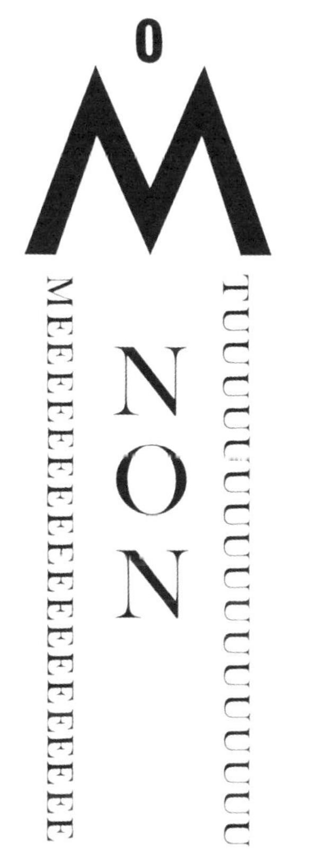

O
M
MEEEEEEEEEEEEEEE
NON
TUUUUUUUUUUUUUUU
MONUMENTO

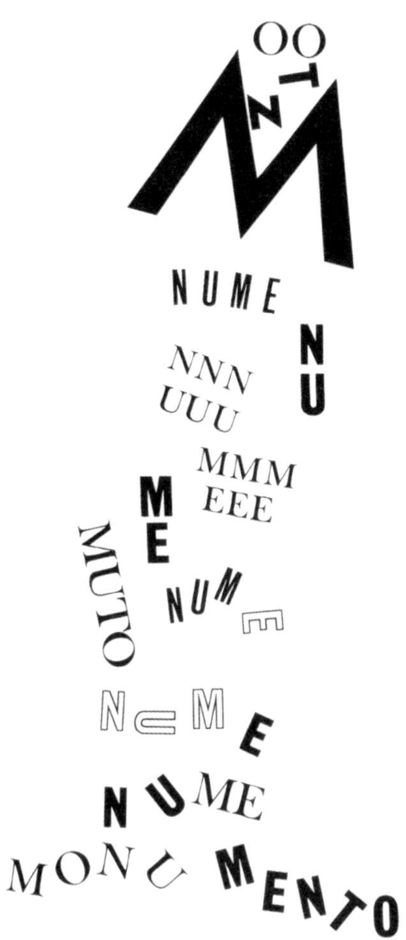

MONUTO
OO
NUME
NU
NNN
UUU
MMM
EEE
ME
MUTO
NUME
NUME
NUME
NUME
MONUMENTO

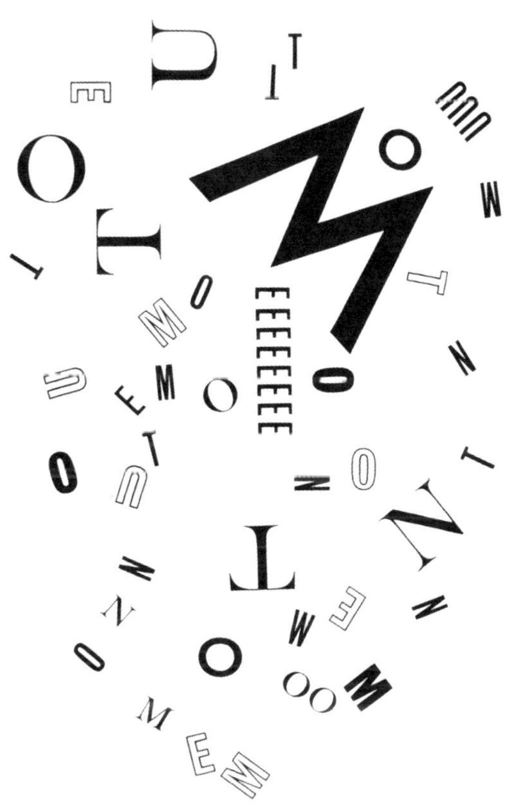

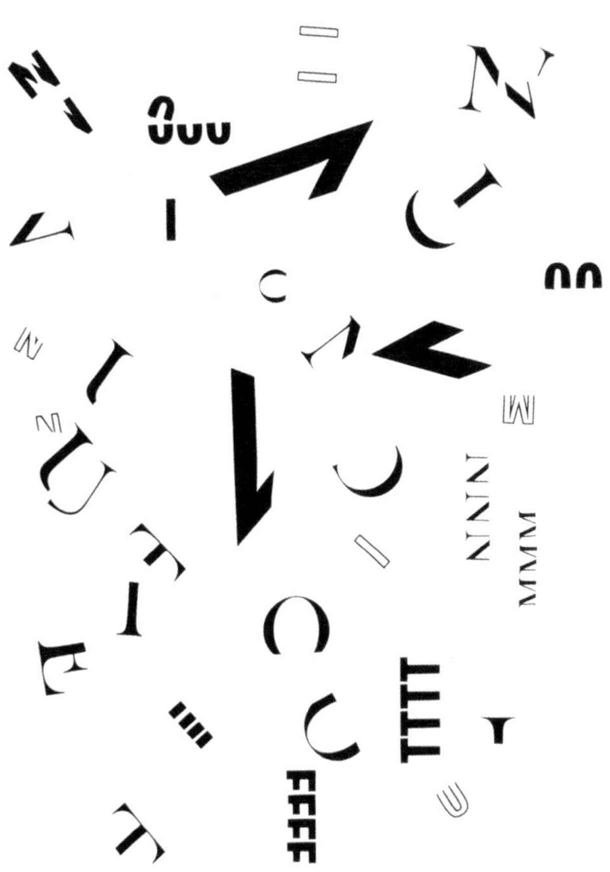

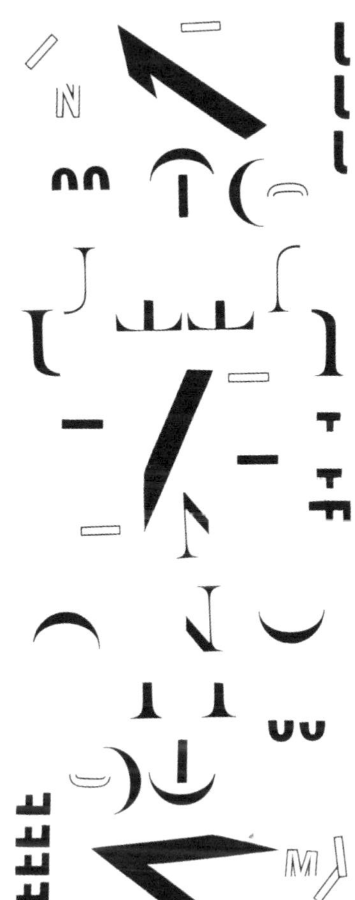

Monument], 1978) (Figure 5), foregrounding their uselessness (the columns serve neither as pedestals for statues nor as structural supports). From a fragment of a street sign knocked down in a traffic accident (*senso unico* = one-way) she creates *Perdita di senso [Loss of Sense]* (1997) (Plate 21), a meditation on the psychic disruptions of city life, as well as a poetic revelation, in the tradition of Marcel Duchamp's *objet trouvé* (found object), of a broader loss of sense within human existence. She writes of another urban intervention, *I muri di Singapore (Walls of Singapore)* (1978) (Plate 11):

> I find "pages" on public walls. The street becomes the location of my visual-poetic messages. I have often assembled and reorganized found objects, giving a poetic order to them, changing their conventional meanings, and so trying to reveal their semiotic potential. I found these torn posters on a wall in Singapore, and simply changed the order so as to obtain my poem *From East to West, from sign to matter,* which suggests a gradual erasure of the word. Little by little the writing disappears and the material support—the wall—reveals itself. From instrumental everyday communication comes a visually ambiguous message.[10]

In this visual poem, Bentivoglio underlines the difference between the elegant, precisely rendered alphabetic signs of the East and a visual language based on the textures and surfaces of physical matter (*materia* in Italian) that informed much Western abstract art.

VI.

The British art historian and critic John Berger wrote that with the invention of photographic reproductions, the aura of a work of art—that quality that resides in the material presence of the object and its location within certain originary rituals—is replaced by new ritual possibilities linked to a myriad of physical locations (the classroom, the student dormitory, the art history textbook, the documentary film, the art gallery).[11] Bentivoglio exploits this aspect of photographic technology, expanding the potential meanings of works of art through replication and relocation. For example, two of her works utilize photographic images of one of the most iconic of Italian Renaissance sculptures, Michelangelo's *Pietà* (1498–99). In the first, *L'altra Veronica (Ecce Mulier) (The Other Veronica [Behold the Woman])* (1992) (Figure 7), the *Pietà* appears in a photograph within a photograph. Bentivoglio writes:

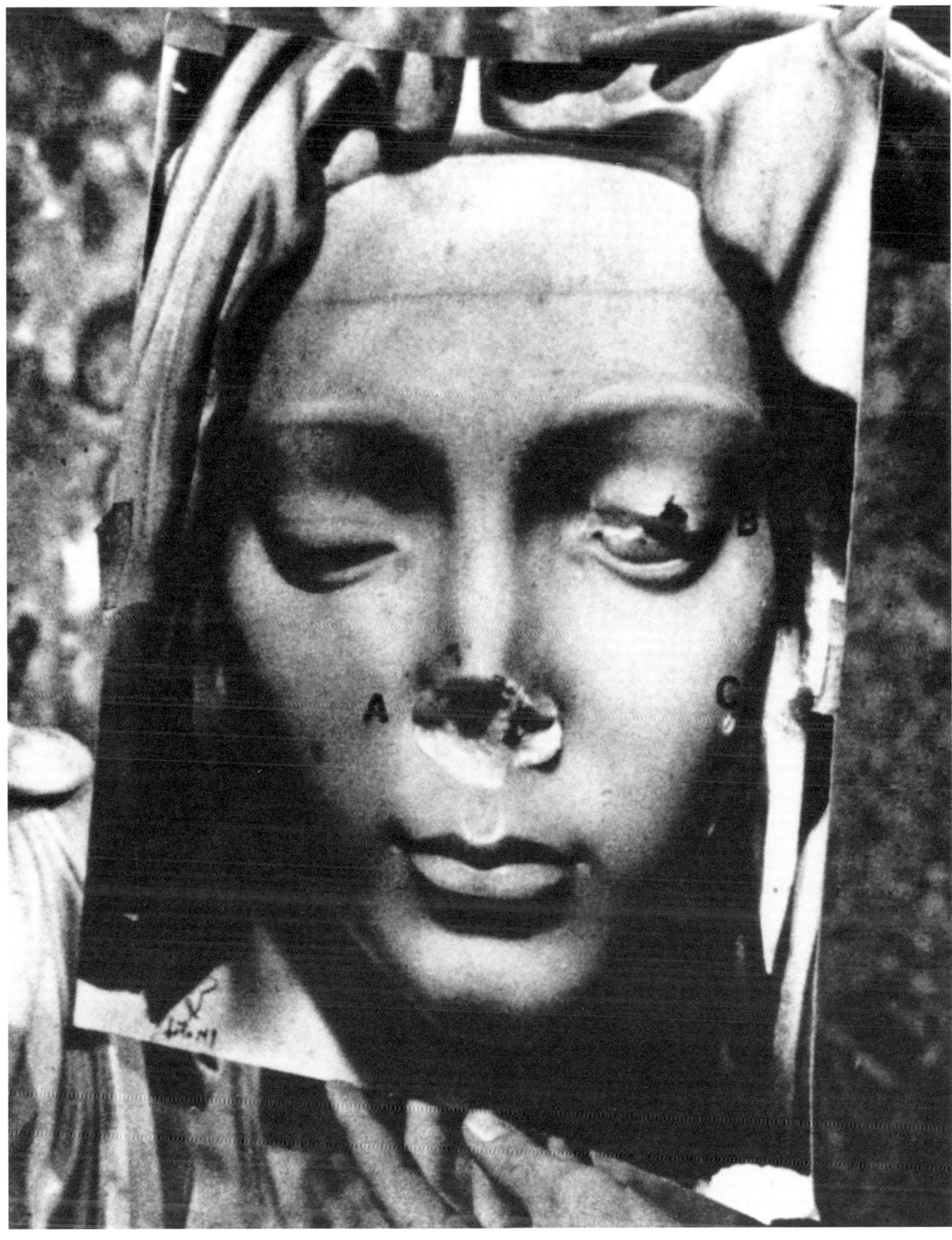

FIGURE 7—
*L'altra Veronica (Ecce Mulier) (The Other Veronica
[Behold the Woman])*, 1992. Photomechanical
print on canvas, 13⅝ × 10⅜ in. (34.61 × 26.35 cm).

Frances K. Pohl

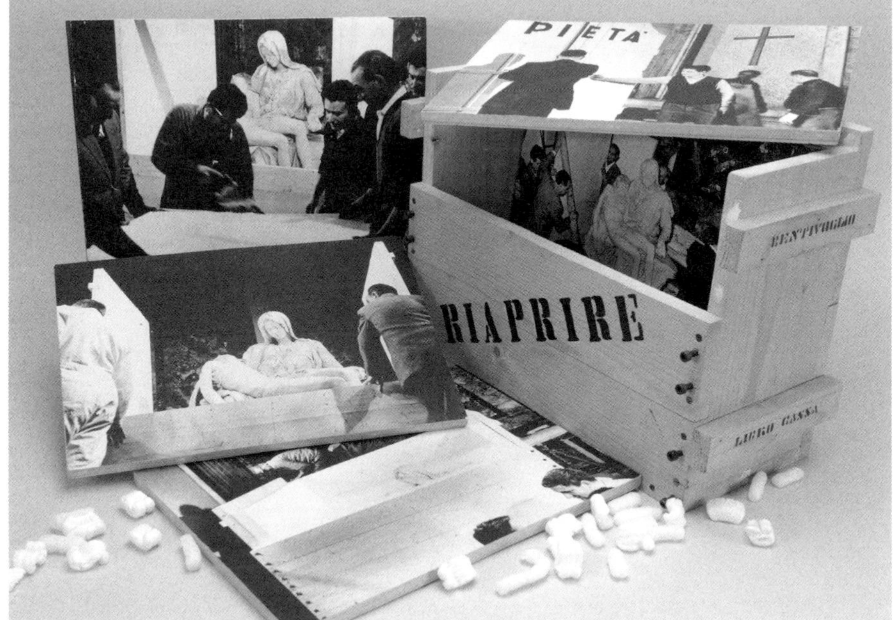

The blows that a madman inflicted in 1972 on the incomparably gentle face of the Madonna depicted in Michelangelo's *Pietà* created a new icon of womanhood. What the blows of that hammer produced can be interpreted as the face of the woman offended by the violence of patriarchy, but also as the portrait of the psychic deformations which derive from the centuries of separation of female roles from active cultural engagement. The image, drawn from a daily newspaper, refers to an anonymous photograph, hung up to dry. It references the traditional religious image of the agonized male face imprinted on the veil of Veronica.[12]

Bentivoglio reproduces the photograph on canvas to reinforce the connection with Veronica's veil. And the subtitle, *Ecce Mulier (Behold the Woman)*, echoes Pontius Pilate's *"Ecce Homo"* (Behold the Man) as he presents the prisoner Christ to the angry mob in Jerusalem, a mob that would ultimately condemn him to crucifixion. Bentivoglio presents to us the innocent woman, brutalized and condemned by our patriarchal culture.

The second work by Bentivoglio that utilizes photographic representations of the *Pietà* is *Riaprire (Open Up Again)* (1989) (Figure 8). Here the photographs trace the disappearance of the statue as a crate is constructed around it for

FIGURE 8—
Riaprire (Open Up Again), 1989. Mixed media installation (wood, photographs, Styrofoam), 13¾ × 19⅜ × 8½ in. (34.93 × 49.21 × 21.59 cm).

its shipping to the United States. These photographs represent the pages in Bentivoglio's crate-book (*libro cassa*), the exterior of which is constructed from the same type of wood out of which the original *Pietà* crate was built and according to the same proportions (the photographs are also mounted on this wood).[13]

In Italian, the word "*pietá*" has two meanings: the primary meaning is "compassion"; a secondary, specialized, and less commonly used meaning is any sculptural or pictorial image of a Madonna holding her dead son. In the last "page" of the crate-book, we do not see the statue, but only the single Italian word on a crate, thus pointing us to the more common meaning of the word "*pietá*." By firmly closing the crate, the packers seem to confine compassion; by titling her work *Riaprire (Open Up Again)*, Bentivoglio rejects this confinement. Her work thus contains both a refusal of compassion and a rejection of this refusal and of the status quo, where compassion has to be suppressed in order not to interfere with the pursuit of material gain. These two words—*pietà* and *riaprire*—function as interpretive keys that allow the photographic sequence, which shows the gradual sinking of the monument into its container, to be read in reverse as a poetic metaphor of that lost feeling: *pietà*.

VII.

In 1977, a year of widespread violence by leftist political organizations in Italy,[14] Bentivoglio, in collaboration with the Italian photographer Francesco Balladore, produced *Egemonia op (Hegemony Op)* (Figure 9). The work consists of two large panels, the left containing 16 photographs of equal size, the right 15 photographs plus a section of text in the lower right-hand corner. The photographs in the left panel, read from left to right and top to bottom, show a man removing the words "*Egemonia Operaia*" ("all power to the working class") from the exterior wall of a building. In the second panel, Bentivoglio reverses the order of the photographs. The text in the second panel reads:

> In 1977 the photographer Francesco Balladore photographed, unseen, the doorman of a distinguished apartment building in the act of erasing, letter by letter, the writing "*Egemonia Operaia*" [All power to the Working Class] from the wall of the block of flats. Mirella Bentivoglio has in turn reversed the order of the sequence, revealing the unconscious of the doorman, as if he is himself in reality tracing the text. The title of the duplicated sequence, *Egemonia Op*, is taken from one of the phases of the erasure/retracing. Op art, or rather optical art, was founded on perceptual ambiguity.[15]

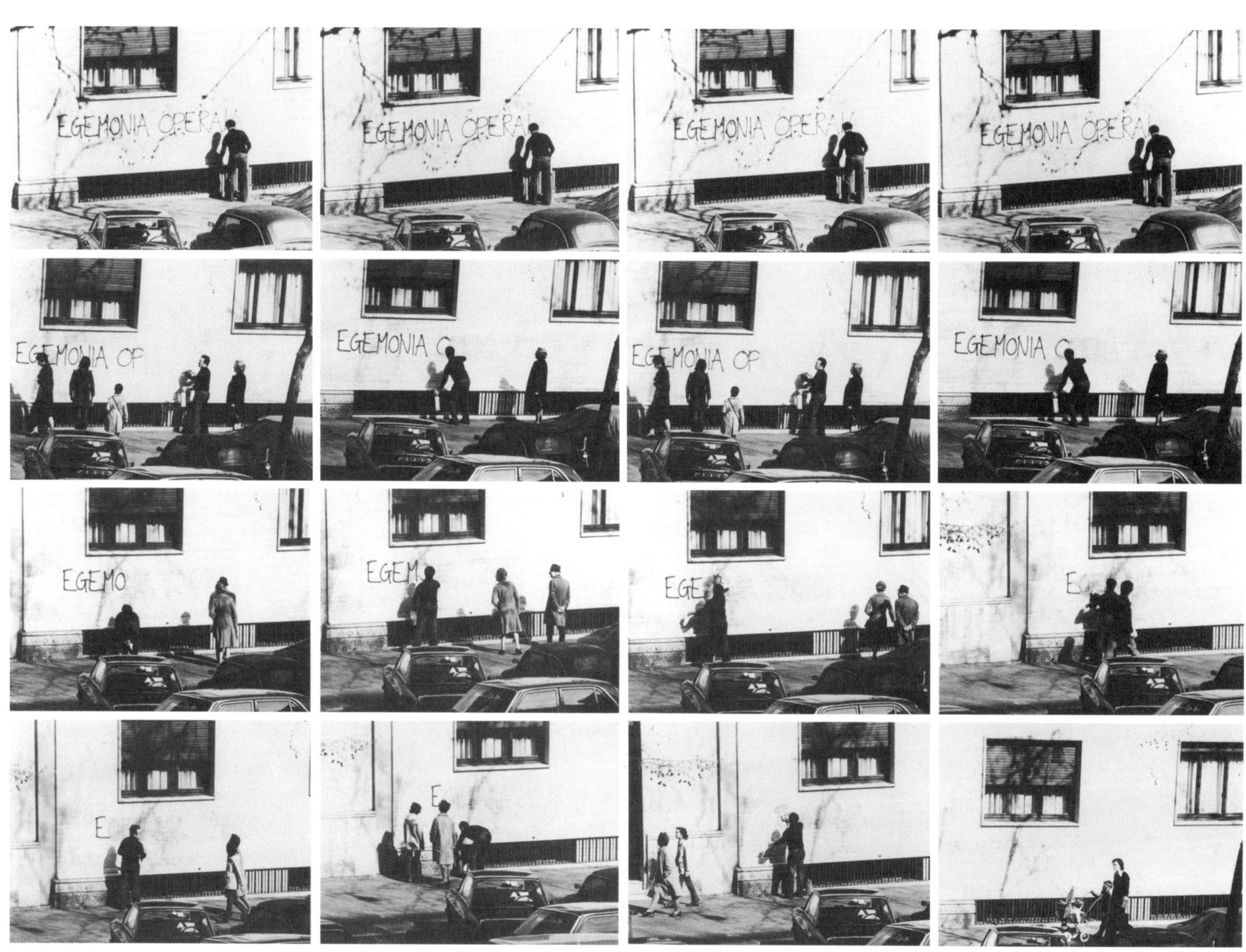

FIGURE 9 —
Egemonia op (Hegemony Op), with Francesco
Balladore, 1977. Two panels of photomechanical
prints, 26 × 36 in. (66.04 × 91.44 cm) each.

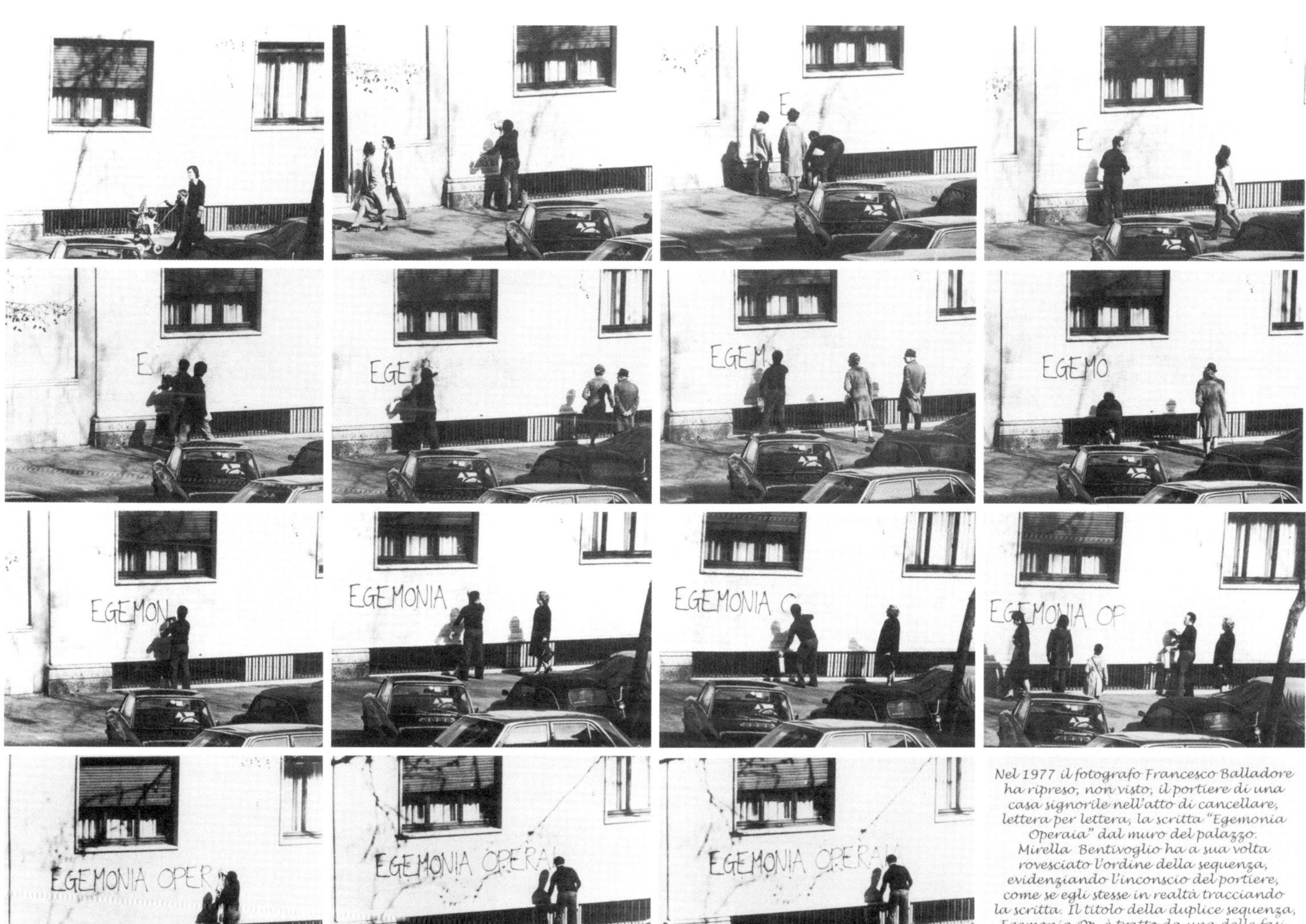

Nel 1977 il fotografo Francesco Balladore ha ripreso, non visto, il portiere di una casa signorile nell'atto di cancellare, lettera per lettera, la scritta "Egemonia Operaia" dal muro del palazzo. Mirella Bentivoglio ha a sua volta rovesciato l'ordine della sequenza, evidenziando l'inconscio del portiere, come se egli stesse in realtà tracciando la scritta. Il titolo della duplice sequenza, Egemonia Op, è tratto da una delle fasi della cancellazione/scrittura.
l'arte op, ossia optical, è fondata sulla ambiguità percettiva.

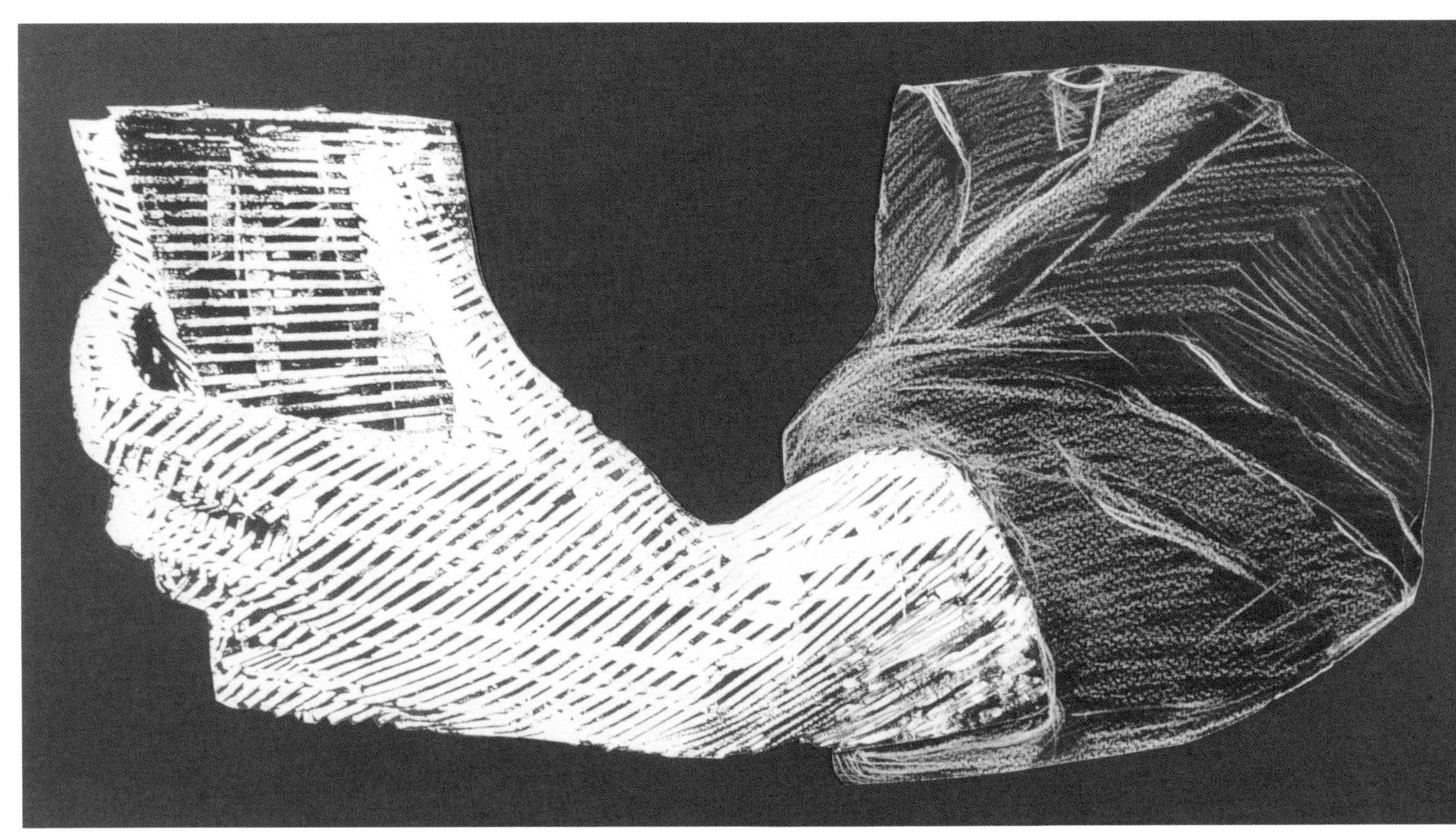

FIGURE 10—
*Anatomia del braccio sinistro della Statua
della Libertà (Anatomy of the Left Arm of the
Statue of Liberty)*, 1992. Photomechanical
print on paper, 8½ × 17 in. (21.59 × 43.18 cm).

Bentivoglio captures this perceptual ambiguity through a narrative reversal (is he writing or erasing?), thus allowing the doorman the option of declaring rather than suppressing his own identification with the socioeconomic class to which he belongs. The photograph from which the title of the work is taken contains the greatest number of onlookers, who reinforce the public—and potentially disruptive—nature of the doorman's declaration of class allegiance in Bentivoglio's version of the narrative.

VIII.

"With words," observes James Gleick, "we begin to leave traces behind us like breadcrumbs: memories in symbols for others to follow.... Writing comes into being to retain information across time and across space."[16] Bentivoglio captures this thought in *Transitorio/durevole (Transitory/Durable)* (Figure 18), a work she created in 2002 with the Brazilian artist Regina Silveira. Silveira prepared the drawing and heavy plastic cutout of the anamorphic shadow, which is based on a backlit photograph of Bentivoglio seated with a book in her hands, reading. The top half of the shadow is attached to the wall, the bottom half to the floor. Bentivoglio's two-dimensional shadow-hands hold a partly open three-dimensional book. On the two pages that are visible, the image of the shadow itself is repeated, as if wall and floor have become pages. "We are passing shadows," reflects Bentivoglio in the latter years of a long life and career, "but our transitory existential experience becomes lasting when it is located in an area of communication like a book."[17]

Un arco di tempo (An Arch of Time) (1980) (Plate 1, frontispiece) is also predicated on the concept of the book. The two photographs have been taken on the same spot in front of St. Mark's cathedral in Venice, one in 1940 and one in 1980, the year Bentivoglio's husband passed away. The words "*un arco di tempo*," written on the upper margin along a hand-drawn arch that springs from the two columns behind the figures, connect the two photographs. "In the book," writes Bentivoglio, "the spine is the arch of time, because when you read, time goes by, not just literally but symbolically, one page after another. The arch is also the entrance to the temple, the temple of life."[18]

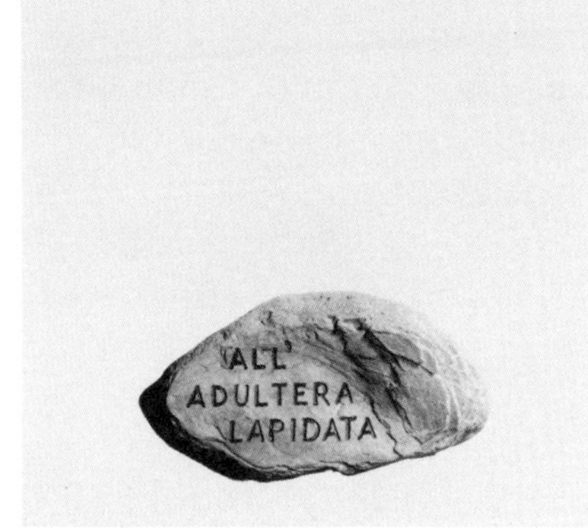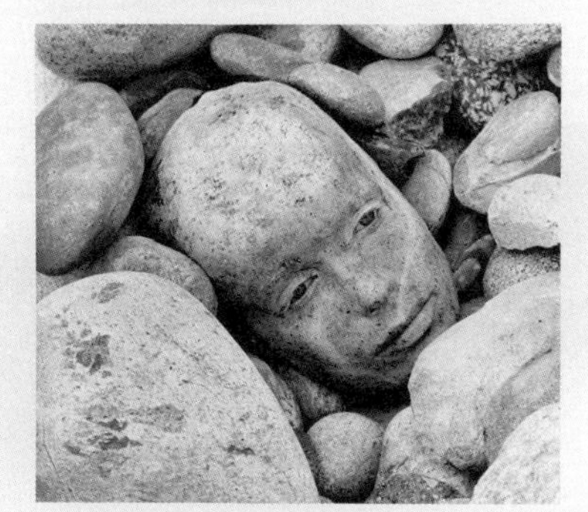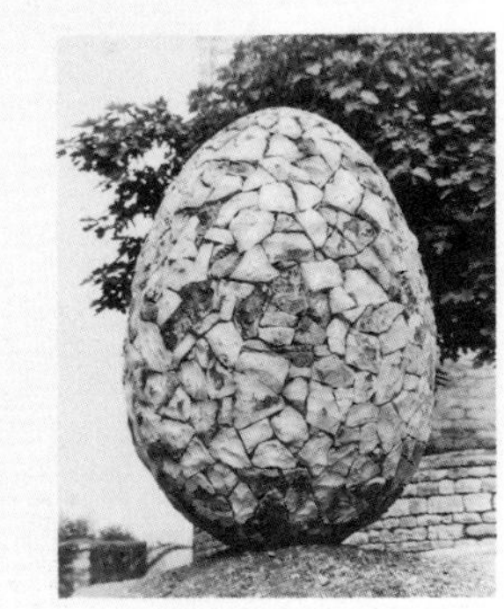

IX.

My work, which began within language with an analysis-metamorphosis of the word, has been gradually narrowing down to the use of a few simple forms and materials, selected for their capacity to communicate at the level of symbols. The letter "o", the initial for the word "origin" and the sign indicating alternative [o in Italian = or] has been gradually converted, in my logoiconic works, into the image of the egg. Simultaneously the use of marble and stones to supply a formal metaphor of the book has led me to recognize in the stone memorial tablet, as understood in the Western world, a sign-image with a multi-semantic potential, contrasting with the meaning of the oval form. My work is now based upon the dual symbology of encounter, clash, exchange, and the reciprocal assimilation of egg and stone tablet: beginning and end, matter and logos, genesis and culture, fragility and fossilization, hidden and clear....[19]

One of Bentivoglio's first works to bring together the egg and the stone tablet was *L'Ovo di Gubbio (The Egg of Gubbio)* (1976) (Figure 12). The sculpture was installed in the medieval town of Gubbio as part of its 1976 Biennial, which was devoted to the theme "Interventions in the Landscape." Just over eight feet (two and one-half meters) tall and weighing approximately two tons, *L'Ovo di Gubbio* was composed of stones embedded in a concrete surface such that the egg appeared to be cracking apart. While the egg form is obvious, the reference to the stone tablet is more subtle. One of the stones bears the inscription *"all'adultera lapidata"* (to the stoned adulteress). In Biblical times women who defied patriarchal law by committing adultery were stoned to death. "My egg,"

FIGURE 11—
All'adultera lapidata—L'ovo di Gubbio (To the Stoned Adulteress—The Egg of Gubbio), 1995. Three photomechanical prints on paper, 14¾ × 16⅛ in. (50.17 × 69.53 cm) each.

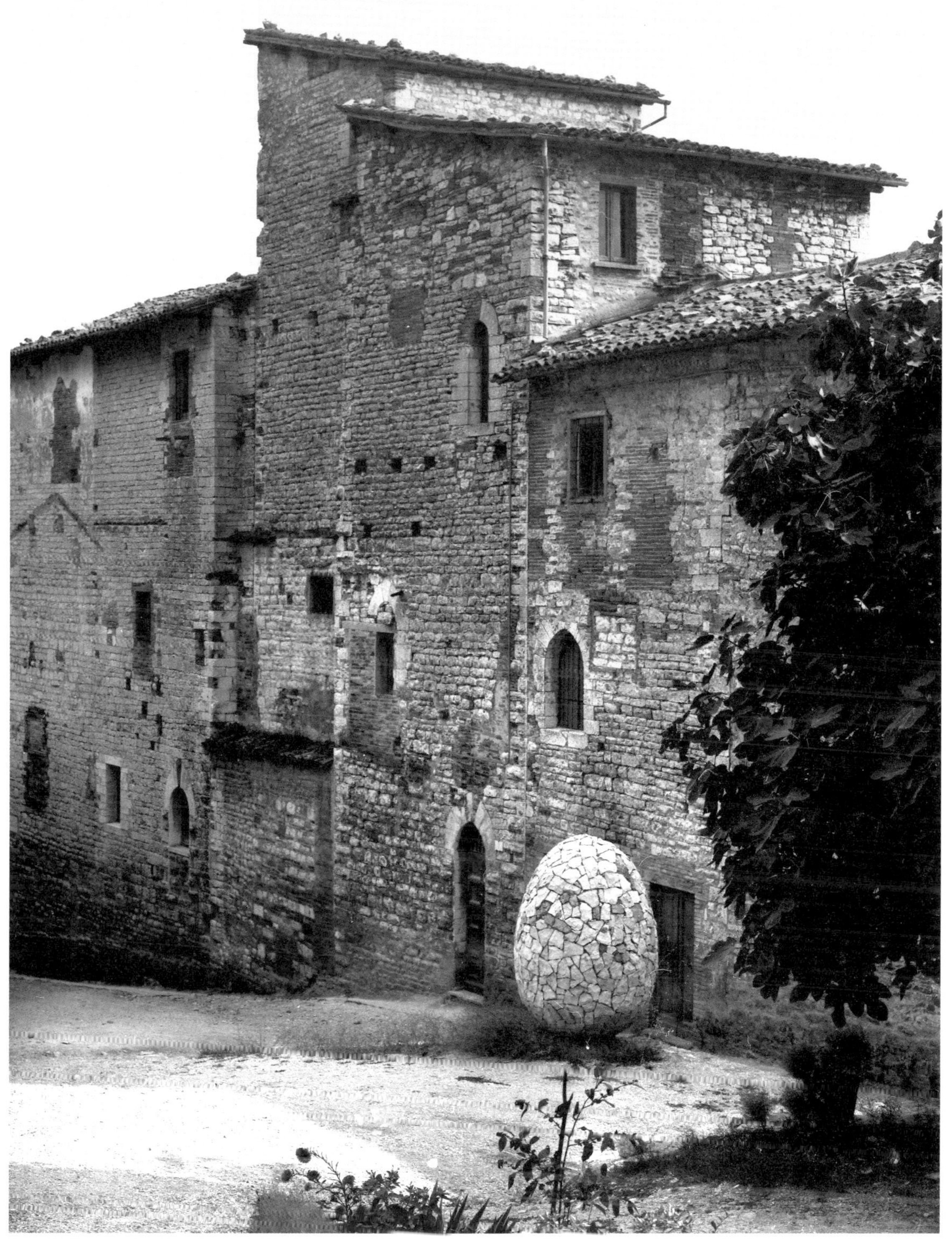

FIGURE 12—
L'Ovo di Gubbio (Egg of Gubbio), Gubbio,
Italy, 1976. Public installation. Stone, 90 in.
(230 cm) high.

comments Bentivoglio, "is a symbol of life made with the instruments of death, the most ancient of weapons—pointed stones. Women were killed with stones, which are, symbolically, fragments of the Tablets of Moses's Law. (If the Law is broken, the fragments of the broken tablets are turned against the lawbreaker.)"[20]

Yet the fragments of the egg also represent a new beginning, for when an egg breaks open a new life emerges. Thus, when a truck backed into *L'Ovo di Gubbio* in 2004, destroying it, Bentivoglio resisted the entreaties of the residents of the town to reconstruct it. (It was initially intended to last only one month, the length of the Biennial, but remained in place for 28 years.) *L'Ovo di Gubbio* lives on in the other works that were inspired by that initial public art project (*All'adultera lapidata—L'ovo di Gubbio [To the Stoned Adulteress—The Egg of Gubbio]* [1995] [Figure 11] and *Nascita Seconda [Second Birth]* [2009] [Figure 13]) and in Bentivoglio's continuing commitment to the exploration of the tensions between the conceptual and the material, language and image, justice and injustice, the individual and the community, and destruction and rebirth. In *Anatomia del braccio sinistro della Statua della Libertà (Anatomy of the Left Arm of the Statue of Liberty)* (1992) (Figure 10), Bentivoglio draws attention to the tablet representing the book of laws that will form the communal framework for the new American nation after its successful revolutionary war, rather than to the much more famous fiery and very rhetorical torch of individual liberty held in the statue's right hand.[21] In *Tavole della legge del consumo (Tablets of the Law of Consumerism)* (1992) (Plate 25), the shape chosen by McDonald's for the initial letter "M" is "revealed" by the artist. The tablets of Moses become the tablets of McDonald's; the spiritual is replaced by the commercial as the source of moral action. Yet in *Davide e Golia (David and Goliath)* (1989) (Plate 4, frontispiece), the power of the egg/beginning breaks through the symbol of consumer society, an echo of the escape from the cage of acquisition encapsulated in the "o" of one of Bentivoglio's earliest works, *Gabbia (Ho) (Cage [I Have])* (1966/1969) (Plate 7).

X.

Gubbio was the site of another "intervention in the landscape" in 1976. In this instance Bentivoglio gave voice not to the stone, but to the tree. In one of her first performance works,[22] she brought into sharp focus the social dimension of the relationships between humans and nonhumans, between men and women on the one hand, and the land they inhabit on the other. Until the second half of the twentieth century, Gubbio was surrounded by fields containing rows of trees specially pruned in the shape of a chalice

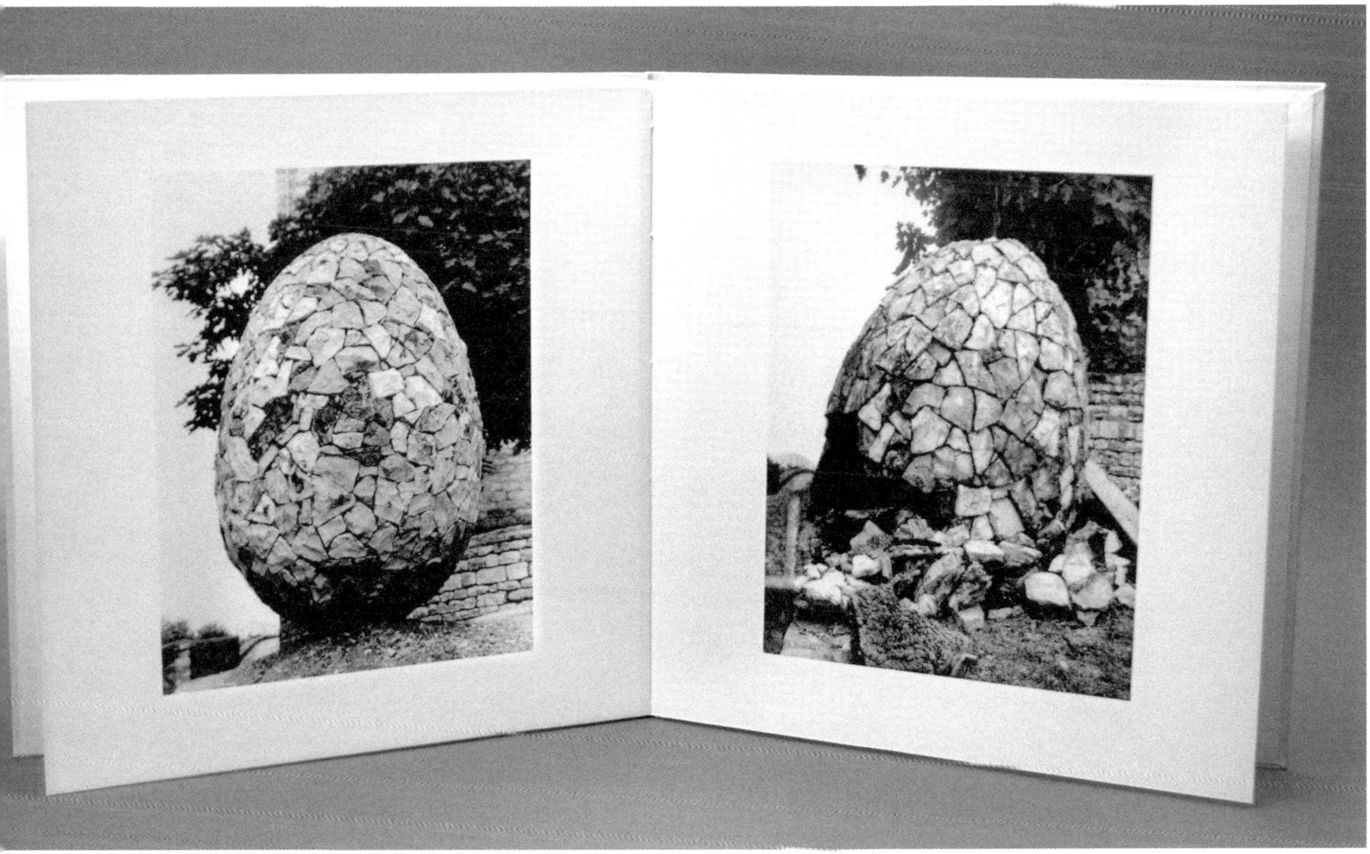

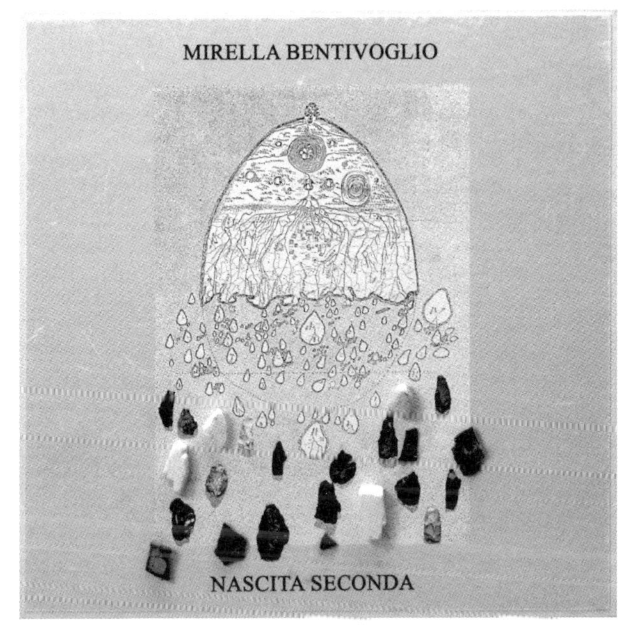

FIGURE 13—
Nascita seconda (Second Birth), 2009.
Book (paper, stone), 11¾ × 11¾ × ¼ in.
(29.85 × 29.85 × .64 cm).

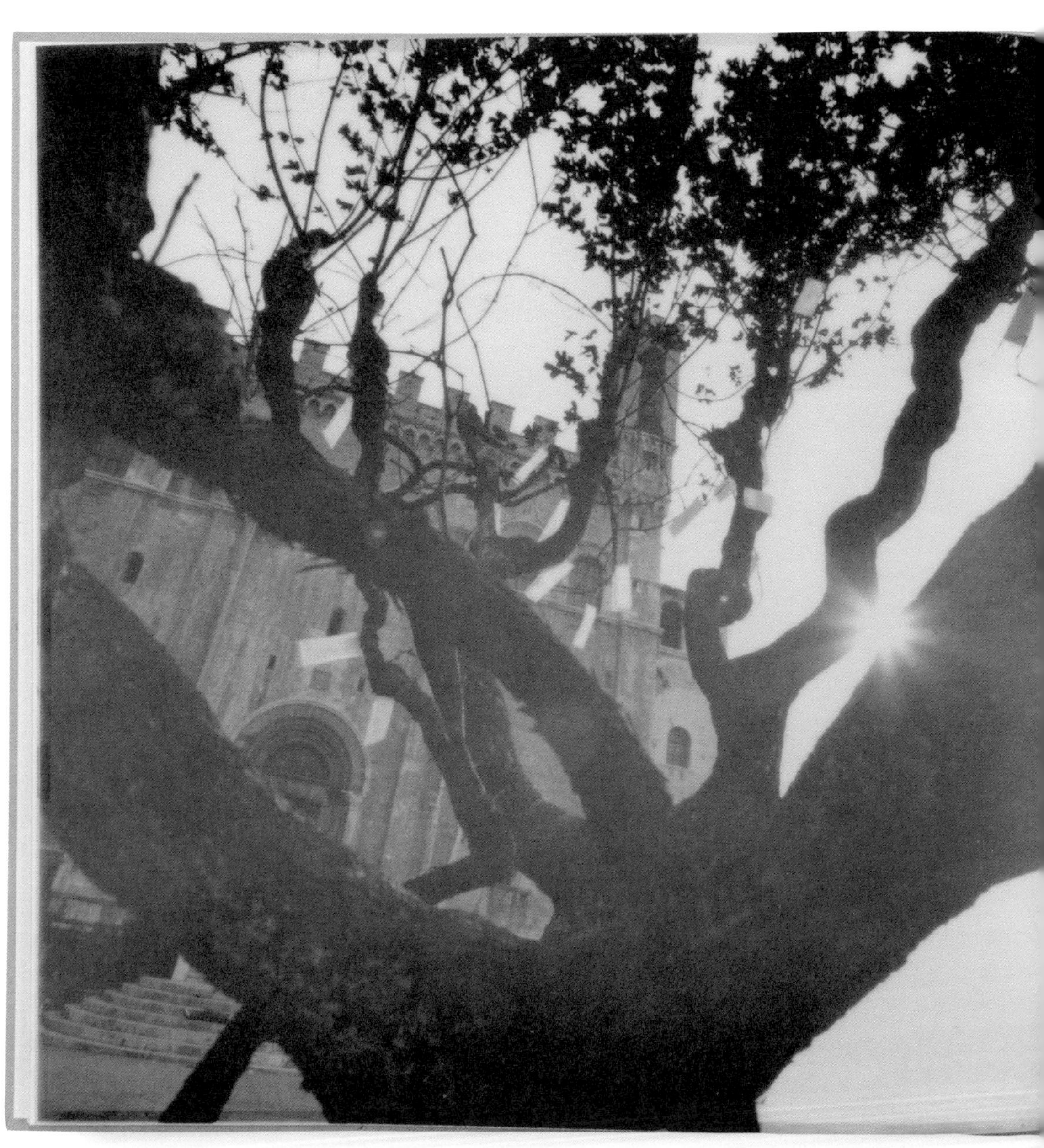

FIGURE 14—
Un albero di pagine (A Tree of Pages), 1992. Book, 12 × 12 in. (30.48 × 30.48 cm).

Sono rimaste sorprese: nella piazza ho notato un albero
fiorito

Mi fa riflessioni con tante malinconia e quando fioriva
di salito e mangiava l'uva

come è bello..!!

FANTASTICO

Per me è molto bello

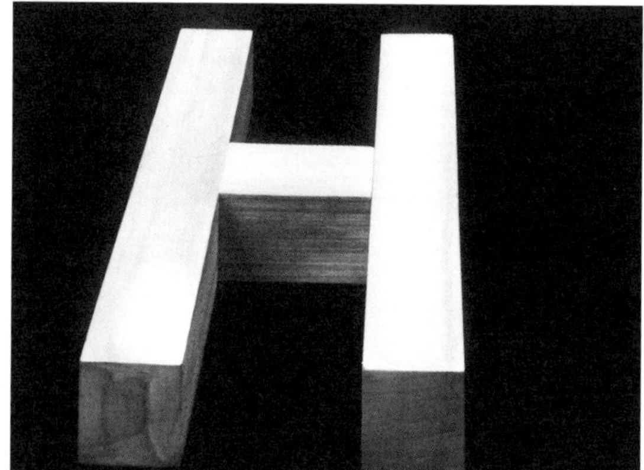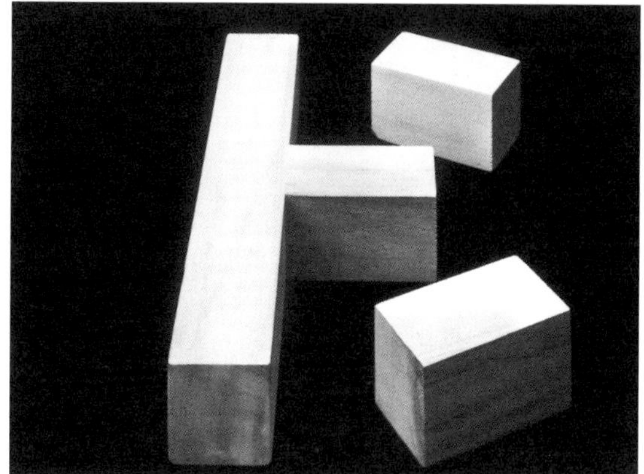

in order to act as supports for the grape vines and to store wood or crops such as corn in the fall. By the early 1970s, however, as part of the mechanization of agriculture, these trees were increasingly uprooted by tractors and replaced by metal supports, which required less maintenance. Rather that standing tall in the flat plains, the trees lay on the ground along the edge of the fields.

Bentivoglio took one of these trees, hoisted it upright in the Piazza della Signoria, and invited passersby to write their responses to the tree on pieces of paper, which were then attached to its branches. The artist then selected several offerings and, without changing any of the words, constructed a poem that could be read beginning from either end. The Italian critic Luciano Cherchi compared the resulting "poem written by a town" to the 1962 publication of Nanni Balestrini's *Tape Mark I*, poetry produced with a computer: "[T]he Tree-poem summarizes and condenses...a change of social perspective; from the technological infatuation of the 1960s to the austerity induced by the political, economic and moral crisis that we are currently experiencing."[23]

In 1992, Bentivoglio commemorated her 1976 *poesia-azione* (poetry-action) *Poem to a Tree* with the publication of *Un albero di pagine (A Tree of Pages)* (Figure 14), which includes not only a record of the performance, but also reproductions of the slips of paper out of which the poem to the tree was composed. These pages pay homage to the tree through both the thoughts contained therein and the very material out of which they are made. The

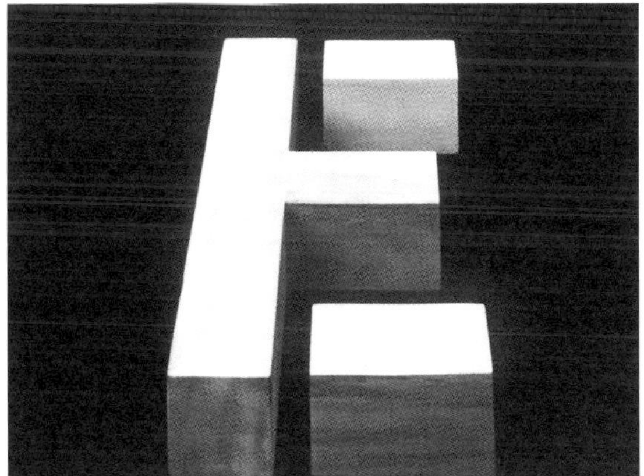 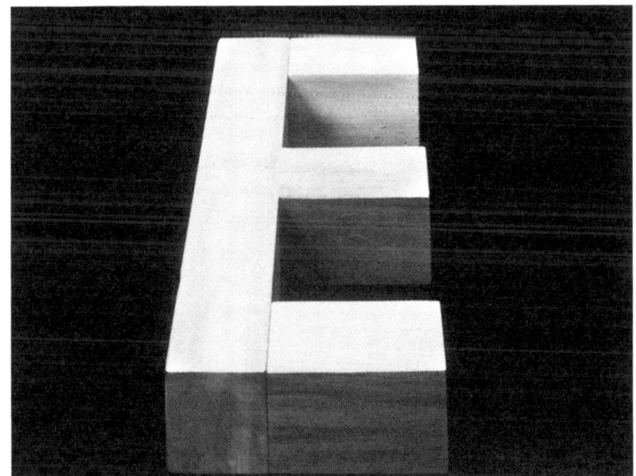

material and the conceptual combine once again in her work to remind us of the indelible interconnectedness of life on this planet.

This commitment to interconnectedness is expressed clearly in her work with the letter "E." "E" in Italian means "and," which for Bentivoglio symbolizes relationship. The challenge for contemporary societies is to find ways to support productive relationships, or, in broader terms, the common good, while still protecting the rights of individuals. For example, in the print *E= congiunzione (E=conjunction)* (Figure 20), the letters form an interconnected mass, yet none of them actually touch. This balance between the individual and the group is difficult to achieve and sustain, and Bentivoglio recognizes this in her *Moduli a E (E Combinations)* of 1977 (Figure 21), several of which embody "wrong conjunctions" or failed relationships. A selection of these *E Combinations* has been reconstructed for this exhibition in the main gallery of the Pomona College Museum of Art. They transform the museum floor into yet another page for the poetic visualization and subversive reimagining of language that is at the heart of all of Bentivoglio's work.

1. John D. O'Brien, "Il libro-campo" (Rome, 2000; Los Angeles, 2014). Unpublished typescript.

2. Federico García Lorca, "Lament for Ignacio Sánchez Mejias," in Francisco García Lorca and Donald M. Allen, ed., *The Selected Poems of Federico García Lorca* (New York: New Directions, 1955), pp. 135–37.

3. Ibid., p. 139.

4. Quoted in James Gleick, *The Information: A History, A Theory, A Flood* (New York: Vintage Books/Random House, 2011), p. 53.

5. Southwell's teachings lived on in his publications, most notably *Mary Magdalene's Funeral Tears* (1591) (ten editions had been printed by 1636) and *St. Peter's Complaint with other poems* (1595) (fourteen editions by 1636).

6. Mirella Bentivoglio to Frances Pohl, June 2013.

7. Thomas Curwen, "His mind is set on brain-like chip," *Los Angeles Times*, February 25, 2014, p. 1.

8. Ibid., p. 12.

9. Italo Calvino, *Invisible Cities*, trans. William Weaver (New York: Harcourt Brace Jovanovich, 1974), pp. 10–11. I would like to thank my colleague George Gorse for bringing this quote to my attention.

10. Bentivoglio to Pohl, June 2013. See also Frances K. Pohl, "Mirella Bentivoglio: Dismantling Images of Power in Italy," *Women's Studies: An Interdisciplinary Journal* 25, no. 3 (1996): p. 252.

11. John Berger, *Ways of Seeing* (London: BBC and Penguin Books, 1972), pp. 7–33.

12. Bentivoglio to Pohl, June 2013. The Hungarian-born Australian geologist Laszlo Toth attacked the statue, installed in St. Peter's Basilica in Rome, with a hammer on May 21, 1972.

13. Bentivoglio obtained the photographs from the carpenter who built the *Pietà* crate and who also built the crate in *Riaprire* (ibid.). See also Pohl, "Mirella Bentivoglio," pp. 260–61.

14. The 1970s in Italy was the decade of the Brigate Rosse, or Red Brigades, a militant leftist organization committed to overthrowing capitalism and the Italian state through violence, including arson, kidnapping, and murder, in order to install a dictatorship of the proletariat and to redistribute the benefits of the country's rapid economic growth of the previous two decades. Between 1952 and 1970, per capita income increased 134 percent and automobile ownership rose from less than half a million to 10 million, yet many still lived in poverty and worked in unsafe conditions (Christopher Duggan, *A Concise History of Italy* [Cambridge: Cambridge University Press, 2004], pp. 263–76). In November 1977 a member of the Red Brigades shot and killed Carlo Casalegno, deputy editor of *La Stampa* newspaper, in broad daylight on a street in Turin.

15. Translation by author.

16. Gleick, p. 31.

17. Bentivoglio to Pohl, June 2013.

18. Ibid. This work on paper is related to a small sculpture Bentivoglio created for the 1980 Venice Biennial. She had been invited to contribute a work to an exhibition titled "Tempo della Museo Venezia" (The Time of the Venice Museum). The two photographs were attached to an open marble book, with the same text as in the work on paper connecting them.

19. Mirella Bentivoglio, *All'Adultera Lapidata* (Rome: Edikon, 1976), n.p. This illustrated pamphlet was published in conjunction with the biennial Gubbio 76.

20. Quoted in J.V.R. and J.J., "All'Adultera Lapidata," *13th Moon* (1978): p. 35.

21. The tablet bears the inscription "July 4, 1776." The statue was a gift of the French government to mark the friendship between the two countries and was designed by the French sculptor Frédéric Auguste Bartoldi and installed on a pedestal designed by the American architect Richard Morris Hunt. Located on Liberty Island in New York City's harbor, it was dedicated on October 28, 1886.

22. Bentivoglio would go on to create several performance works over the next three decades, a number of which took place in or near Gubbio (e.g. *E = congiunzione [E = Conjunction]* in the Campo Santo Spirito in Gubbio, in 1981, and *Operazione Orfeo [Operation Orpheus]*, Stage 1, at nearby Monte Cucco, in 1982).

23. Luchiano Cherchi, untitled catalog essay in *Mirella Bentivoglio: Simbolo Come Struttura*, originally written for Bentivoglio's exhibition, "Poesia-azione," at Spazio Alternativo, Rome, in 1978.

PLATE 6 ——
Moduli a E: Predominio sull'altro (E Combinations: Predominance Over the Other), Gubbio, Italy, 1980. Wood. Each "E" 90 in. (230 cm) high.

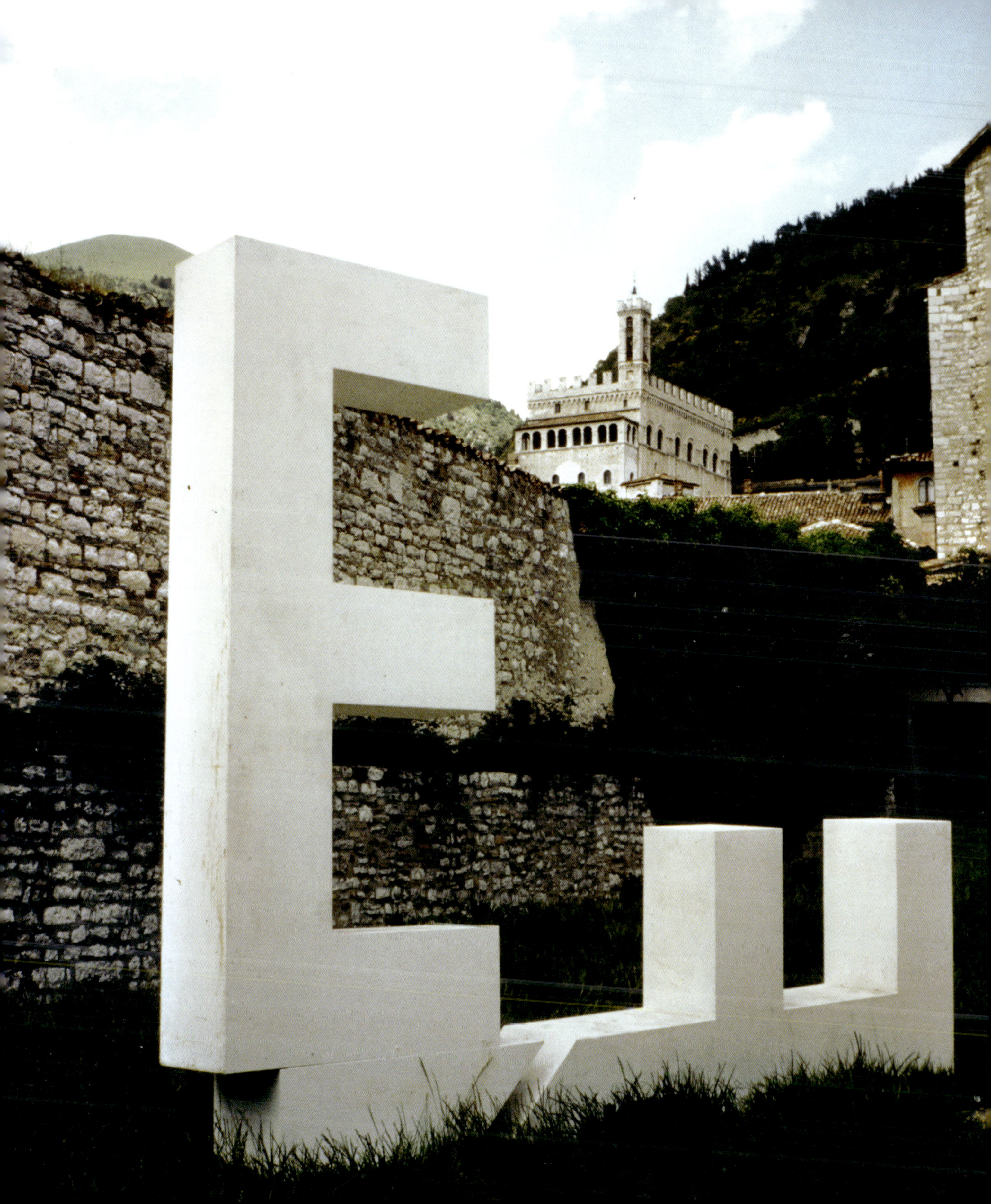

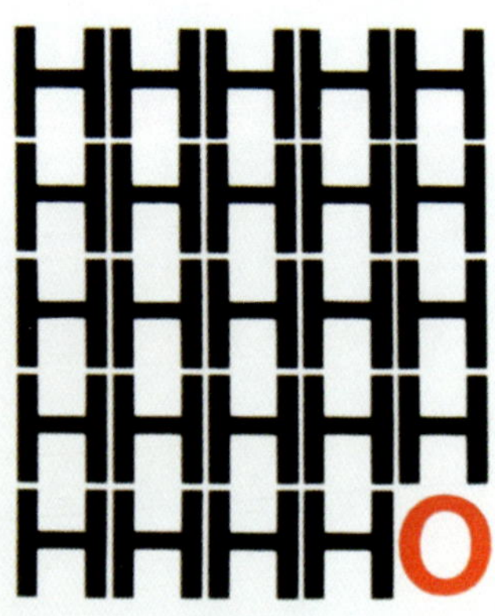

gabbia (:HO)

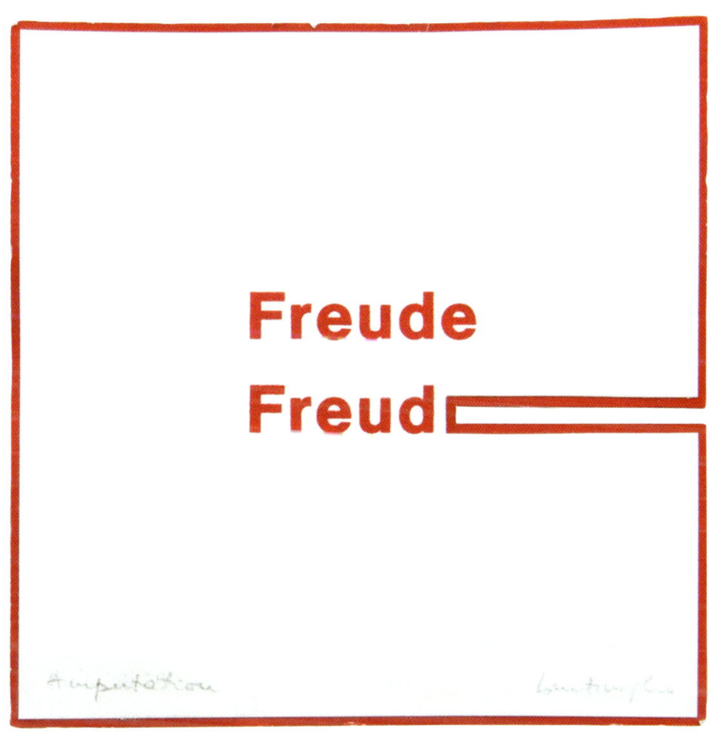

PLATE 8 ——
Amputazione (Amputation),
1971. Serigraph on paper,
5⅝ × 5⅝ in. (14.29 × 14.29 cm).

Freude is German for joy

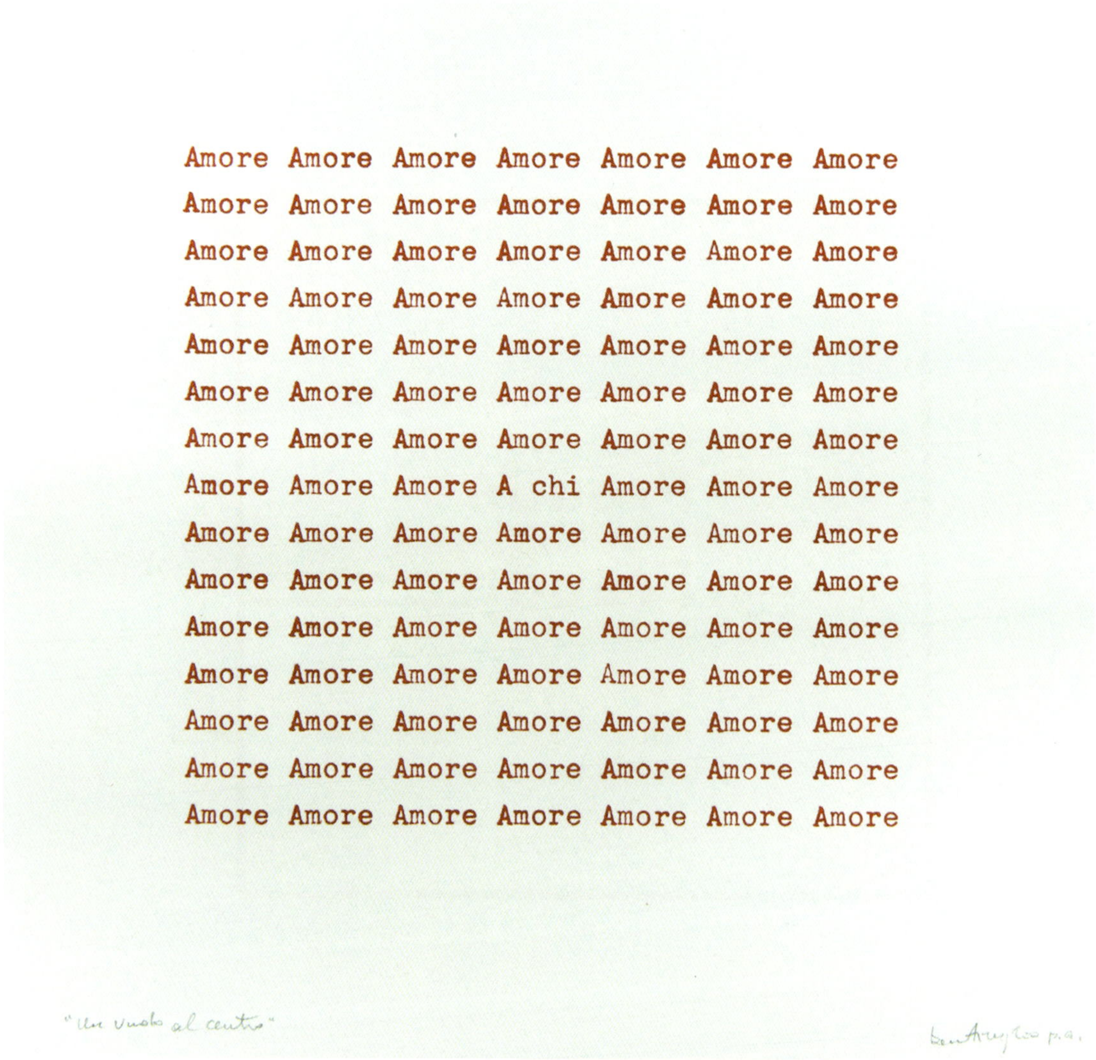

PLATE 9 —
Vuoto al centro (Void in the Center),
1966. Serigraph on paper, 16½ × 17 1/16 in.
(41.91 × 43.34 cm).

amore = love; *a chi* = to whom

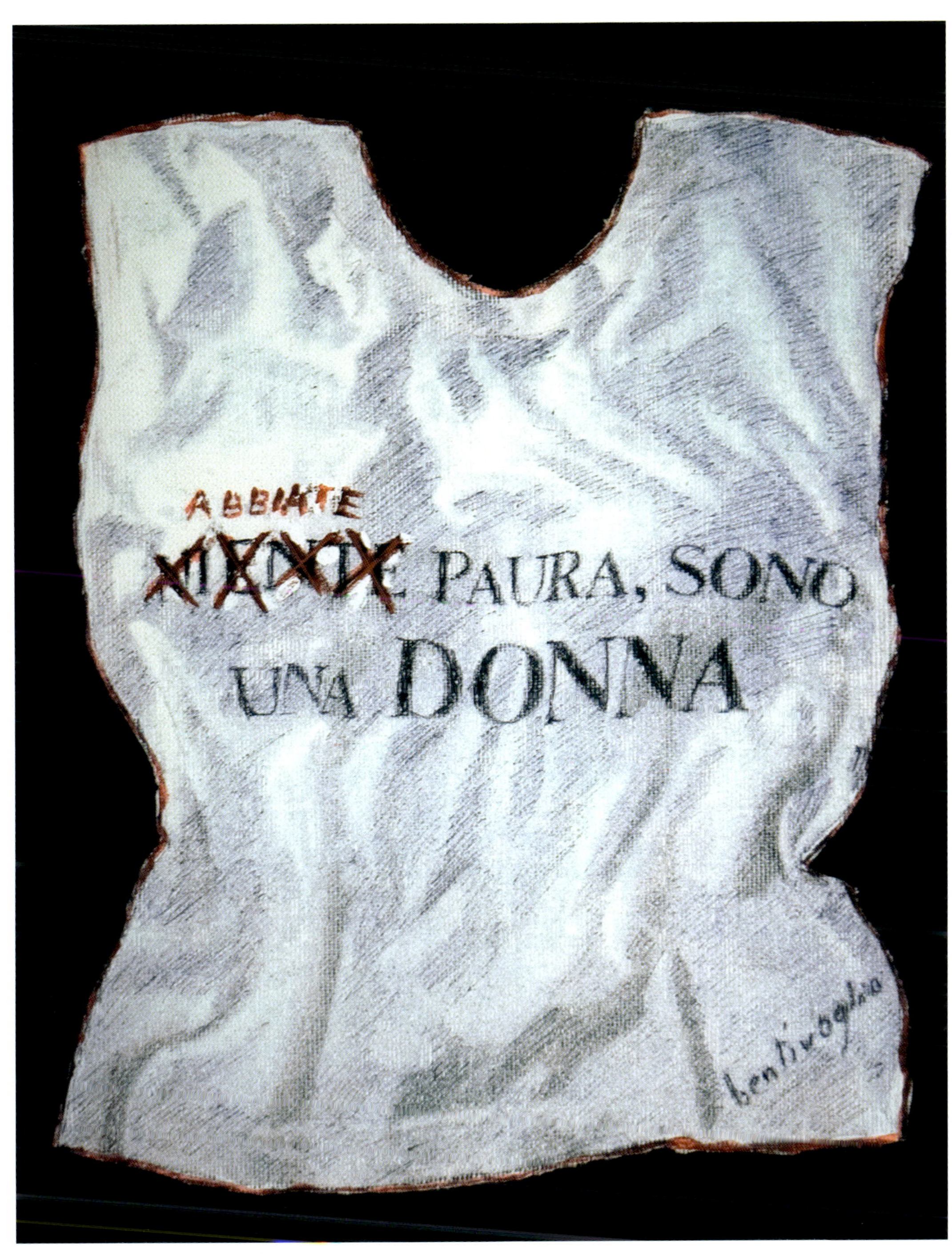

Correzione (Correction), 1985.
Photomechanical print on paper,
17 × 16 in. (43.18 × 40.64 cm).

Niente paura, sono una donna = Have no fear, I am a woman;
Abbiate paura, sono una donna = Have fear, I am a woman

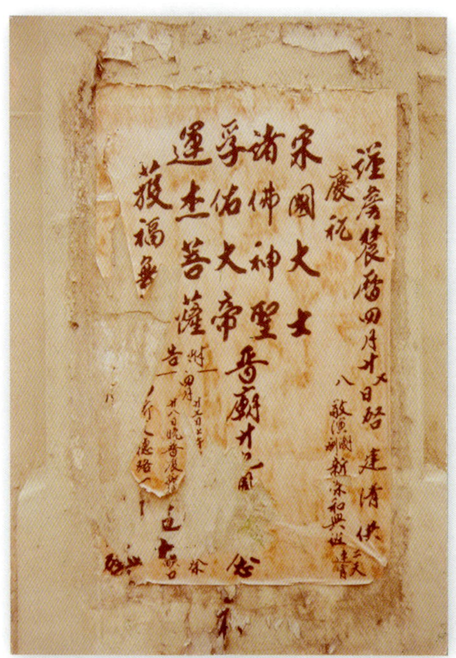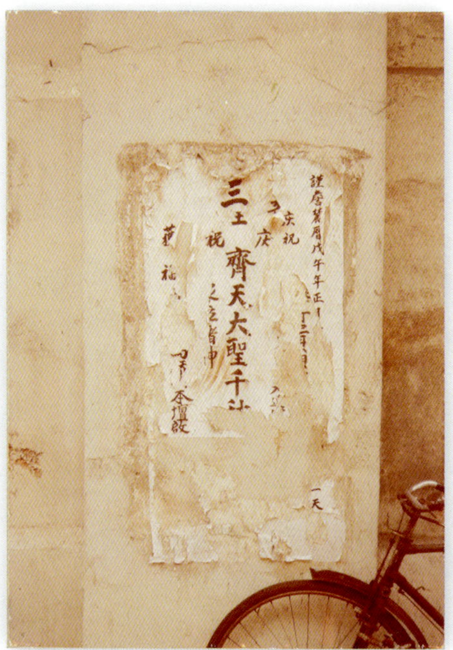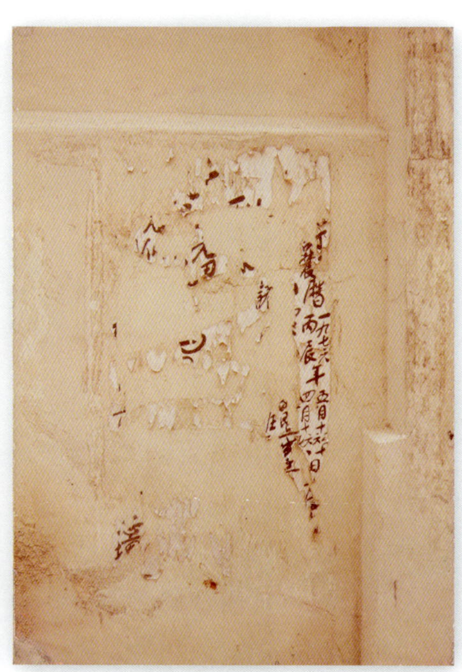

PLATE 11 —
I muri di Singapore (Walls of Singapore),
1978. Six photographs on wood panels,
6⅝ × 4⅝ in. (16.8 × 11.7 cm) each.

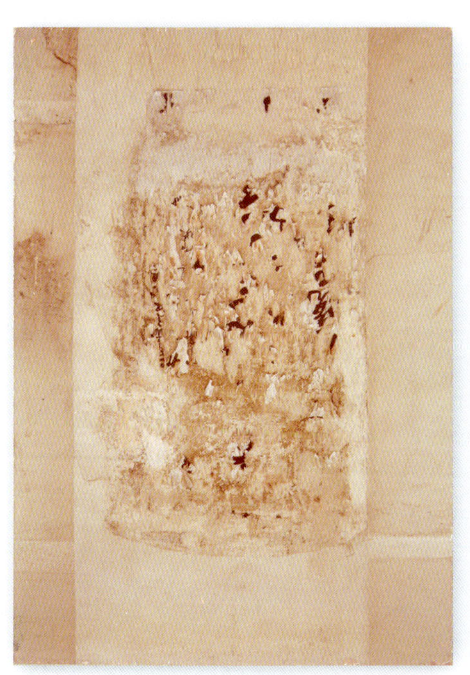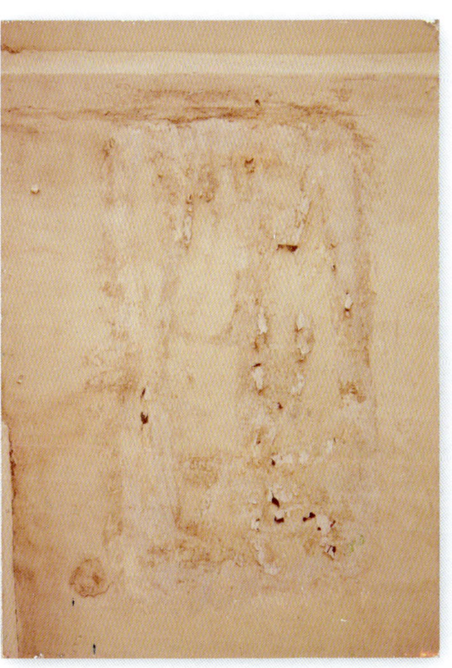

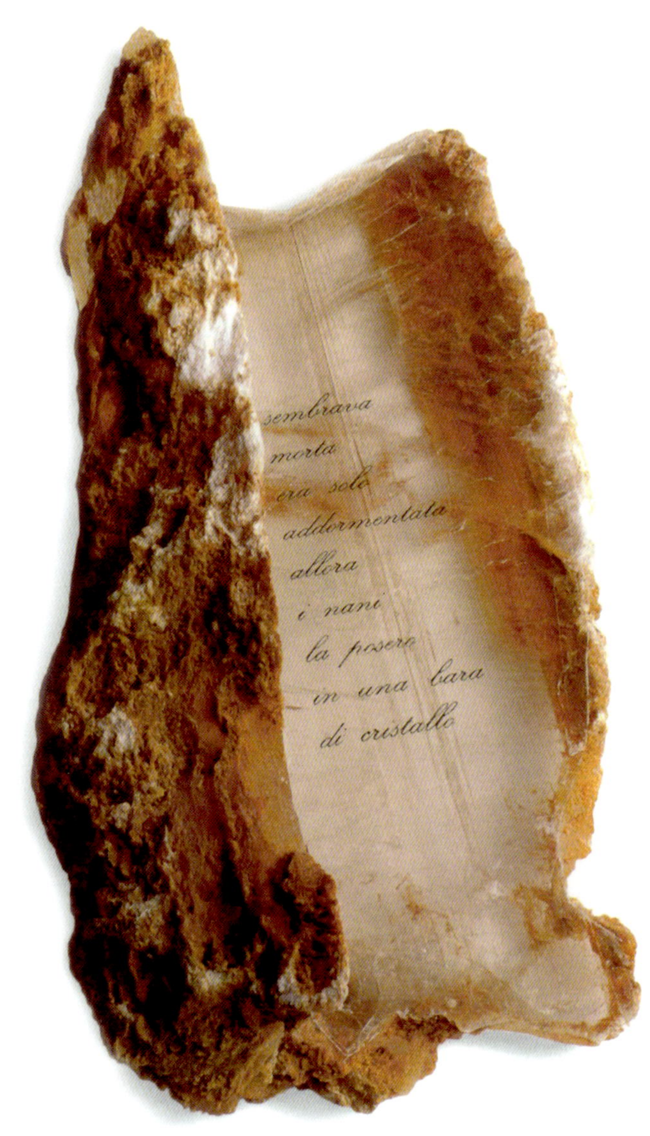
sembrava
morta
era solo
addormentata
allora
i nani
la posero
in una bara
di cristallo

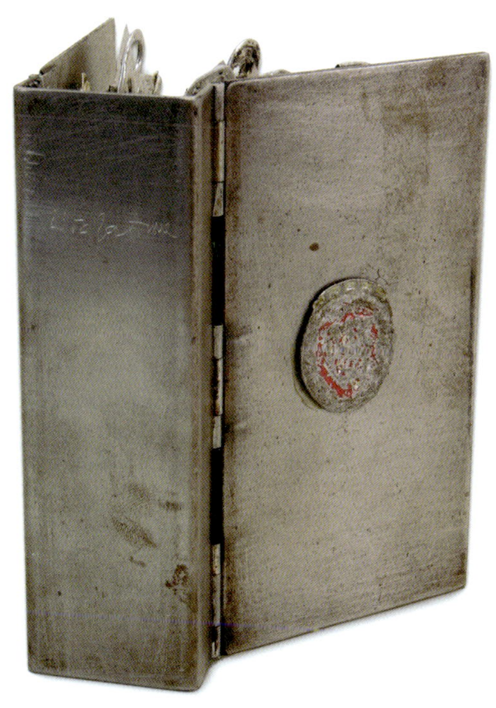

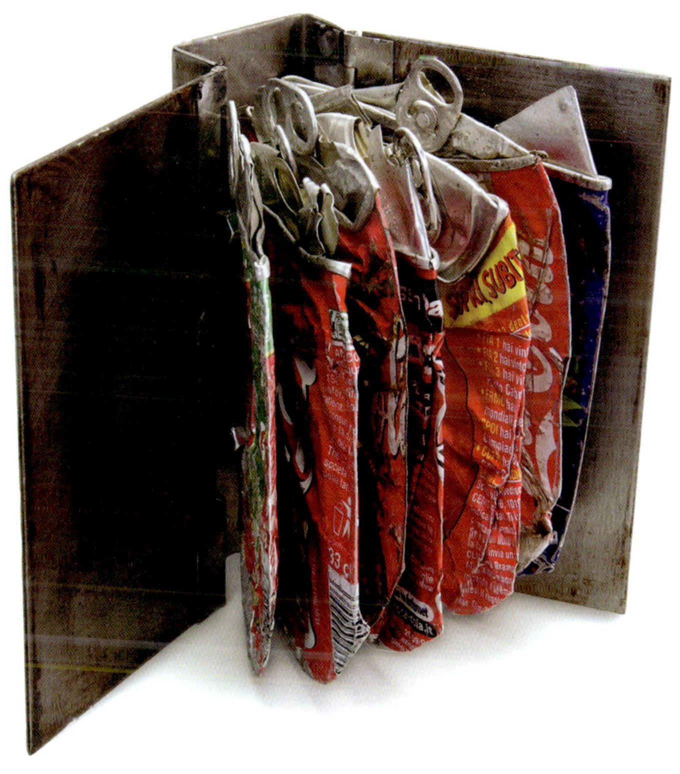

PLATE 13 —
Litolattine (Tin Book), 1995.
Tin and aluminum, 5⅝ × 3⅞ ×
2⅛ in. (14.29 × 9.84 × 5.4 cm).

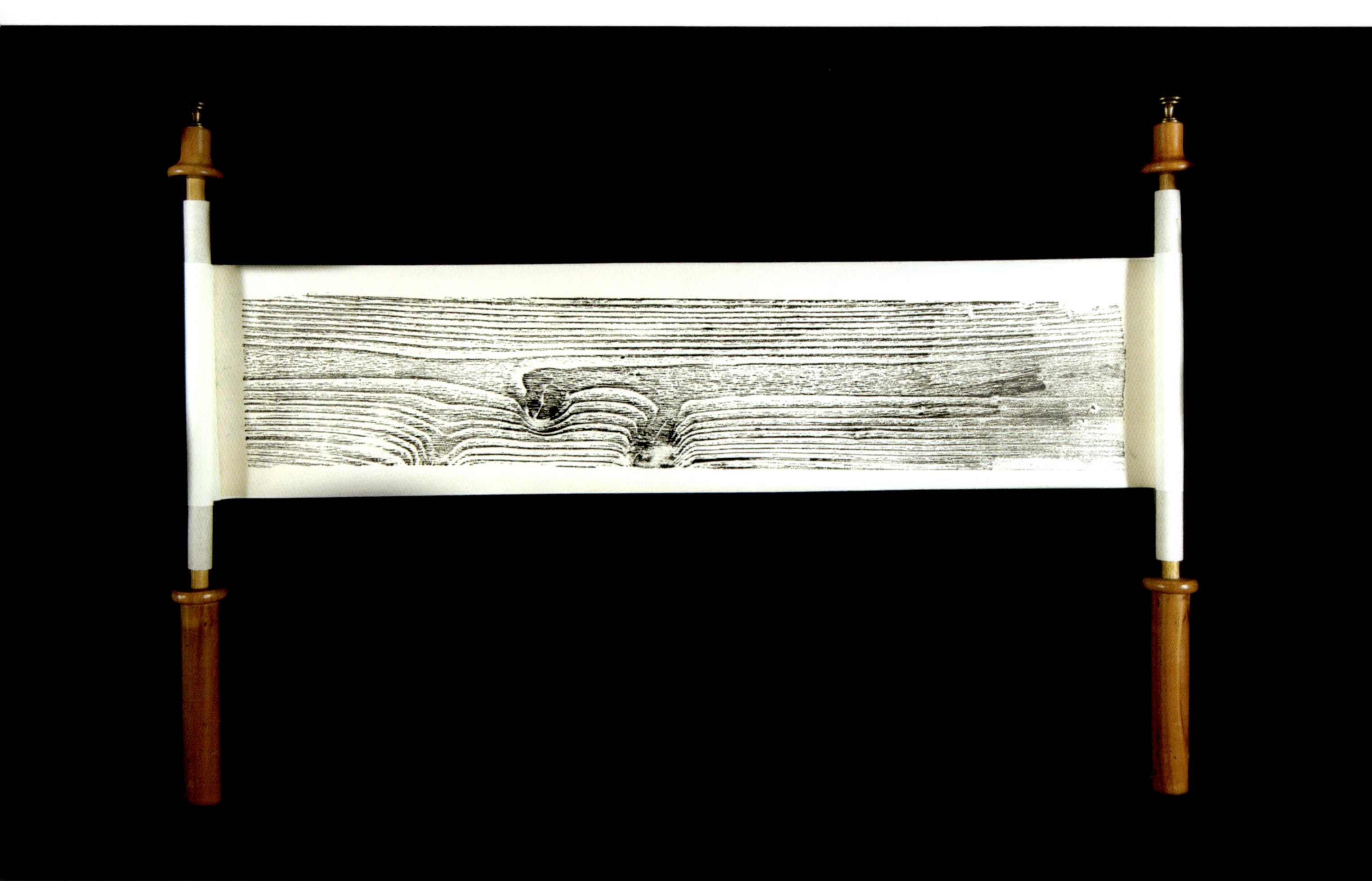

PLATE 14 ——
Leggere l'albero (Read the Tree), 1990.
Xylography on paper, 16½ × 24¾ in.
(41.91 × 62.87 cm).

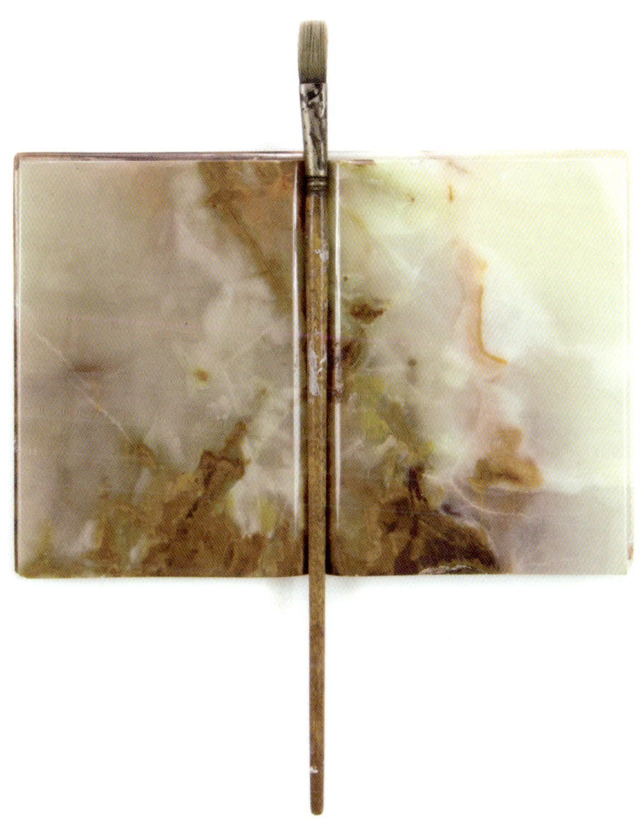

PLATE 15—
*Lapide alla pittura (Tombstone
to Painting),* 1975. Marble and wood,
11¾ × 9½ in. (29.85 × 24.13 cm).

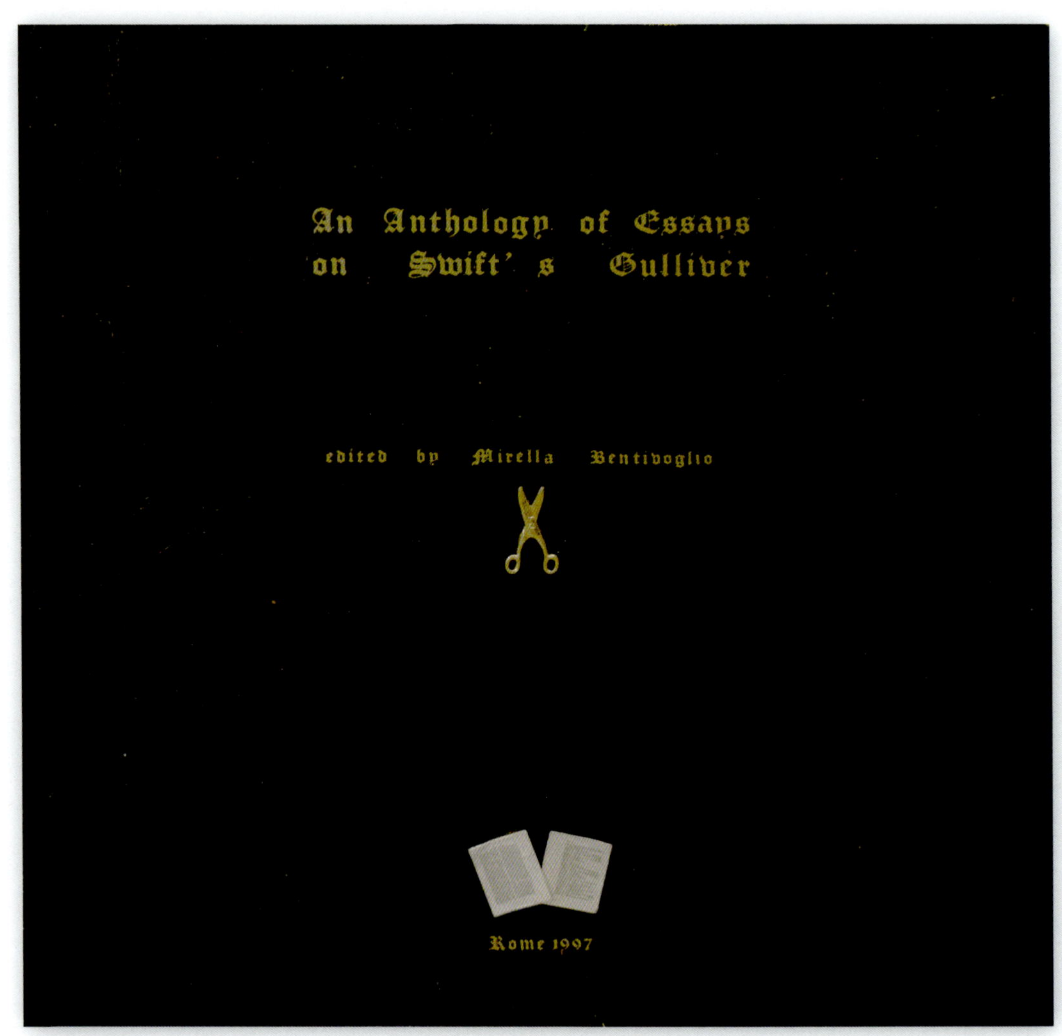

PLATE 16 —
An Anthology of Essays on Swift's Gulliver,
1995. Closed (left) and open (right) view.
Mixed media, 13⅝ × 13⅛ × 2⅛ in. (34.61 ×
33.34 × 5.4 cm).

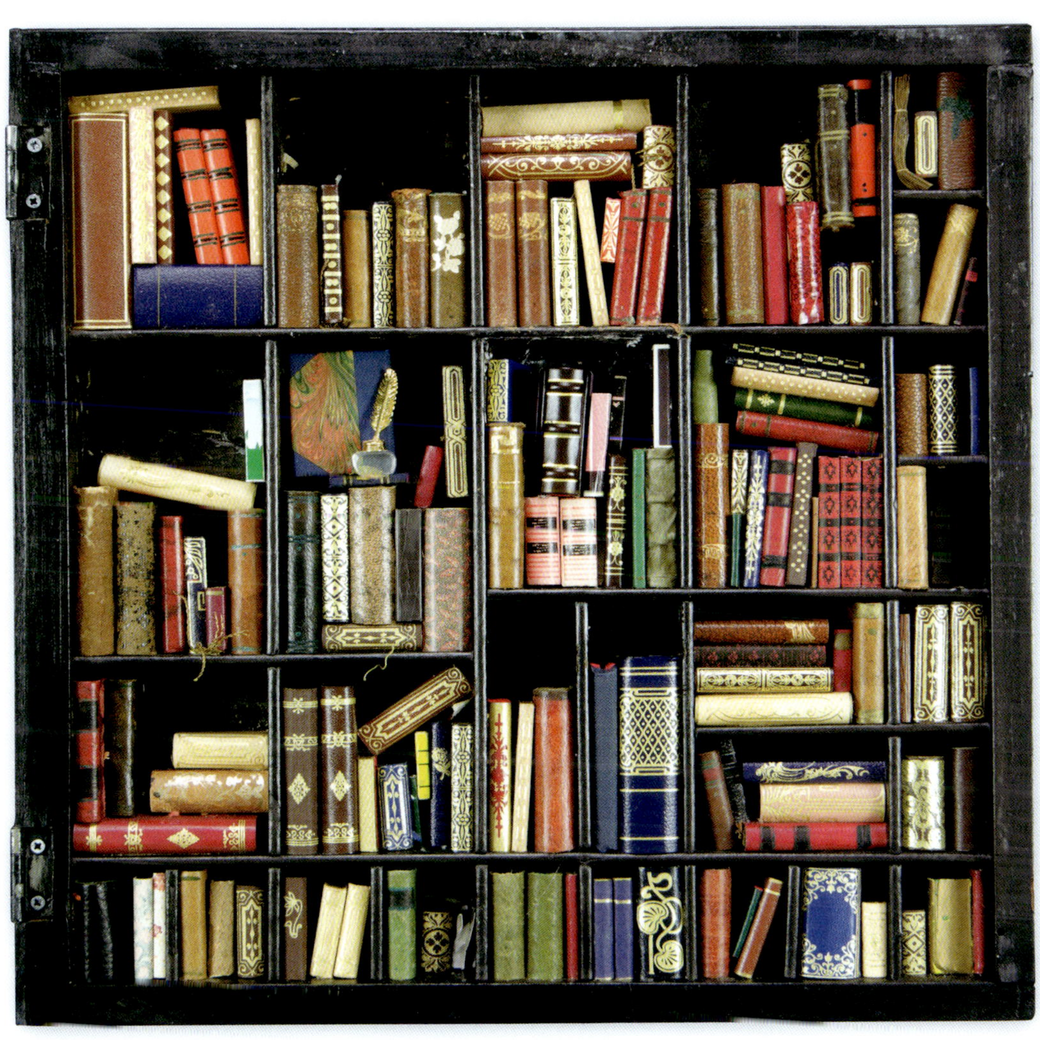

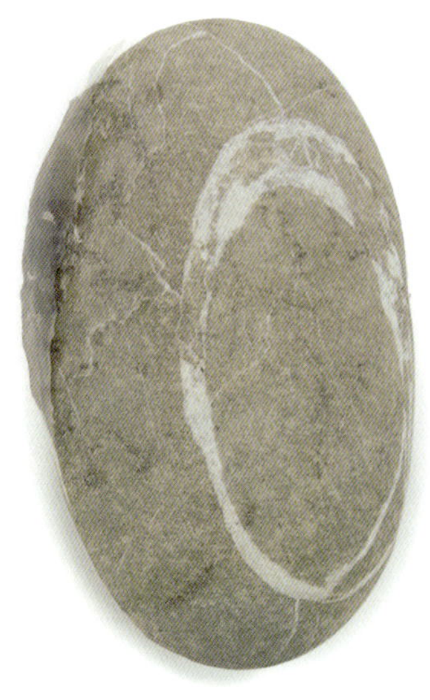

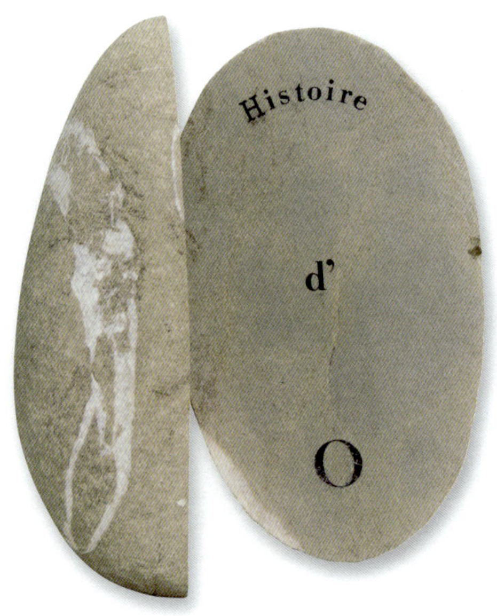

PLATE 17 ——
Histoire d'O (Story of O), 1985.
Ink on stone, 3¼ × 3⅝ × 1¼ in.
(8.26 × 9.21 × 3.18 cm).

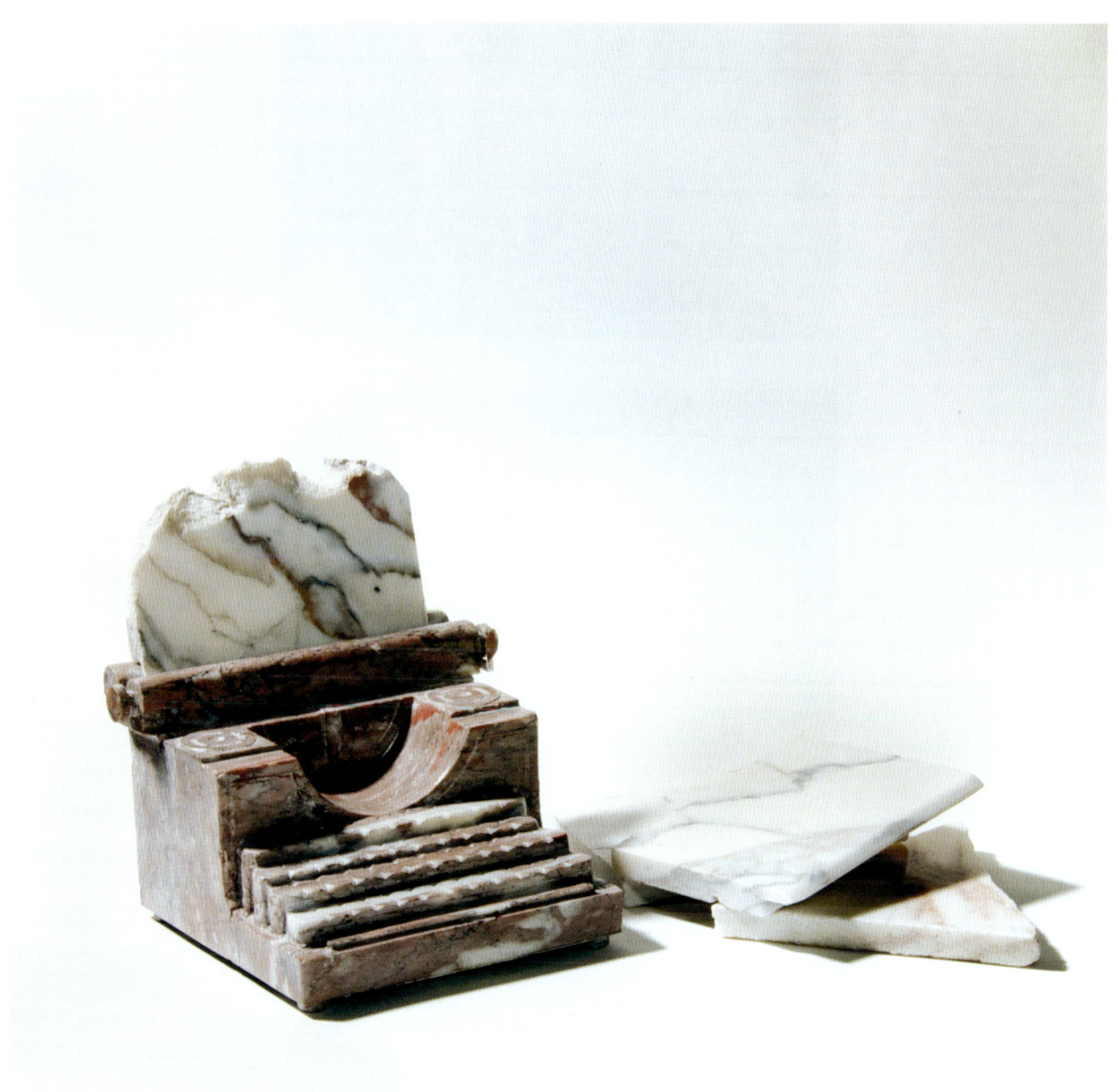

PLATE 18 —
La macchina da scrivere di Dio (God's Typewriter), 1988. Photomechanical print on paper, 15⅝ × 15⅝ in. (39.69 × 39.69 cm).

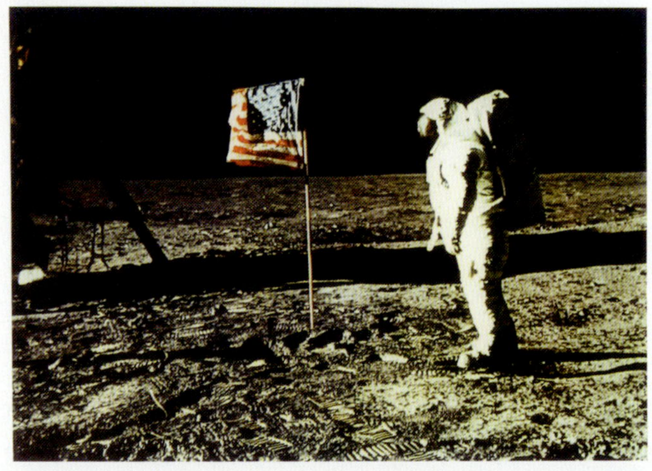

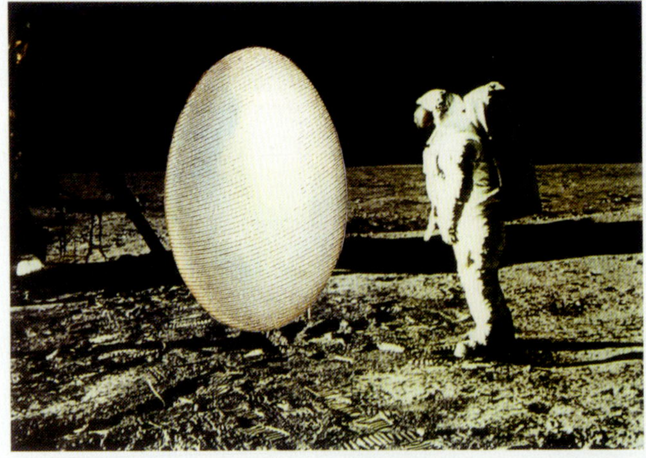

Moon/ument

In one of its phases, the moon seems to take the shape of an egg. Thus, the story told to children that the moon is the place where children come from. Astronauts on some future lunar voyage are invited to take along the white shell of an uninflated, oval ball, and then, with suitable instruments, once having reached their destination, to fill it with oxygen and to set it up, erect, at a suitable place on the moon's surface. A sign of the planet of life, from which derives the fragment which constitutes the moon. No more the flags that signal the subdivision of the earth! A sign of provenance. A symbol of the secret of the cosmos.

Moon/ument, 2011. Photomechanical print on paper, 17¾ × 8½ in.
(45.09 × 21.59 cm).

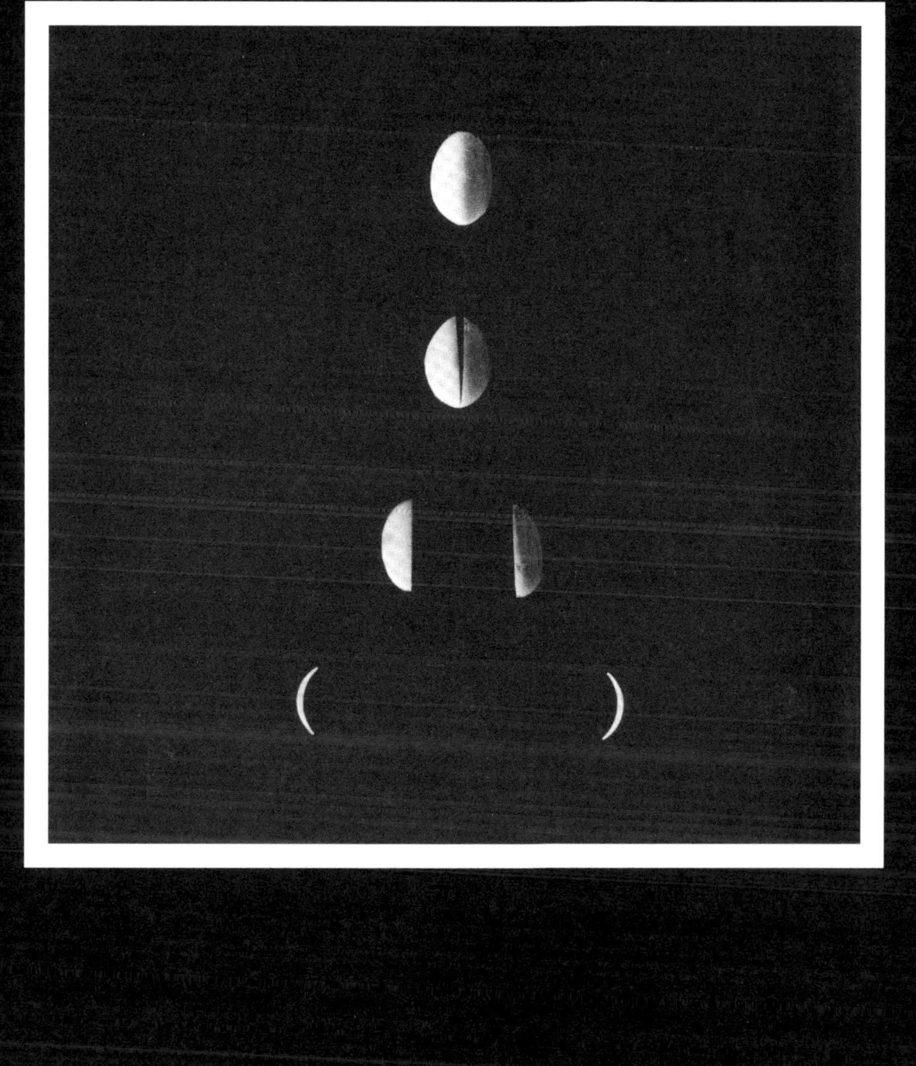

FIGURE 16—
Eclissi (da simbolo a segno) (Eclipse [from Symbol to Sign]), 1981. Photograph, 8⅝ × 8⅝ in. (21.91 × 21.91 cm).

INTERVIEW WITH MIRELLA BENTIVOGLIO

Benjamin Kersten

INTERVIEW WITH MIRELLA BENTIVOGLIO

Benjamin Kersten

—

The following interview took place in Rome at the home of Mirella Bentivoglio on June 3 and June 8, 2013.

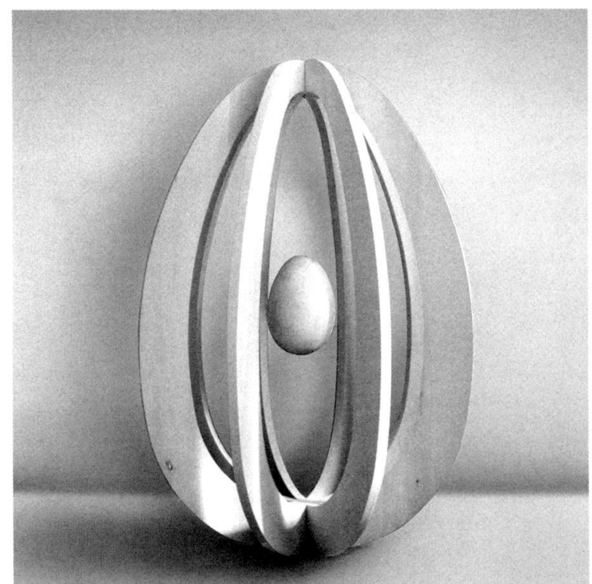

——BEN KERSTEN——

You are an artist who works in many genres—as a poet, sculptor, performance artist, concrete poet and visual poet. Do people who write about your work tend to emphasize one part of your artistic practice over another? How would you describe the relationship between your various bodies of work?

——MIRELLA BENTIVOGLIO——

Art critics who write about my work generally consider it Visual Poetry, in spite of its having resemblance to sculpture. There is a continuous back and forth in my work from meaning to form. For instance, my large wooden *Hyper Ovum* (1987) (Figure 17) is a sort of sculptural version of my graphic work *Eclissi (Eclipse)* (1981) (Figure 16), where the disappearance of the egg creates the parentheses. In the three-dimensional version, this idea has become an egg of air, whose contours are a number of parentheses. If I have to sum up my various bodies of work in one word, I will choose the word "poetry."

——BK——

Have you found any one particular medium (e.g. stone, metal, paper) more suitable for conveying the relationship between image and word? Is there a medium you have yet to experiment with that you would like to try?

——MB——

Yes, I have found a particular medium that I consider very suitable to my poetic world. It is stone, the crust of our planet. The veins of the stone are the writings of earth. And there are no media with which I did not try to work if I was interested in them.

——BK——

You often use found objects or materials from the world of consumer culture in your work. When did you start to do this, and why?

——MB——

I started at once, in the middle of the sixties, when I left painting and verse poetry. The withdrawal of objects or materials from the world of consumer culture allows me to turn upside down the given meanings in a concentrated way. What I am looking for is always "coincidence."

FIGURE 17—
Hyper Ovum, 1987. Wood, 90½ in. (230 cm) high.

—BK—

You deal with the world of consumer culture when it comes to products like Coca-Cola (Plate 24). Do you deal with the consumption of art as well?

—MB—

Yes, I did some ironic works that contained criticisms about considering art on the basis of its financial value within the art market, considering it just as a good investment, in some cases even condemning it to silence inside the obscurity of a safe-deposit box. But I did not mean to criticize the existence of an art system itself. Without a free market, art would be controlled by political powers, as happened in the Soviet Union, with the awful results that we all know.

—BK—

Your work does raise questions about systems of authority (e.g. religious, political, economic). Do you think it is possible for artists to alter these systems through their work?

—MB—

I hope so. It takes a great deal of time, but using this new kind of poetry to stimulate people's sense of criticism of such established structures may be productive.

—BK—

In particular, much of your work deals with legal, religious, medical, and social challenges faced by women in a patriarchal culture. Is this work informed by any particular feminist writers or artists, by your own personal experiences, or both?

—MB—

Feminist writers have influenced my work, but I have learned a lot from my personal experiences. I had to give up many opportunities for communication with a large audience because of my role as a mother and wife. In the seventies, I could not accept a grant from the Harkness Foundation, which would have allowed me to visit American museums. That grant would have placed a car and a secretary at my disposal for a whole academic year. But I had three children and all of the corresponding domestic duties, so I could not accept the grant.

—BK—

You have created works for public spaces that do reach large audiences. What is important, for you, about the public nature of these spaces? What do you think are the key differences between viewing a work in a public space as opposed to a private space (a gallery or home)?

—MB—

The works I made for public spaces are strictly bound to the character of those spaces. For small works, the context is not important. It may be private or public, with no influence on their various levels of meaning.

—BK—

Have you explored in your art or your writing the role that language plays in the distribution and reception of art?

—MB—

Certainly, language always has been the way to explore art. It plays a big role in our reception of art, but the works have to be experienced by feeling. Afterwards, rationality and knowledge may explain how that feeling was reached.

—BK—

You are also an art historian and an art critic. How has this work influenced your artistic practice?

—MB—

As a poet, I have a critical approach to the society we have built, so I do not distinguish between my so-called creative work and my critical thought.

—BK—

Your art is very open and rich in meaning. Do you often begin with one idea and change your mind in the process of making a work? Also, have you found that the meaning of a work, for you, has changed over time?

—MB—

Yes, I often start with one idea and then change my mind in the process of making a work. The process shows me where that first seed of an idea wanted to take me. Some American conceptual

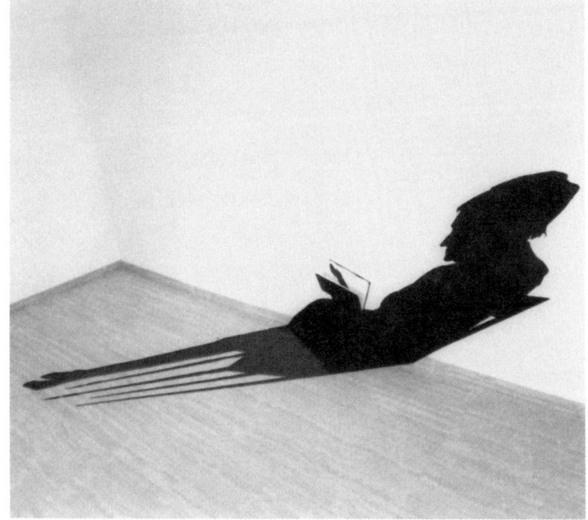

artists declared that the work is all in its plan. This is absolutely wrong. Only the meeting with reality, with physicality, permits the project to reach a poetic result. And I have often found that my work contained a deeper meaning of which I had not been conscious when it started.

——BK——

Transitorio/Durevole (Transitory/Durable) (2002) (Figure 18) uses the book to capture history. Do you see books and records of performances as answers to the transient nature of time?

——MB——

All art and poetry is an answer to the fleeting nature of time, particularly the installation *Transitorio/Durevole*, which is about survival. We are transitory shadows, but our transitoriness becomes durable when it is expressed on the pages of a book, as happens here.

——BK——

As you said, the book is important for preservation, but it has also been a powerful tool for shaping the world in which we live. Many people accept what they read in non-fiction books as objective facts, rather than as information shaped by the views of the author. Can you talk about how your work challenges our understanding of the book?

——MB——

The book is an object deeply imprinted in our psyche. It is a symbol. We swear on closed books, not on open pages. Additionally, the book is a tangible object. We have to experience it physically if we read it. We touch its pages, we hear the sound of turning them. I often realized poetic metaphors of the book. My *Libro campo (Field Book)* (1998) (Figure 1) is made of earth. It tries to express jointly the creativity of nature and of the human mind.

——BK——

Your art often includes monuments or other works of art from the past. Do you think your art is able to influence the way we view the past?

——MB——

I hope so. Many artists of the near or far past seem to me to be more "modern" than the art historians who write about them today.

——BK——

Are there any particular artists, either working today or in the past, who have inspired you?

——MB——

Certainly, many artists of the near and far past have influenced me. When I painted and wrote verse poetry, I encountered the work of the Russian-American artist Ben Shahn, who often utilized words in his paintings. I started to feel that I had to overcome the arbitrary subdivisions of codes. Not through addition, combining distinct images and words, as was done by Shahn, but through coincidence. Shahn was not a poet. He was a painter, still operating in a "unidisciplinary" way, but his work gave me the first push towards a new way to consider expression. Then I contacted the Brazilian founders of the so-called Concrete Poetry movement, and gave up both painting and verse poetry. I started experimenting in Concrete Poetry, and then in other currents of verbo-visuality, particularly with Visual Poetry,

FIGURE 18 —
Transitorio/durevole (Transitory/Durable), with Regina Silveira, 2002. Installation, heavy plastic and wood; 65 × 168 × 80 in. (165.1 × 426.72 × 203.2 cm).

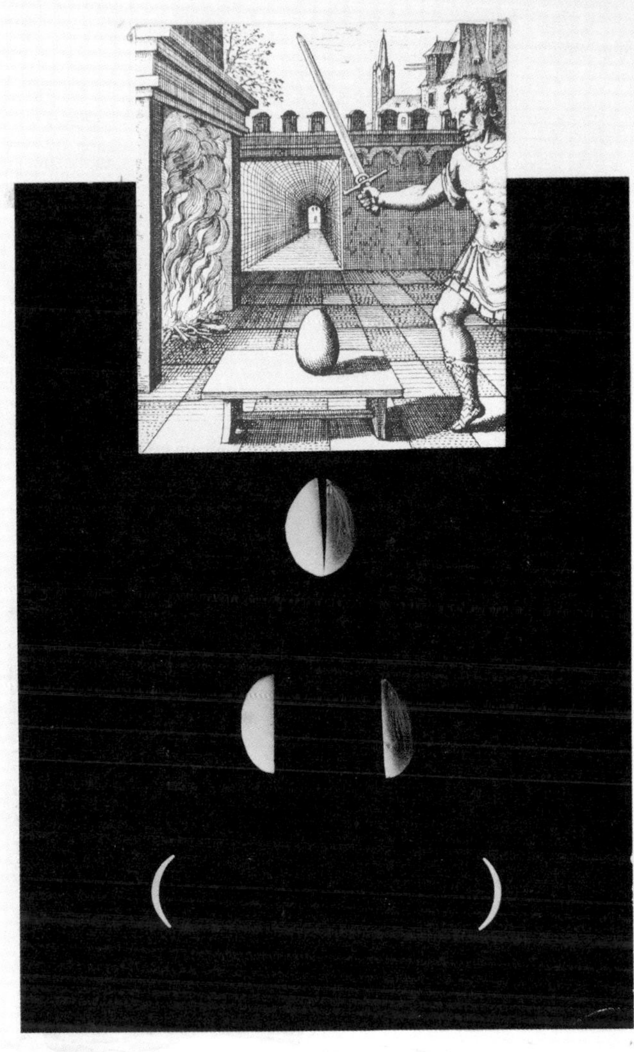

FIGURE 19 —
Eclissi alchemica (Alchemic Eclipse), 1995.
Photomechanical print on paper, 14⅞ ×
10¼ in. (37.78 × 26.04 cm).

62

which was thriving in Italy in the 1970s. So, indirectly, all twentieth-century international avant-gardism that nourished the research of those Brazilians and that inspired Italian *poesia visiva* [Visual Poetry] have influenced me, like Futurism and Dadaism. I was especially interested in the study of the Futurist concept of words-in-freedom. It captured the visual value of letters in part by overcoming all mechanisms of syntax and grammar. I also discovered some relationship between my work and the seventeenth-century alchemists (Figure 19), the first visual poets, who stated that art had to be transformation and not creation.

——BK——

What made you start exploring East and West in works such as *I muri di Singapore (Walls of Singapore)* (1978) (Plate 11) and *Rima: oriente e occidente (Rhyme: East and West)* (2003) (Plate 28)?

——MB——

Rima: oriente e occidente is a work I did with Chima Sunada, a Japanese calligrapher and poet. She communicates in Japanese, and I in Italian, so our bridge is English. The work focuses on the letters "h" and "y," which rhyme visually, just as the Italian words *oriente* and *occidente* (East and West) rhyme phonetically. I am not only enchanted by the mystery of the cosmos, but also by the complementarity, with one another, of all the different human cultures that have so richly developed on the surface of earth.

——BK——

You want to close the show with *Moon/ument* (2011) (Plate 19). How does this relate to your interest in cosmic problems?

——MB——

I am not an astrophysicist, nor a biologist, nor a prophet. I am a visual poet. *Moon/ument* is in some way the spatial counterpart of my *Operation Orpheus* (1982–85) (Figure 32). With *Operation Orpheus* I had concealed the symbol of life in the depth of an underground cavern, where not even an H-bomb could have reached and destroyed it. With *Moon/ument*, I wanted to export poetry into space, out of our planet, to imaginatively sow the symbol of life where there is no life. And with that image, I meant to celebrate the unity of the cosmos in the most primary reachable context, where there are no nations.

——BK——

You have been a practicing artist for over fifty years. What do you think are the biggest changes that have taken place in your work over this time? Have there been any key discoveries or turning points in your career?

——MB——

The biggest changes in my work? From painting to poetry. From play of words to sculpture. My work has not become deeper, weaker, or more detached from reality. There has only been a kind of enlargement, not of the work itself but of the source of inspiration. To illustrate this, I am now most interested in "cosmic" problems. I think that achieving the means to explore cosmic space may open a new era, if our planet will not be destroyed by our own foolishness.

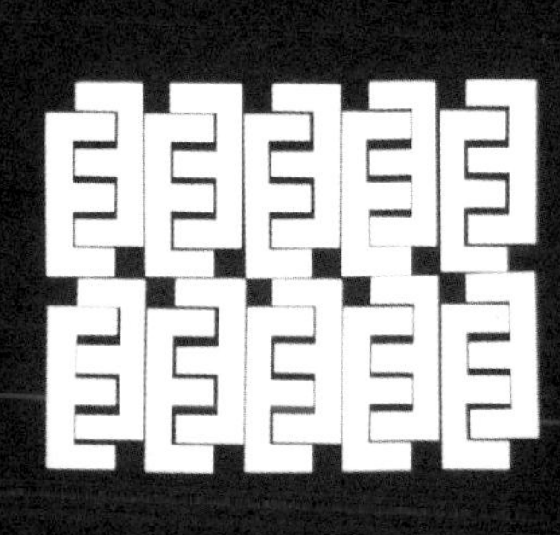

BACK TO THE PICTOGRAM: AN INQUIRY INTO THE NATURE OF COMMUNICATION

Franca Zoccoli

When one grows old, ancient memories flash back with unwonted clarity. Mirella Bentivoglio remembers a seemingly insignificant episode from her early childhood. Once—she must have been three or four years old—she ran away. Not because she was angry or as a protest of any kind, but simply for the pleasure of walking in the streets unaccompanied, of looking at people, choosing her way. It was an omen of what her life as an artist was going to be: a long journey away from the secluded domestic sphere and even the quiet realm of libraries, into public space, trying to give such space fresh meaning by discovering new metaphors and overthrowing outdated symbols.

In all the stages of her career, from the initial Concrete to Visual Poetry, from the object-books and the sculptural letters to the works in sequential pages, Bentivoglio never wanted to belong to a group in a formal sense, since she wished to be free from all rules, to take from here and not there, to mix codes to her own liking. One of her early works, *Gabbia (Ho) (Cage [I Have])* (1966/1969) (Plate 7), is in many ways a summation of this position, a refusal of limitations: even a label identifying you with a particular art movement is something you possess and that may hamper the freedom of creativity.

The street is always, for Bentivoglio, a source of inspiration and a destination—real or ideal. The works made with crushed cans (Plate 13), pieces of asphalt, or traffic signs (Plate 21) answer the same compulsion. "It is like the drive," says the artist, "which pushes graffitists to write on public walls their words, even the most intimate. Mine is an orderly graffiti, which does not do damage."[1] The artist was also struck by the rhetorical bombast of monuments located along the streets or in the middle of squares celebrating men (not women) who were often responsible for the death or ruin of multitudes: generals who had won great battles, statesmen and politicians who had learned "to quench the blushes of ingenious shame" (as Thomas Gray already complained in the middle of the eighteenth century). Throughout her career, Bentivoglio has expressed her dissent with such monuments and has suggested instead more vital symbols: the early portfolio *Monumento (Monument)* (1968) (Figure 6), in which the monument is deconstructed and crumbles, to

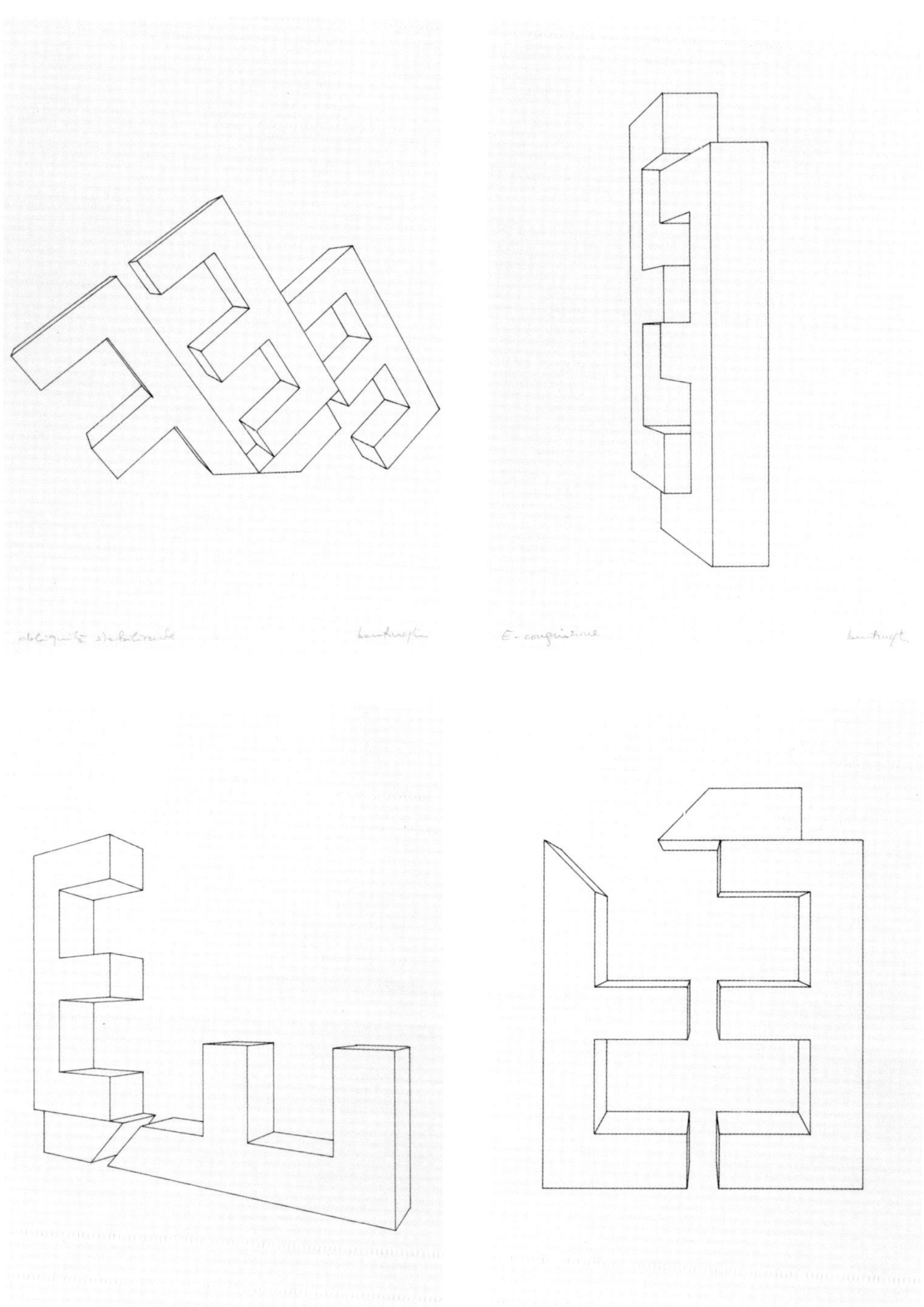

FIGURE 21—
Moduli a E (E Combinations), 1980. Ink on paper drawings after 1977 wooden constructions, 11⅝ × 8¼ in. (29.53 × 20.96 cm).

Clockwise, from top left: *Obliquitá stabilizzate (Stabilized Obliquities)*; *E = congiunzione (And = conjunction)*; *Mutilazione per accentuazione (la porta dell'essere) (Mutilation for Accentuation [The Door of Being])*; *Predominio sull'altro (Predominance Over the Other)*

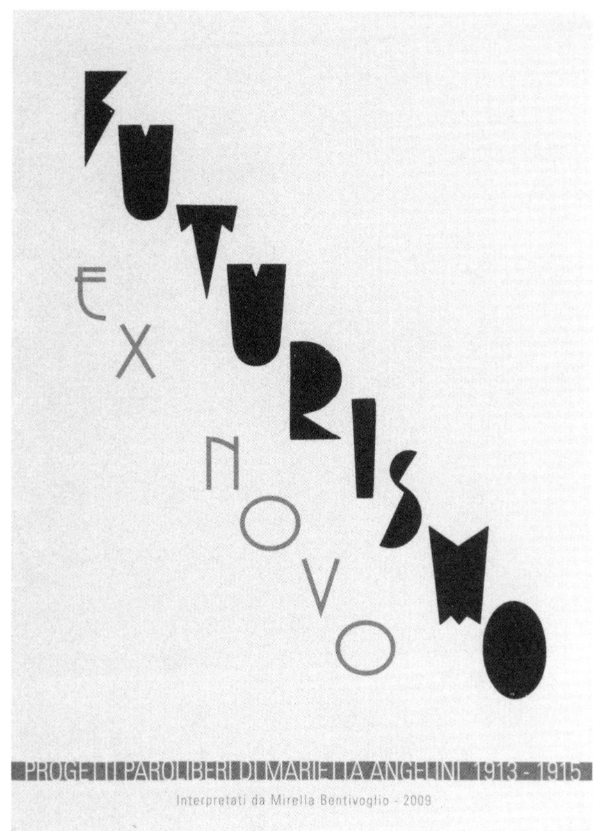

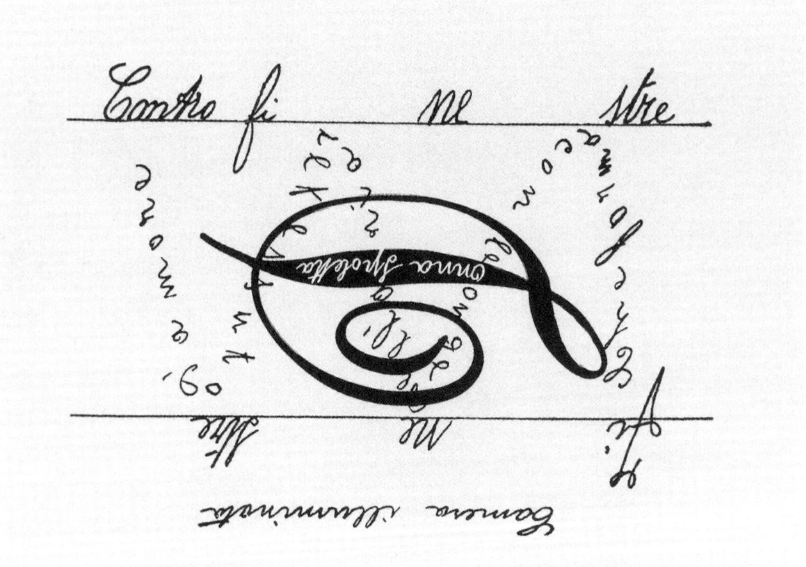

FIGURE 22 —
Futurismo ex novo (Futurism Anew) (frontispiece
and interior page), 2008–10. Offset lithography
on paper, 13¼ × 9½ in. (33.66 × 24.13 cm).

be born again as something different; *JeruSalem* (2012) (Figure 24), the *monument trouvé* for the witches of Salem, a huge water-tank right on the top of the hill, the site of their martyrdom; and finally, the *Moon/ument* (2011) (Plate 19), a symbol of life, brought to that celestial body. As Martin Heidegger emphasized, a work of art is always an allegory, a key to interpreting the surrounding reality.

When Bentivoglio felt the need to conquer the third dimension and passed "from page to space," she seldom used words but, rather, single letters. Most of the time they are vowels, and among the five vowels, her favorites are "o" and "e," which in Italian are complete words (conjunctions), while "u" has no autonomous value and "a" and "i" are respectively a preposition and an article and therefore need the support of a noun. The artist eradicates the letter she has selected, so as to extract its hidden essence. "O" ("or" in Italian), the initial of "origin," becomes an egg or a womb, in straightforward metaphors legible to all (Figure 12). "E" ("and" in Italian), set in various combinations, investigates the dynamics of relationships, as in her series *Moduli a E (E Combinations)* (Figure 21). In her voyage to the root of things, Bentivoglio went from words to letters and then back to the pictogram, a move that parallels the appearance of contemporary icons within our computerized world. In this way, the Stone Age and the digital era combine in her work: the heaviness of materials— marble, bronze—and the ethereal substance of the web.

"The society of the image" was an expression commonly employed in the 1970s. Sight had become the privileged sense, continuously stimulated by advertising and other kinds of visual messages; the prevalence of the identification of a word with an image, however, where an icon takes the place of a word or a short sentence, is a much more recent phenomenon. An example is the widely used "emoticon," which finds an old precedent in the universal symbol of a heart meaning "I love." When Pope Benedict XVI resigned at the end of February 2013, several banners were seen showing "the sad face," with the lips turned downward, among the crowd that filled St. Peter's Square to express their sorrow. This might at first have appeared disrespectful, but it was simply the language of our global, multiethnic world: whatever the country from which they came, everyone could understand it. Bentivoglio foresaw this need to overcome the impending disasters brought about by the new Tower of Babel (Plate 32), and sought a remedy by studying the tools and devices of communication and going deep into their super-imposed layers to find their innermost secrets and meanings.

There are also several works in which Bentivoglio sets aside altogether both words and individual letters, but maintains her ever-present playfulness.

Her book-objects are among the most notable in this category. Made of marble or other natural materials, they are open as if ready to be read yet dried-up like fossils, thus allowing no consultation (Plate 15). Here, it is the shape itself that speaks, being automatically associated with learning. But writing slips in here too, unobtrusively: veins, string-like drawings, patches, and rounded bulges suggest mysterious texts from time immemorial.

The artist alternates her work as a visual poet and as a critic, which reciprocally feed each other. In the latter field, the contributions of women to art have always been her central concern. Over the span of three decades, Bentivoglio has worked strenuously to expand our knowledge of women artists working in the area between language and image; she has organized hundreds of exhibitions in almost every country in Europe, as well as throughout the world, from North to South America and from Asia to Australia. The purpose of this engagement was not primarily to document gender-specific features within women's art but rather to correct the imbalance between the two sexes in public exhibitions and museum collections. Bentivoglio's attitude toward feminism is the same as that toward any organized group or movement: she rejects strict militancy, even as she acknowledges that the movement has nourished her work.

The discovery that a written word, besides being a container of meaning and sound, has a shape, and therefore constitutes an image, has a long history, dating back to the early Middle Ages. The real forerunners of Visual Poetry, however, were the Futurists of the early twentieth century, with their free-word compositions and other graphic and typographic experiments. One can therefore understand Bentivoglio's great interest in the women artists of that movement, who ventured into the area "between word and image." She examined each of them in two books, rediscovering or reassessing artists who often were almost unknown.[2] Even though Futurism had a misogynistic bias (often contradicted, however, by its founder Filippo Tommaso Marinetti), it advocated change and dismantled, among others, the stereotypes of womanhood. Bentivoglio wanted to pay special homage to Futurist women by compiling a portfolio, *Futurismo ex novo (Futurism Anew)* (2008–10) (Figure 22), using typefaces of that time period to reproduce some of their preliminary projects and including a commentary in which she attempts to interpret and revive interest in their work.

More recently, Bentivoglio has favored sequential works. We no longer find individual monuments but rather ongoing stories that proceed through what Gilles Deleuze called *la répétition différente*.[3] Rather than book-objects, upturned trees, or huge eggs of stone, in these works, sheets follow one another, such as the series dedicated to Lina Cavalieri (*Lina e il cavaliere [Lina and the Knight]*, 2012 [1978]) (Figure 23) and *Facce Murate (Walled Faces)* (2005) (Plates 22 and 23), in which Borrominian faces are lined up along a street in Prague, inside niches normally used for advertising. These "wrathful countenances of rock"[4] (the gigantic posters frame only the central portion of the face) stand motionless above the incessant flow of traffic. It is as if Bentivoglio felt the need to recover the page that she once had abandoned, and close the circle of her long journey with works open to interpretation, seasoned with the salt of irony, and in tune with our time of frantic evolution, whose outcomes can hardly be foreseen.

—

ENDNOTES —

1. Mirella Bentivoglio, conversation with author.

2. See Mirella Bontivoglio and Franca Zoccoli, *The Women Artists of Italian Futurism—Almost Lost to History* (New York: Midmarch Arts Press, 1997); and Mirella Bentivoglio and Franca Zoccoli, *Le futuriste italiane nelle arti visive (The Women Artists of Italian Futurism in the Visual Arts)* (Rome: De Luca Editori d'Arte, 2008). The Italian publication was an expanded version of the earlier English language version. Bentivoglio wrote the first section in both books ("*Da pagina a spazio*" [From Page to Space]), while Zoccoli wrote the second ("The Shape of Speed," in the 1997 version, and "*I colori e le forme dalla pittura alle arti applicate*" [Colors and Forms from Painting to the Applied Arts], in the 2008 publication).

3. Gilles Deleuze, *Difference and Repetition*, trans. Paul Patton (New York: Columbia University Press, 1995 [1968]).

4. Mirella Bentivoglio, conversation with author.

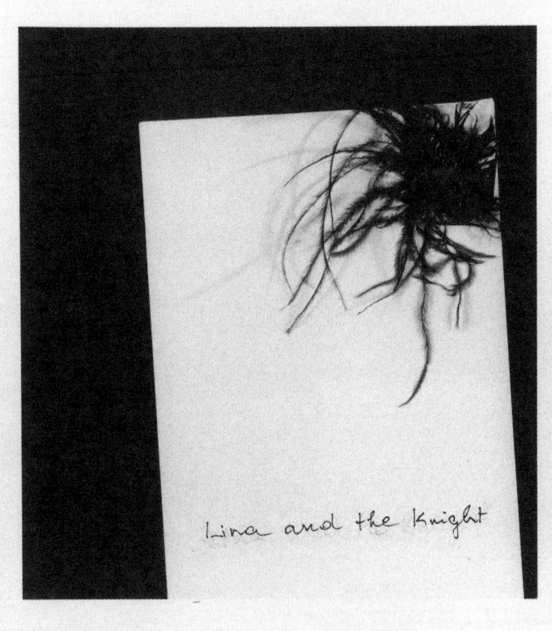

A poetic strip by Mirella Bentivoglio, 1978, from Michetti's photograph
"Lina Cavalieri".

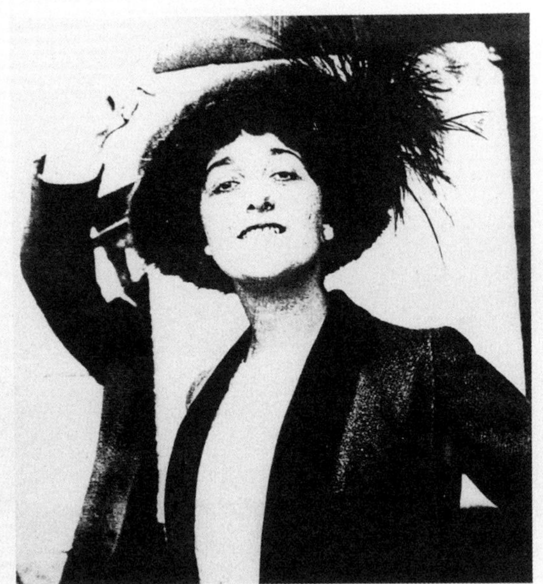

Michetti's photograph. The knight peeps out of a cloth which he holds up
behind the figure of Lina. Is photography too crude a medium for the
celebration of a woman? He mediates the photograph.

FIGURE 23 (facing page and following spread)—
Lina e il cavaliere (Lina and the Knight), 2012
(1978). Eight photomechanical prints on
paper, 15½ × 11⅝ in. (39.37 × 29.53 cm) each.

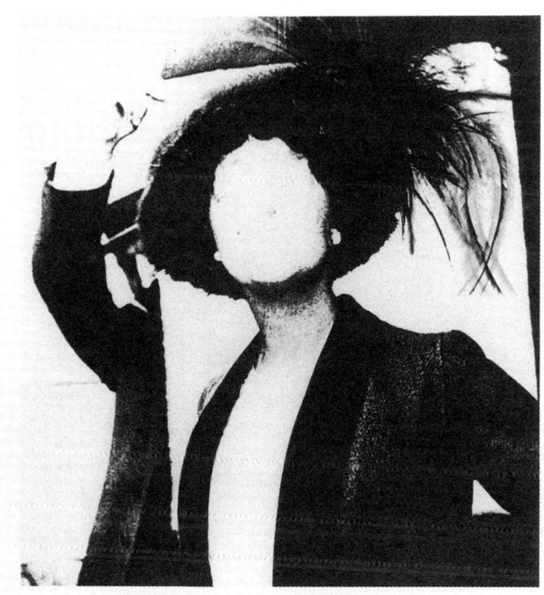

The cloth suggests the painter's canvas. Woman is an abstraction, an icon created by man. Lina is absent, the protagonist is woman.

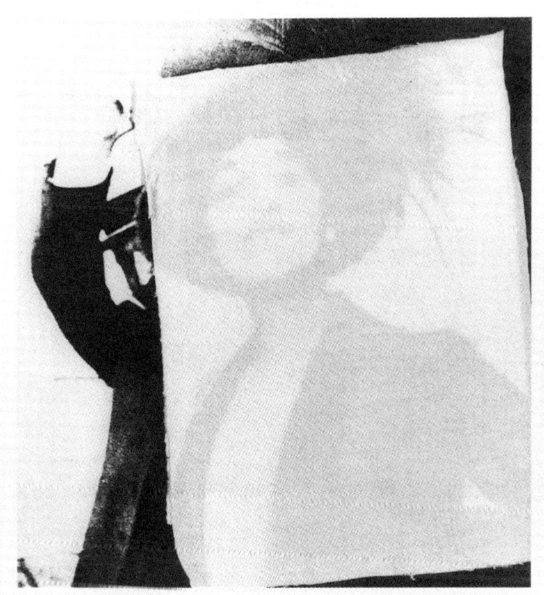

If Lina is only a ritual image, the cloth really covers the person Lina. A pictorial phantom appears through it.

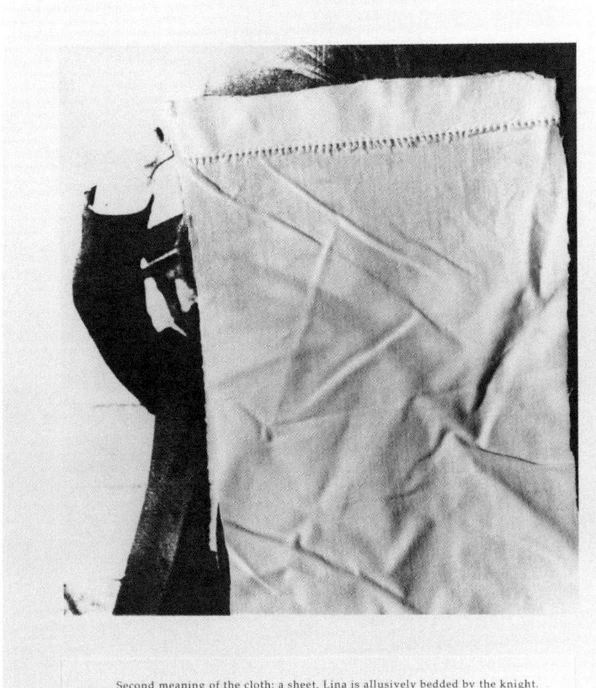

Second meaning of the cloth: a sheet. Lina is allusively bedded by the knight.

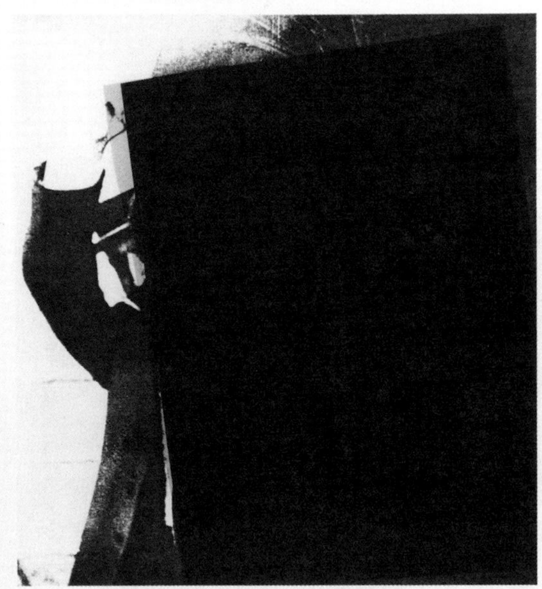

Lina is therefore only a symbol, a madonna, or only an object, a body, and the cloth is the sum of the cancellations of Lina.

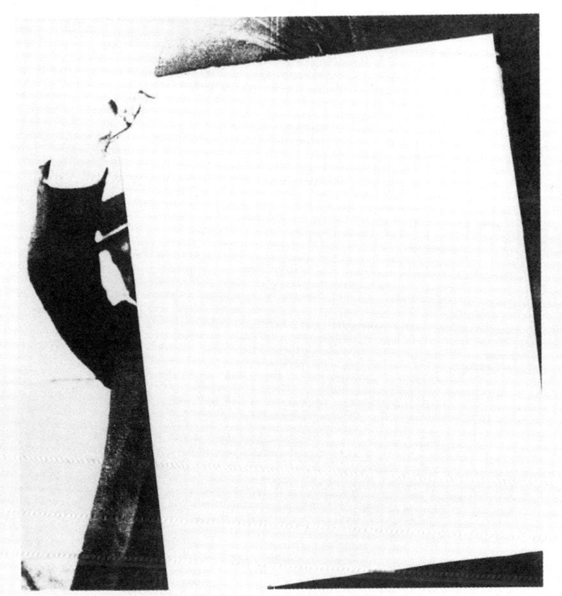

Today the cloth is the white flag of the knight ready to surrender to the reality of Lina. Or is it the blank page on which Lina is going to write her own chapter?

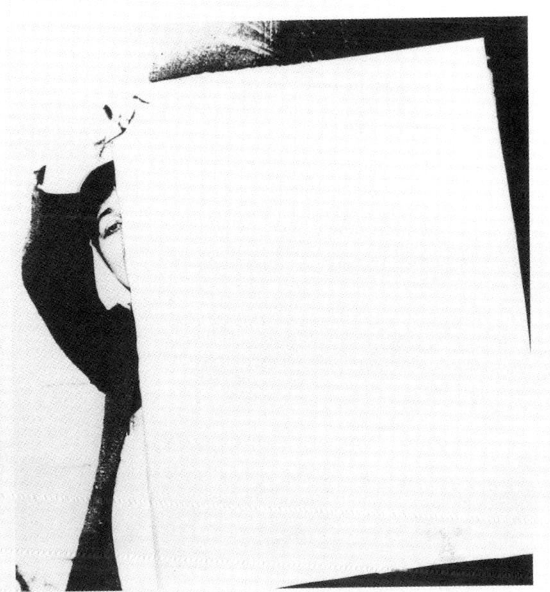

No, the page on which Lina will write herself can only be held by Lina. Behind the cloth she now peeps out from real space.

JeruSalem

Text by Mirella Bentivoglio, photos by Amelia Etlinger

In 1977, in Massachusetts where I was the guest of Amelia
Etlinger, the two of us made a trip to the nearby town of
Salem, as though on a pilgrimage. Towards the end of the
17th century, fourteen women accused of witchcraft had
been executed there, by hanging.
According to the documents, the scaffold had stood on the
hill on the city's outskirts. We knew that the place displayed
no marker in memory of the event.

FIGURE 24 (facing page and following page)—
JeruSalem, 2012. Five photomechanical
prints, 10¾ × 7¹¹⁄₁₆ in. (27.31 × 19.53 cm) each.

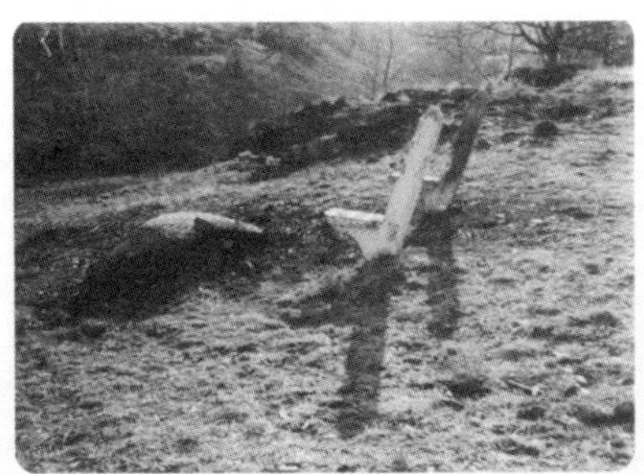

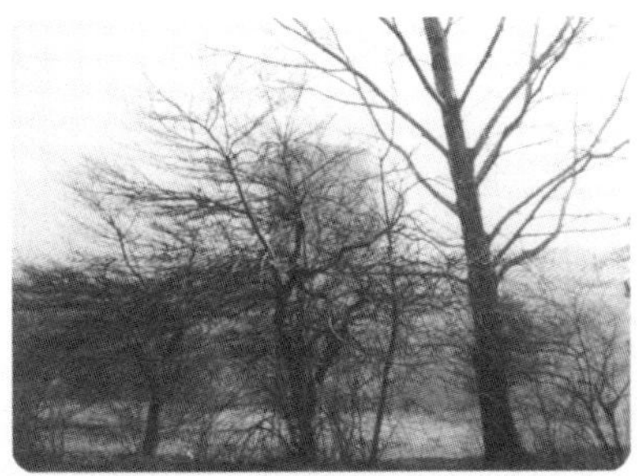

We could find no easy path uphill. In the midst of the thicket at its base, no trail could be discerned. We walked to a rise that faced the hill, and noticed a strange bench, with no backrest and no seat: a bench for ghosts, half-sunk into the soil of the underbrush.

I managed somehow to sit there, while Amelia took photographs. I looked off into the distance before me. From exactly that point, something on the hill in front of me seemed to come into view behind a dense group of trees.

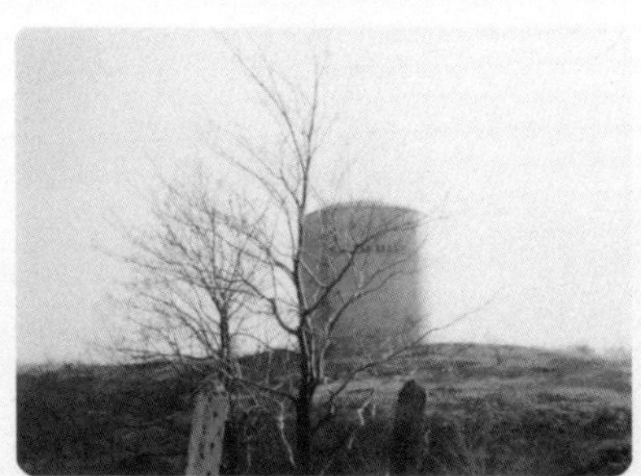

This felt to us like an invitation. We made our difficult way up the ravine that divided the rise from the hill, and at its summit we saw a gigantic cylindrical container which from no point before had been visible.

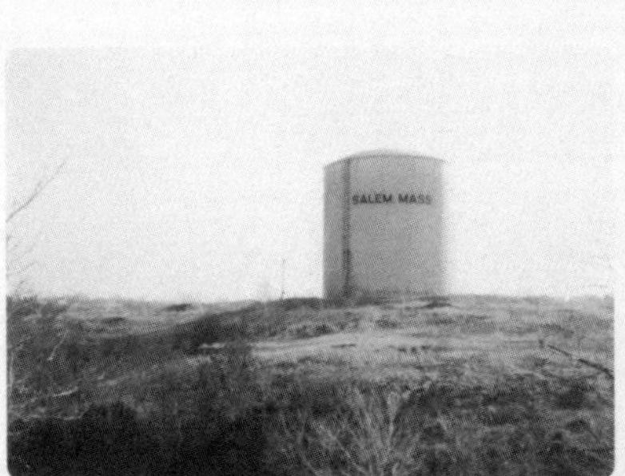

Woman and water: primary elements. That, precisely, must have been the site of the execution! Placed by chance, and ready for us to recognize it, stood that crypto-monument with its inscription "Salem, Mass". Water, with which, as well, to put out the fires of all witches' pyres. Water, for the washing of history.

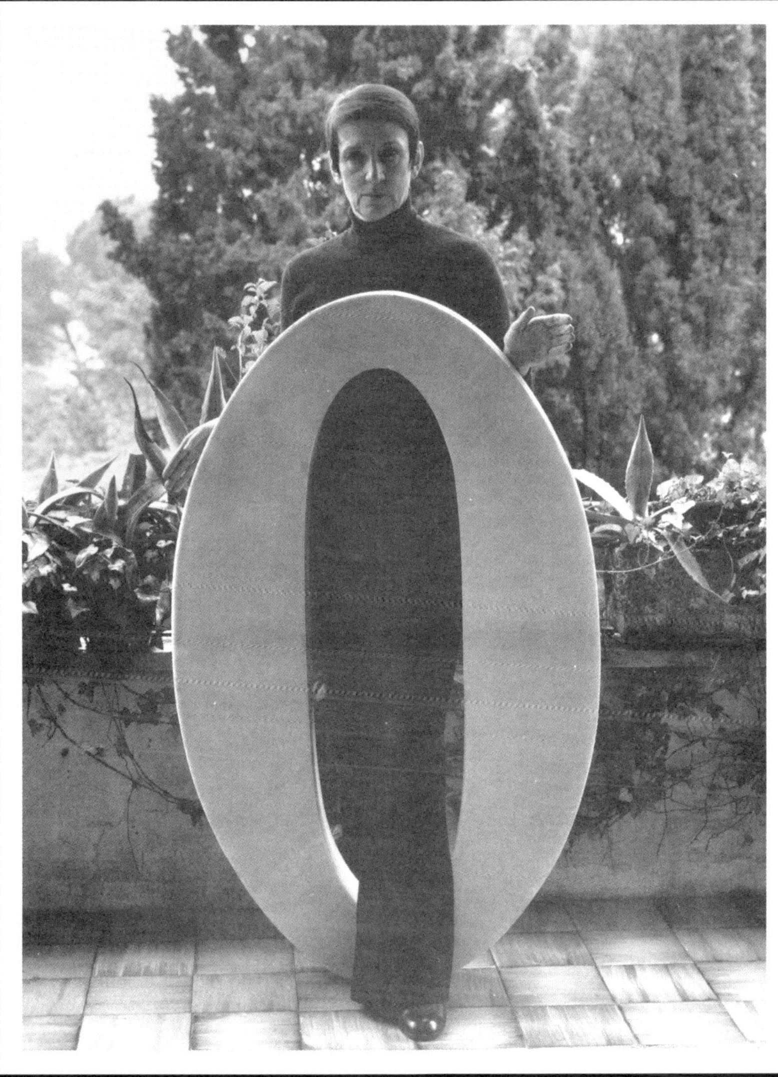

FIGURE 25—
Io (Me), Mirella Bentivoglio in the 1970s.

CURATORIAL PRACTICE AND THE LANGUAGE OF ITALIAN FEMINISM IN THE WORK OF MIRELLA BENTIVOGLIO

Leslie Cozzi

In the late 1970s, Mirella Bentivoglio produced a strikingly idiosyncratic photograph of herself standing within a chest-height letter "o" (Figure 25). The resulting image compressed the figure of the artist and her work into a single word: "*io*"—the first person pronoun and a noun meaning ego or self in Italian. Bentivoglio's image is more than a witty pun on the tautological nature of self-portraiture. Rather, it is a demonstration of the centrality of language to her practice and a confident declaration of her prominence and visibility as an artist at a time when the very possibility of female artistic accomplishment was hotly debated.

Bentivoglio's self-recognition was a matter of practical, and not merely theoretical, concern, as her multifaceted practice as an artist, curator, critic, and historian was deeply tied to the changing status of women. Since the 1970s, Bentivoglio has organized over two dozen exhibitions that explored the connection between image and text in work by both male and female artists. Of particular significance for this essay are her women-only exhibitions of the 1970s that engaged with contemporary feminist concerns and presented works by women artists to a broad audience. Between 1971 and 1981 alone, Bentivoglio curated fourteen different installations that spanned four countries and three continents.[1] Thanks in large part to her efforts as a curator, a sizeable number of women began to be taken seriously within the Italian art world and continue to enjoy international recognition.

Dovetailing with her larger curatorial program, Bentivoglio's own work challenged both gender norms and disciplinary boundaries. Her early work was characterized by an interest in language as a malleable, material substance. She began her career as a poet, but by the late 1960s abandoned traditional linear verse poetry for the relatively young and experimental fields of Visual and Concrete Poetry—interrelated hybrid art forms employing both text and image, often in the form of collage. Derived from earlier forms of experimental, imagistic poetry, Visual and Concrete Poetry freed words from the traditional formal requirements of structure and syntax in order to gain expressive freedom, disrupt normative modes of communication, and render language more corporeal. Though they differed in their approach to language—Visual Poetry generally combined word and image, whereas Concrete Poetry treated words *as* images—they shared an iconoclastic spirit and an emphasis on the formal components of language.[2]

Many of Bentivoglio's early works deconstruct and reassemble a single word or phrase in order to illuminate meanings buried within the text. In the 1966 silkscreen *Gabbia (Ho) (Cage [I Have])* (Plate 7), for instance, Bentivoglio rearranges the letters in the Italian word *ho* to resemble a prison. The stark black vertical and horizontal lines of the capital "H's" appear as bars, while a single letter "o" at the bottom right, in a rich red, forms a trap door that both punctures and punctuates the structure. Along the bottom margin of the work, Bentivoglio provides the viewer with a miniscule line of text: "*gabbia(:HO)*." This phrase functions not only as a title, but also as a key to deciphering the work.

"*Ho*" translates as "I have," and thus the arrangement of the letters implies that people are imprisoned by their own desire to possess. Yet the word "*ho*" is also often employed in idiomatic expressions that use the equivalent of the English verb "to be." "*Ho fame*," "*Ho sete*," and "*Ho sonno*," for example, mean "I am hungry" or thirsty, or sleepy, respectively. "*Ho*" is not an incidental word, but rather a common way to capture an individual's subjectivity by describing one's physical state. Deconstructing the word allows Bentivoglio to release its hidden connotations, which she refers to as "ellipses" or "illuminating contractions."[3] By arranging the word "*ho*" in the form of a prison, Bentivoglio acknowledges the limitations of language as a tool for self-expression. At the same time, by imbuing the word's physical arrangement with significance, she seeks to transgress those boundaries. Bentivoglio's project can be compared with the French poet Stéphane Mallarmé's search for "a hypothetically or mythically original language, ideally and miraculously expressive, such that everyday language *is not*."[4] Refuting the arbitrariness of signs, Bentivoglio instead suggests an intimate, physical link between the formal substance of language and the thoughts it is capable of expressing.

In several early works, Bentivoglio used language as a vehicle through which to illuminate the idiosyncrasies of human relationships. The silkscreen *L'(assente), positivo/negativo, segno/figura (The Absent One, Positive/Negative, Sign/Figure)* (1971) (Figure 26), for example, depicts the Italian definite article "the" in stark white on a black background. This version of

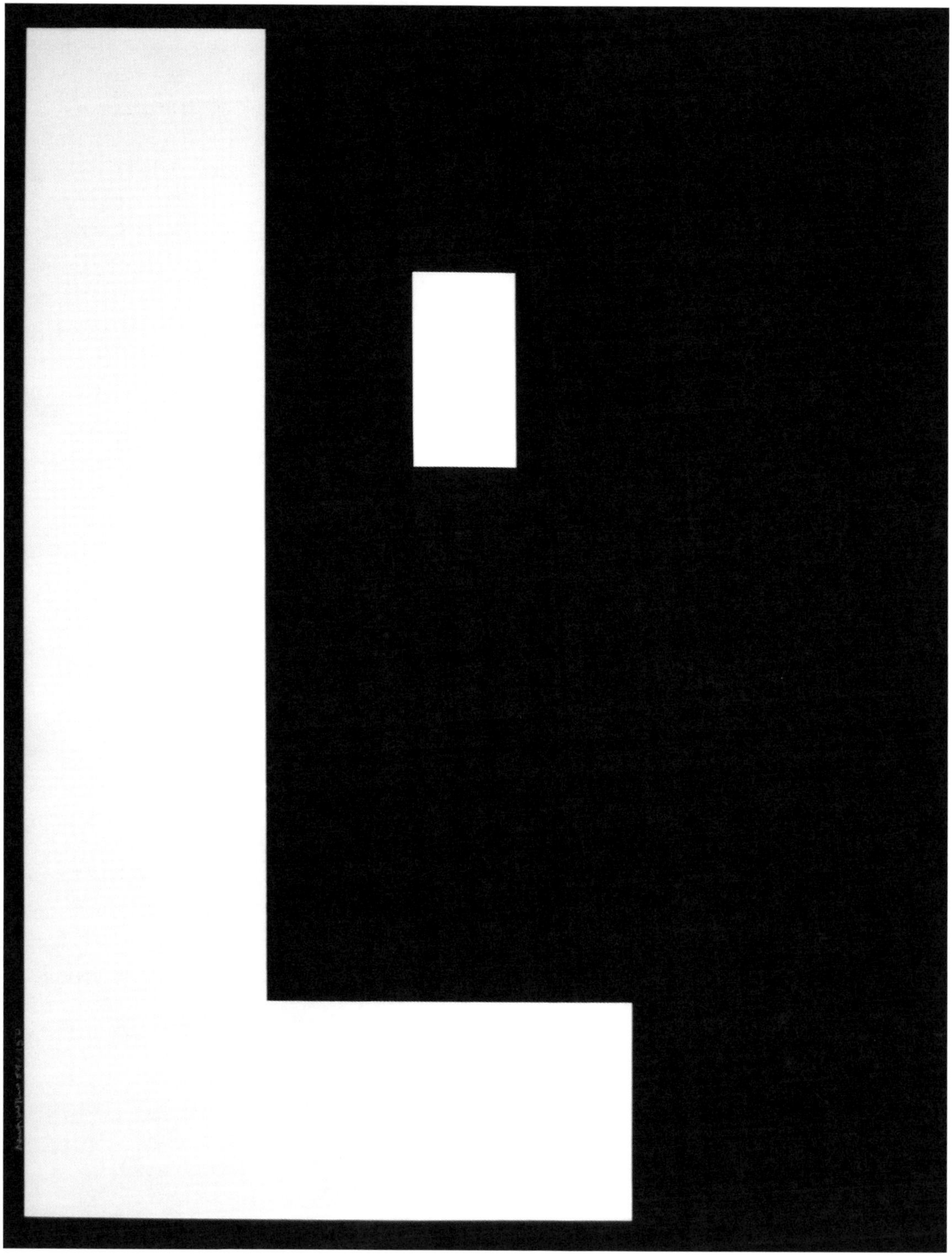

FIGURE 26 —
*L'(assente), positivo/negativo, segno/figura (The
Absent One, Positive/Negative, Sign/Figure)*, 1971.
Serigraph on paper, 24⅝ × 19 in. (62.55 × 48.26 cm).

l' = the

the definite article is always used in cases where the noun begins with a vowel, such that the article attaches to the word itself (for example, *l'automobile* [the car] as opposed to *la donna* [the woman]) and is incomplete without it. But Bentivoglio has left the corresponding noun out of the image. Here she again uses the title of the work as a key to its interpretation, since *"assente"* in Italian refers to someone or something that is missing. The white letter and apostrophe on black ground reverse the color scheme of traditional printed text, allowing the black ground to stand in for the absence to which the title of the work refers. And the black absence that functions as the painting's parenthetical subject resembles the abstracted profile of a human face.

Bentivoglio, who recognized that absence implied a departed human presence, called *L'(assente)* an "ideogram of suspension. The current human situation."[5] *L'(assente)* plays with the notion of absence not just as a formal principle of composition—that is, by suggesting emptiness as an inevitable precondition of any figure/ground relationship—but as a metaphor for human coupling. The work epitomizes two persistent and interrelated tendencies in Bentivoglio's work—on the one hand, treating words as compositional elements whose form is central to their meaning and, on the other hand, imbuing language with personal and political significance. As her engagement with feminist concerns grew, Bentivoglio united these two impulses through a diverse spate of exhibitions in order to promote women's capacity for self-expression.

At issue within Bentivoglio's ongoing curatorial project was the relationship between men and women in the institutionalized art world—a subject that prompted various, and occasionally opposing, responses.[6] In 1970, the art critic Carla Lonzi and the artist Carla Accardi founded *Rivolta femminile*, a consciousness-raising group that produced some of Italy's most influential feminist theory. *Rivolta femminile* advocated for a separatist model of creative production, attempting to positively define and explore female difference through women-only cultural formations.[7] Others rejected separatism as an economically damaging and politically naïve response to the problem of women's marginalization. Writing in the introduction to Simona Weller's 1976 census of women in the Italian art world, the poet Cesare Vivaldi assessed the barriers to women's advancement in terms of career success. For Vivaldi, participation was a prerequisite for professionalism, which was the true litmus test of artistic achievement:

> The dilettante whose works do not induce anyone to buy them or listen to them or to see them or to read them earns neither real social prestige nor a true personal identity. Such things are reserved for whoever makes the effort, to whoever acquires the competence and the experience to become a professional.[8]

Vivaldi suggests that women who were not respected by the mainstream art establishment were not only relegated to second-rate status as artists, but also limited as human beings. Arguing for integration, he rejects the self-imposed division advocated by separatist theorists.

It would fall to Bentivoglio to bridge these opposing strategies regarding women's cultural importance through her curatorial practice. Over the course of the 1970s and throughout the next several decades, she organized a number of landmark touring exhibitions of women working with text and image in a variety of formats. Fulfilling the goals expressed by both separatists and those who favored participation in the mainstream art world, Bentivoglio exploited the logic of what she dubbed the "ghetto show" to establish art world parity while exploring the unique nature of women's creativity.[9] Bentivoglio organized her first exhibition of all-women artists in 1971, the same year she held her first solo show. One year later, she curated an exhibition at fellow visual poet Ugo Carrega's alternative art space Centro Tool. The idea for the exhibition rested on the premise that, due to the scarcity of women artists, such a show would fit the small space comfortably. Indeed, in Italy in 1972, it appeared that there were few women artists to be seen.[10]

Bentivoglio's early curatorial program propelled female visual poets into mainstream recognition. She was, in fact, part of a growing contingent of artists who were, as Gabriele Schor has explained, "conscious of the fact that women had to claim their terrain, to self-consciously live their lives as artists."[11] In self-consciously living her life as an artist, however, Bentivoglio simultaneously critiqued the very terrain she was claiming. In *La firma (The Signature)* (Figure 27), for example, a collage she created in 1973, she furnishes a wry exploration of the way artistic gestures are imbued with financial value and symbolic importance. In the piece, Bentivoglio cuts her last name out of a 1,000 Lira bill—then the average price for a piece of Concrete Poetry—and places it at the center of the composition against a black ground. However, the artist omits the final two letters from the central design, instead substituting them for the signature at the bottom right of her collage. "*Io*," as discussed at the beginning of this essay, is the Italian first person pronoun, which exists in the work both alongside and in place of the artist's name. Conflating the work's subject with its author, "*io*" ceases to function

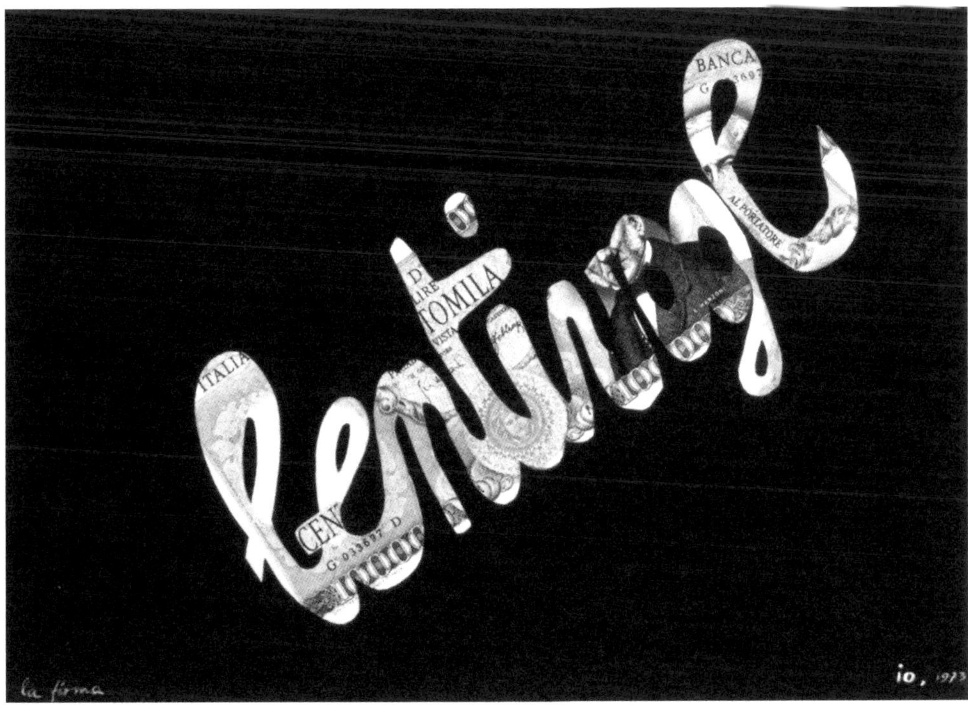

as a universal part of speech and instead self-reflexively refers to the artist herself. In a sense, "*io*" functions as an artist's monogram, an early form of establishing artistic copyright. In discussing this work, Bentivoglio insisted:

> I am the person who has mutilated my name, substituted my signature for the work, placed the money inside the name, put the pronoun in place of the signature. I am the individual who can express her liberty only through contradiction, and breaks the rules of the game by playing along.[12]

The artist declares her presence through a self-reflexive circuit of fragments. With one deft slice, she implicates the art market as part of the mechanism of exclusion that she must confront in order to subvert.

The annual exhibitions of women visual poets that Bentivoglio oversaw in the early years of the decade were so successful that by 1978 the mere existence of women artists in Italy was no longer in doubt. In the exhibition *Materializzazione del linguaggio (Materialization of Language)* (Figures 28 and 29), which Bentivoglio was invited to curate for the Venice Biennial, the roster

FIGURE 27 —
La firma (The Signature), 1973. Collage on paper, 19¾ × 27½ in. (50.16 × 69.85 cm).

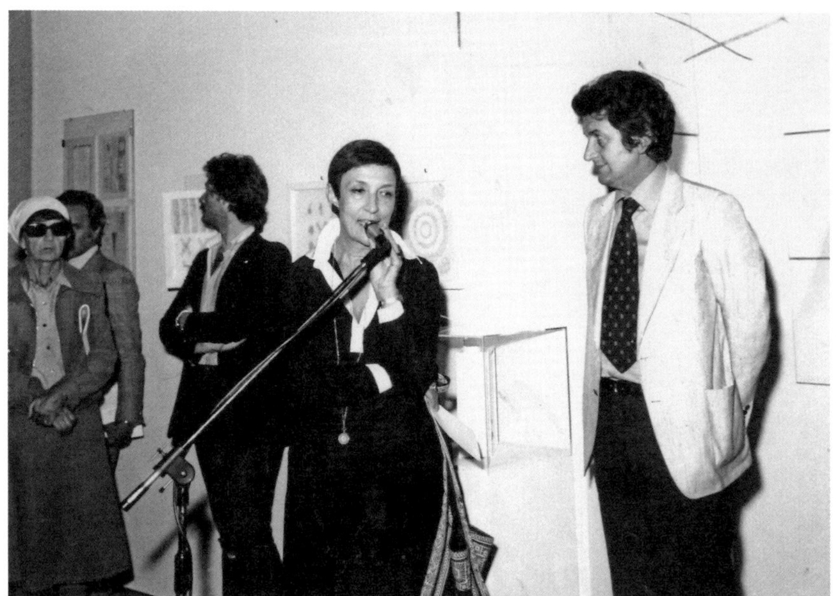

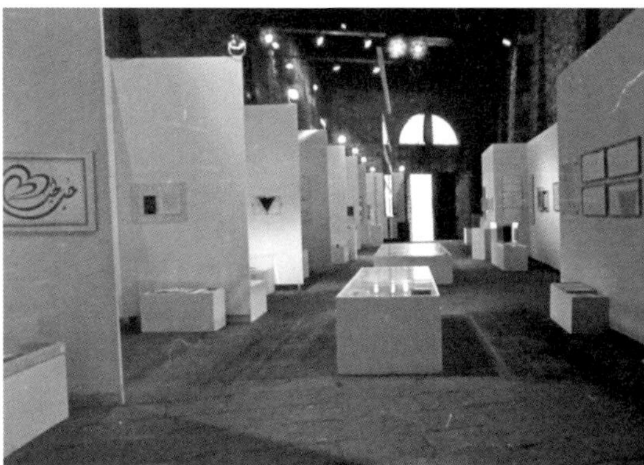

had expanded to include over 80 female contributors. *Materializzazione del linguaggio* was the first historical retrospective of women's art ever mounted at the Biennial, and the only exhibition that year to feature Soviet Bloc artists. It would go on to tour New York and the 1981 São Paolo Biennial, among other venues. Bentivoglio's subsequent shows continued to broaden in scope, as her curatorial reach expanded to include more historical as well as contemporary artists and to focus on more discrete subtopics, such as the concept of thread in work by women artists.[13] Her aims also changed as she began to articulate a more nuanced and complex understanding of female subjectivity in relation to language, which drew heavily on the concepts expressed in her early works. For Bentivoglio, establishing women as artists meant more than just adding their names to the art world rolls. Rather, it entailed recognizing and appreciating the novel and creative ways in which women's work responded to historical, theoretical, and social constraints.

Bentivoglio was not the only artist occupied with the question of how to understand women's relationship to culture once the anonymity to which they had been assigned was lifted. This question was being confronted throughout the 1970s in Italy as well as internationally, and it would become

FIGURE 28 ⎯
Opening of *Materializzazione del linguaggio (Materialization of Language)* exhibition, Venice, 1978. Far left: Futurist artist Maria Ferrero Gussago; center: Mirella Bentivoglio; right: Mario Rigo, mayor of Venice.

a cardinal concern of Italian feminist theory.[14] In this respect, Bentivoglio's recurring fascination with the term "*io*" was prescient. As subsequent Italian critics would explain, that familiar word "*io*" not only functions as the first person pronoun regardless of the gender of the speaker, but also corresponds to the masculine noun meaning ego or self. Thus a simple, two-letter word contained an example of the mechanisms by which the masculine gender assumes a position of neutrality. Here is Adriana Cavarero, a pivotal Italian gender theorist, confronting this conundrum:

> The "I" of discourse, that same discourse that now (I) am thinking and writing in Italian, is unconcerned with its being of the male or female sex. As a noun, I [the word "self"] belongs to the masculine gender but, extraordinarily, a sexuation is not included in it. "I am a woman," "I am male": here the "I" sustains and gathers sexes indifferently, being in itself neutral."[15]

Language functions as both a form of alienation (because the female gender is repeatedly subsumed under the fictive objectivity of the male universal) and as a tool for self-expression (since literature allows women a means to represent their alienation from these existing codes). Although Bentivoglio's *La firma* predates Cavarero's text by over a decade, Bentivoglio's contention that she can "express her liberty only through contradiction" acknowledges this paradox. She manipulates the physical appearance of words in order to disrupt the meanings traditionally attached to them and to explore the ramifications of an artistic subject—*io*—no longer defined exclusively as male.

Bentivoglio's "I" did not merely refer to the artist as an individual creator but rather confronted the larger question of one's relationship to language—in other words, the "I" problematized in feminist discourse. In the photograph introduced at the beginning of this essay, Bentivoglio shows herself literally composing the word "*io*" with her body and a sculpted, slightly flattened letter "o." The composition is remarkably self-contained; she forms the letter "I" with her body and lifts her hands in a gesture of self-presentation. Her gaze is direct but does not convey any particular sentiment. The work is a tautology, a visual equivalent of the statement "I am me," rather than a vehicle for expressing psychological interiority. Forcing the word "*io*" (me) to signify a female subject in this particular action is a radical gesture. It challenges the assumed masculinity of the word while reinforcing Bentivoglio's status as an artist.

For a 2010 exhibition of self-portraits by women artists presented at the Uffizi Gallery in Florence, the curator Giovanna Giusti featured yet another

FIGURE 29 (facing, right)—
*Materializzazione del linguaggio
(Materialization of Language)* exhibition,
Venice, 1978. Installation view.

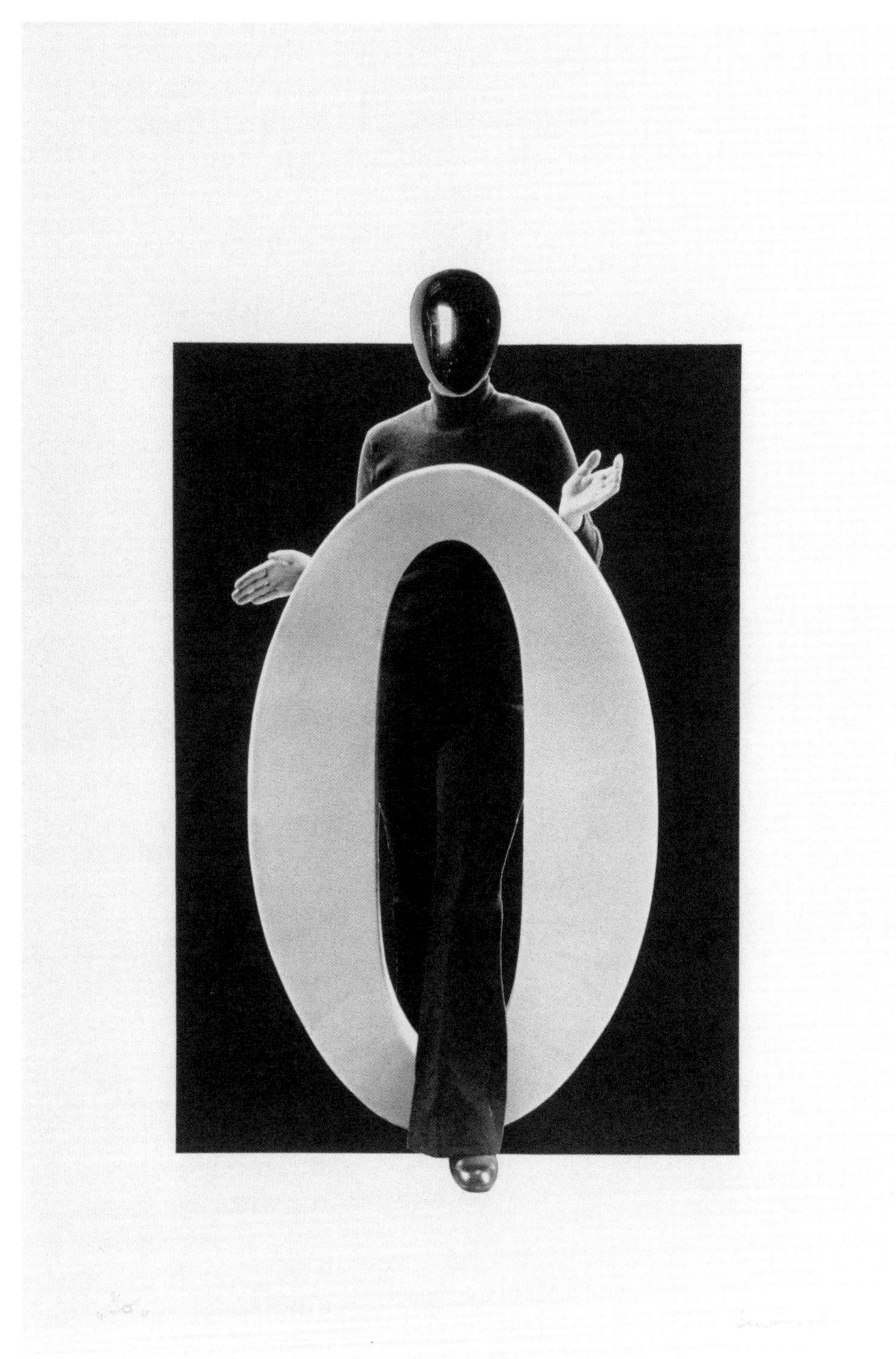

Io (Me), 1979. Photomechanical print
on paper, 23⅝ × 15¾ in. (60 × 40 cm).

version of Bentivoglio's "*io*"-themed works.[16] In this collage from 1979 (Figure 30), she manipulated the photograph discussed above by montaging an image of an egg over her face. The egg had become a central motif in Bentivoglio's work (one of the best-known examples is *L'Ovo di Gubbio [The Egg of Gubbio]* of 1976 [Figure 12]), and she identified it with the feminine, corporeal roots of language and with origins. Thus "*io*" also signifies a broader concept of artistic agency, of new beginnings in a world transformed by feminist theory and the work of women artists.

Bentivoglio was a driving force in changing the Italian art world of the 1970s. For the first time in the century, not only were large numbers of women recognized as artists, but their participation in the mainstream art world would also remain consistent over the following decades.[17] Surveying her activity twenty years later, Bentivoglio recognized the importance of her own contributions, remarking, "The ghetto-shows of the seventies bore fruit. They allowed for close study of the quality of women's work and began an exchange of information."[18] The continued interest in artists that she championed over forty years ago is one index of her lasting success; the international prominence of many Italian women artists who came after her is another.[19] Bentivoglio's recent donation to the MART (Museo di Arte Moderna e Contemporanea di Trento e Rovereto), Italy's premier modern and contemporary art museum, and the exhibition and catalog that accompanied the gift represent the capstone of her three decades of achievement as a curator. The collection, which she amassed largely through gifts from artists, comprises over 300 works by 112 women from 22 countries.[20]

Bentivoglio's curatorial endeavors transformed the art world by making connections among women—what Italian feminists refer to as "*fare cultura fra donne*" or creating culture among women.[21] Believing that women would achieve uncompromised self-expression in the realm of culture more so than on the battleground of politics, Bentivoglio has explained:

> It is customary in Italy to have a political party for protection. …My connection with other women is my party—just friendship. We give to each other, we analyze each other. …It's a network.[22]

Extending across linguistic and national boundaries, her curatorial network provided a catalyst for profound institutional change. The power and success of this network will remain one of Bentivoglio's most enduring legacies.

1. For a full list of Bentivoglio's curatorial work exclusively featuring women artists, see *Poesia visiva: La donazione di Mirella Bentivoglio al Mart* (Milan: Silvana Editoriale, 2011), pp. 200–201.

2. See Frances Pohl, *Love and Joy About Letters: The Work of Ben Shahn and Mirella Bentivoglio* (Claremont: Pomona College Museum of Art, 2003), pp. 22–30; Mary Ellen Solt, *Concrete Poetry: A World View* (Bloomington: Indiana University Press, 1968), p. 7; Vittorio Fagone, untitled essay, in Gillo Dorfles, Vittorio Fagone, Filiberto Menna et al., *La Poesia Visiva (1963–1979)* (Florence: Vallecchi, 1979), pp. 17–19; and Achille Bonito Oliva, "La parola totale," in Gabriella Belli et al., *La parola nell'arte: Ricerche d'avanguardia nel '900. Dal Futurismo a oggi attraverso le collezioni del Mart* (Milan: Skira, 2007), pp. 17–19.

3. Quoted in *Mirella Bentivoglio: La poesia fatta pietra* (Macerata: Coopedit Macerata/Pinacoteca e Musei Comunali, 1984), p. 7.

4. Gérard Genette, "Valéry and the Poetics of Language," in *Textual Strategies: Perspectives in Post-Structural Criticism*, ed. Josué Harari (Ithaca: Cornell University Press, 1979), p. 363.

5. Quoted in *Mirella Bentivoglio: La poesia fatta pietra*, p. 7.

6. In 1971, the year Bentivoglio organized her first all-female exhibition of Visual and Concrete Poetry, Linda Nochlin's groundbreaking essay "Why Have There Been No Great Women Artists?" was the cover story of the January issue of *ARTNews* (*ARTNews* 69, no. 9, January 1971, pp. 22–39, 70–71). Nochlin contended that for centuries women had been systematically excluded from the professional training necessary to function as an artist of any caliber, let alone a great one. The full essay was translated into Italian in 1976 (Linda Nochlin, "Perché non ci sono mai state grandi artiste donne," *nuova dwf* 1, no. 4 [1976], pp. 149–57).

7. See Judith Russi Kirshner, "Voices and Images of Italian Feminism," in *WACK! Art and the Feminist Revolution*, ed. Cornelia Butler (Los Angeles: Museum of Contemporary Art, 2007) pp. 386, 392; Rivolta femminile, "Manifesto di Rivolta femminile," in *I movimenti femministi in Italia: La nuova sinistra*, ed. Rosalba Spagnoletti (Rome: Edizioni Samonà e Savelli, 1971), p. 90; Lucia Chiavola Birnbaum, *Liberazione della donna: Feminism in Italy* (Middletown: Wesleyan University Press, 1986), pp. 80–87; and Carol Lazzaro-Weiss, *From Margins to Mainstream: Feminism and Fictional Modes in Italian Women's Writing, 1968–1990* (Philadelphia: University of Pennsylvania Press, 2011), pp. 33–64.

8. Cesare Vivaldi, introduction to Simona Weller, *Il Complesso di Michelangelo: Ricerca sul contributo dato dalla donna all'arte italiana del novecento* (Pollenza-Macerata: La Nuova Foglio Editrice, 1976), p. 11.

9. Mirella Bentivoglio, "Post-Scriptum," in Anna Maria Fioravanti Beraldi, *Post-Scriptum: Artiste in Italia tra linguaggio e immagine negli anni '60 e '70* (Cento [FE]: Siaca Arti Grafiche, 1998), p. 4. Bentivoglio's tactic, in its attempt to use sexual difference as a positive tool that would allow women to express their creative and social agency, can be compared to strategic essentialism as articulated by Gayatri Spivak, wherein essentialism is deployed as a self-conscious manoeuver in order to address questions of subjectivity and recover a speaking subject that has been written out of conventional historiography. Bentivoglio's conception of female creativity was, after all, provisional—it was articulated largely in response to a social situation she wanted to rectify, thus upholding the distinction Spivak draws between strategy and

theory. See Diana Fuss, *Essentially Speaking: Feminism, Nature, and Difference* (New York: Routledge, 1989), p. 31; and Gayatri Spivak with Ellen Rooney, "'In a Word': Interview," in *The Second Wave: A Reader in Feminist Theory*, ed. Linda Nicholson (New York: Routledge, 1997), p. 358.

10. Mirella Bentivoglio, "Una Testimonianza di Mirella Bentivoglio: Dieci Collettive al Femminile," *Informazioni Arti Visive* (December 1980), pp. 20–21.

11. Gabiele Schor, "The Feminist Avant-Garde: A Radical Transformation," in *Donna: Avanguardia femminista negli anni '70 dalla Sammlung Verbund di Vienna* (Verona: Electa, 2010), p. 25.

12. Quoted in *Mirella Bentivoglio: La poesia fatta pietra*, 16.

13. Bentivoglio, "Una Testimonianza di Mirella Bentivoglio," pp. 20–21.

14. See Section 4, "The Aesthetic," in *Feminism—Art—Theory: An Anthology, 1968–2000*, ed. Hilary Robinson (Oxford: Blackwell, 2001) for an introduction to these debates.

15. Adriana Cavarero, "Per una teoria della differenza sessuale," in Cavarero et al., *Diotima: Il pensiero della differenza sessuale* (Milan: La Tartaruga, 1987), p. 43.

16. Giovanna Giusti, *Autoritratte: Artiste di capriccioso e destrissimo ingegno* (Florence: Edizioni Polistampa, 2010).

17. Maria Antonietta Trasforini, "Ritratti di Signore: Una generazione di artiste in Italia," in *Arte a parte: Donne artiste fra margini e centro*, ed. Maria Antonietta Transforini (Milan: FrancoAngeli, 2000), pp. 145–47.

18. Bentivoglio, "Post-Scriptum," p. 4.

19. Artists that Bentivoglio championed early in their careers are still gaining international notice. Both Irma Blank and Maria Lai were included in the 2009–10 exhibition "elles@centrepompidou," for example, and Ketty La Rocca was recently featured in a 2014 solo exhibition at Wilkinson Gallery in London. Meanwhile, younger practitioners, including Vanessa Beecroft, Monica Bonvicini, Paula Pivi, and Elisabetta Benassi, all have well-established international reputations. See Camille Morineau, *elles@centrepompidou: Women Artists in the Collection of the Musée National d'Art Moderne, Centre de Création industrielle* (Paris: Centre Pompidou, 2009).

20. Mirella Bentivoglio, "I segni del femminile," in *Poesia visiva: La donazione di Mirella Bentivoglio al Mart*, p. 15.

21. Wendy Pojmann, "'We're right here!,' The Invisibility of Migrant Women in European Women's Movements: The Case of Italy," in Pojmann, *Migration and Activism in Europe Since 1945* (New York: Palgrave Macmillan, 2008), p. 195. For a brief introduction to some distinctive cultural elements of Italian feminism, see Lesley Caldwell, "Italian Feminism: Some Considerations," in *Women and Italy: Essays on Gender, Culture and History*, Zygmunt G. Baranski and Shirley W. Vinall, eds. (New York: St. Martin's Press, 1991), pp. 95–116.

22. Quoted in Judy Rosenberg, "Visual Poetry: The Avant-Garde in Italy," *Women Artists News* 6, nos. 2–3 (Summer 1980), p. 8.

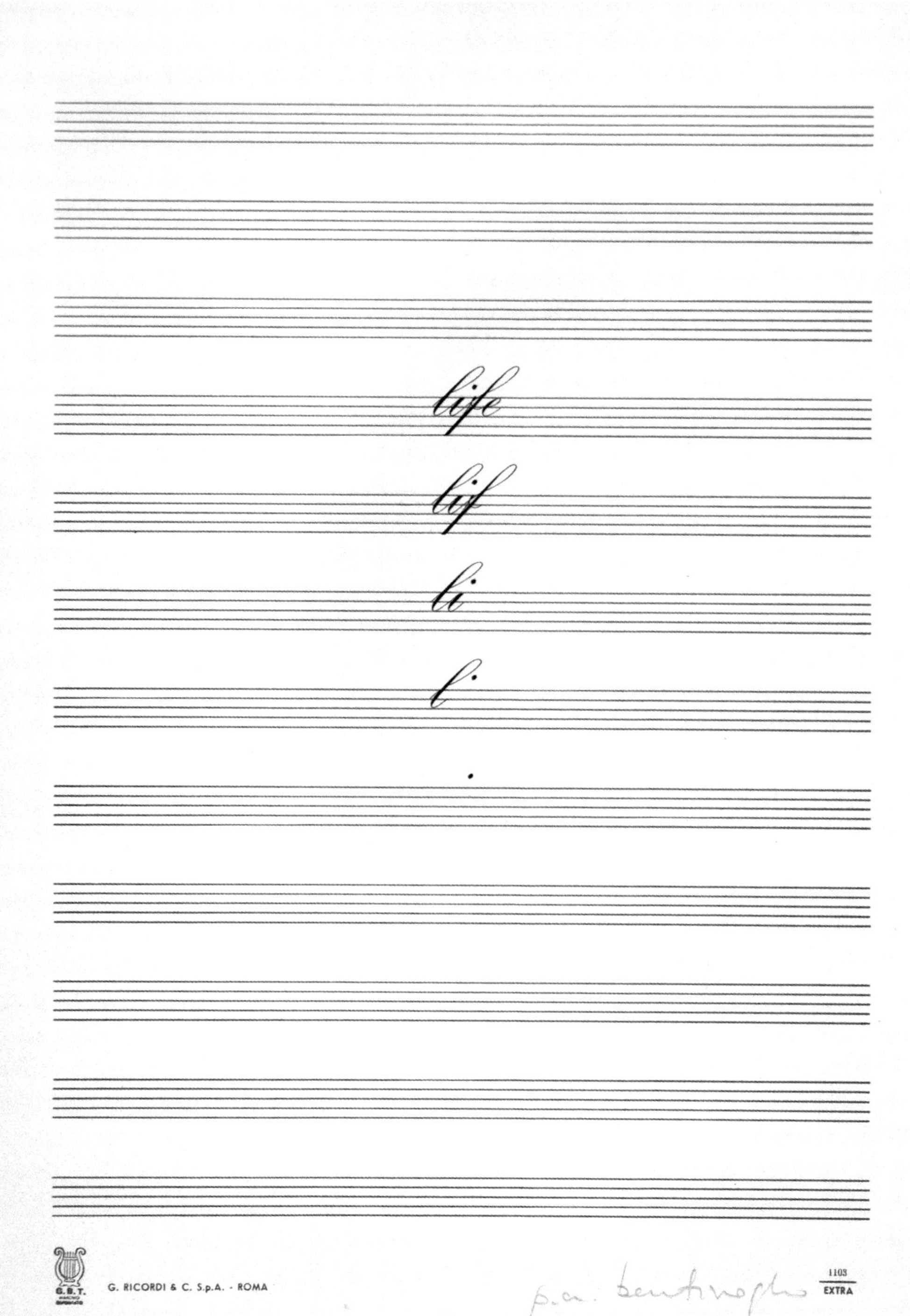

PLATE 20 —
Da punto a nota (diminuendo musicale) (From Point to Note [Musical Diminuendo]), 1971. Lithograph on paper, 12⅝ in. × 9 in. (32.07 cm × 22.86 cm).

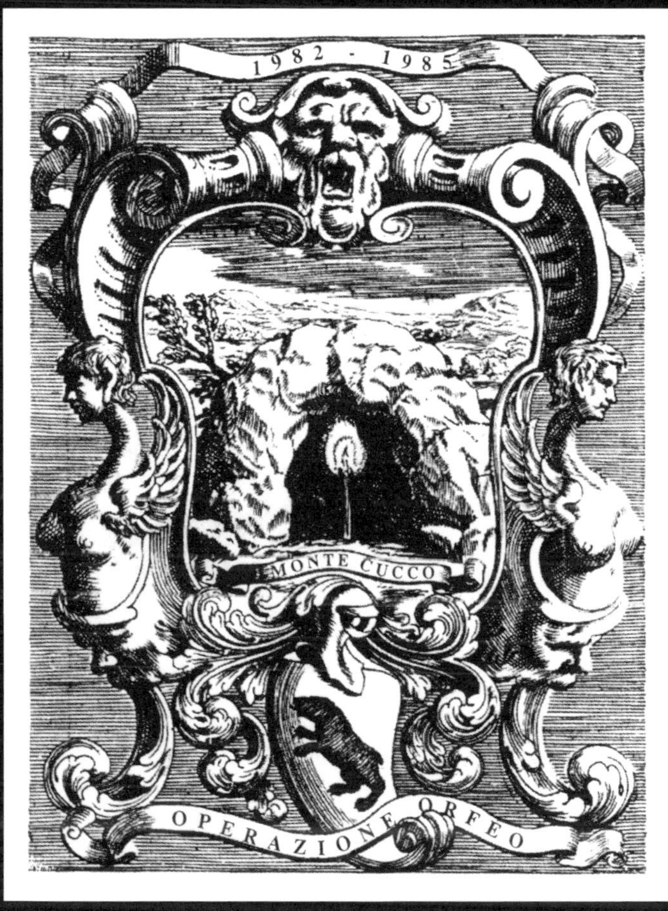

FIGURE 32—
Operazione Orfeo (L'uovo nella caverna) (Operation Orpheus [The Egg in the Cavern]), 1982–85. Six photomechanical prints on paper, 10⅝ × 8⅛ in. (26.99 × 20.64 cm) each. Continues on page 97.

OPERATION ORPHEUS

Mirella Bentivoglio

OPERATION ORPHEUS

Mirella Bentivoglio

In 1982, Gubbio was shaken by a powerful earthquake, and I was certain of its having toppled the large symbolic structure, nearly two and a half meters tall, which, in 1976, I had built with the help of local craftsmen in one of the smaller squares of this ancient Umbrian town. Its form had led the people who lived in its neighborhood to call it simply *L'Ovo*—"the egg" (Figure 12). It had been born as an act of defiance of the laws of gravity: tons of stone balanced on a few square inches of terrain. But I knew that the form of the egg—the form that nature has chosen for the protection of every incipient life—is particularly resistant. And the breaking of an egg, in any case, I thought, is a vital event: a birth.

Telephone lines weren't working, and for days I could get no news. But finally I learned that in fact the egg was still intact, without so much as a crack or fissure.

I decided to thank the earth for having spared it. To do so, I would place a smaller egg in the depths of the cavern of Monte Cucco, the earthquake's epicenter. This gift could also take on other meanings: an act of protecting the symbol of life by setting it up in a place where nothing can reach it to destroy it; an inversion of the valence of the realm of shadows, by seeing it as the place of germination; a proclamation of the maternity of the earth, by way of an emblem that exclusively belongs to the world of the feminine.

Closed to the public, the cavern of Monte Cucco is dark and dangerous, and penetrates into the mountain for kilometers at almost a hundred meters below the ground. It is reached from the summit of the mountain: the last town before its entrance, significantly enough, is named Sigillo: "the seal."

Thanks to the interest and intervention of the speleophotographer Pietro Livi, I was able to obtain the keys to the entrance gate from the National Center of Speleology. Pietro Livi and the artist Toni Bellucci, both from Gubbio, then also gave me invaluable help in preparing for and carrying out the expedition. In speleologists' suits and miners' helmets, we lowered the sling that was laden with the heavy *ex voto* down into the cavern, and then began our steep descent along the dowels that served as steps, fixed permanently into the face of the rock.

This egg was some 60 centimeters (23 5/8 inches) tall. It had been made in Rome, in the workshop of Sandro Coccia. In cement. Very rough. With an armature inside it. I had chosen this material carefully. The stones of the mammoth egg in Gubbio—*L'Ovo*—adhered to an inner layer of cement, and it was right for this sort of *ovum filius* to find its outside surface in that first epidermis, just as birds are born without feathers. In the midst of the cavern's sinuous limestone walls, this cold, gray cement would implicitly declare the date of the intervention: a modern-day material in a context as old as the earth itself.

I entitled the event "Operation Orpheus." The two initial "o's" allude to the form of the egg and the curves of the subterranean vaults around it; but as well, in a certain sense, they repeat the "o's" at the start and end of the name of the mother-egg: that structure in Gubbio, which the local population had re-baptized as *L'Ovo*.

Up until this time I had always seen the oval as a semiological figure that belonged to the area of *mater*: as both "matter" and "mother." I had used this form in opposition to the signs of *logos* (books, or constructed urban spaces) and the results produced had amounted to a kind of all-embracing short circuit. But now the egg discovered itself in a primary context—a "prebirth" context, as it were—and was made of materials that, quite to the contrary, implied technology. A linguistic sign in a prelinguistic context: a contrast. A symbol of knowledge that, like a printed title, transformed its surrounding environment into poetry. And thus an emblem of *logos*, once again for the purpose of underlining—but here in the opposite way—that link between nature and culture that has shaped our world, no less than it has shaped our brain.

One of the works of René Guénon, the French anthropologist of the first half of the twentieth century, contains a chapter on the virtual "Egg in the Cavern." Thus, thanks to the earthquake, I had quite concretely traced my way along some of the paths of what this author saw as "symbols of sacred science." But in the course of that first descent into the cavern, my cement egg could only be positioned, not fixed into place. Livi took photographs to send to the Center for Speleology for the purpose, as agreed, of obtaining their permission later to bolt the object to the outcrop of limestone I had chosen for its base. Having thus concluded this speleological site inspection, we hauled our burden back up to the surface. So, until now the work remained no more than a project, a trial, a first draft.

The permit arrived. But given the effort that the operation demanded, I hesitated. I already had the photographs; the operation had been publicized by way of an illustrated pamphlet (the images of which would make their way

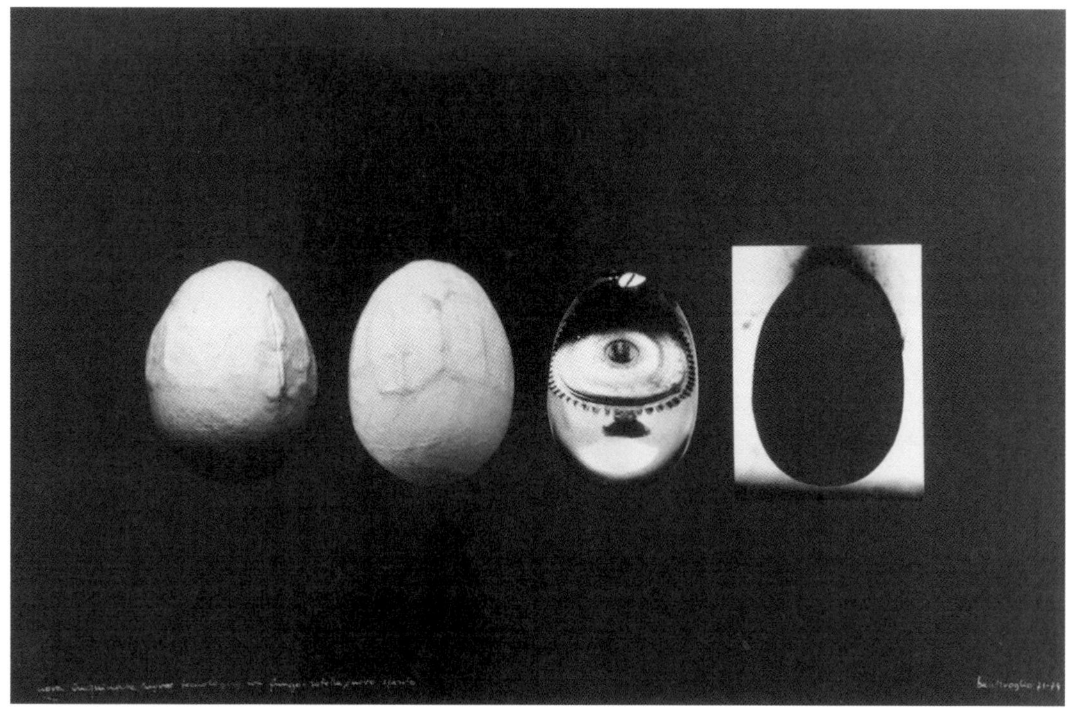

FIGURE 33 —
Da uovo a zero (From Egg to Zero), 1974.
Gelatin silver print on paper, 6¹⁵⁄₁₆ × 9⅜ in.
(17.62 × 23.81 cm).

into subsequent catalogs); so, why do it all again in such an impervious place, inaccessible to nearly everyone?

In 1984, a second, more violent earthquake struck the little Umbrian town and reminded me that promises must be kept. I decided to conclude the operation, and in the summer of 1985 the cement egg was permanently restored to the dark subterranean space for which it had been constructed. The photograph where all of us are seen intent on the operation of bolting it into place, snapped in the dim reddish light of a hand-held torch, resembles ancient nativity scenes illuminated by candlelight.

My memory returned on that occasion to a detail of a work I did in 1974, entitled *From Egg to Zero* (Figure 33): an egg in transparent acrylic resin that contains a bolt and a cogged wheel and which thus insists on that thought of technology as an absence of life.

But now the bolt had issued from its sterile nest, and *Homo Faber* was employing technology to insert a sign of poetry into the most natural possible context. To screw it into place, we repeatedly rotated the cement egg, again and again, and this movement appeared to me to have been prophesied by the cogged wheel in that previous work. All of my work thus seemed to be linked together. As though the technological egg of 1974 had been the unconscious harbinger, in object form, of the action in which I was now engaged. In the course of which, primal life and culture, no longer in the opposition in which before I had set them up, definitively coalesced.

The documentation of this second expedition was also, in part, the work of Alessandro Alimonti, who had joined the group, which had grown more numerous. His final photo of the cement *ex voto*, upright on its limestone pedestal, seemed to portray a human torso, devoid of lineaments and "gender": both man and woman, with a slight covering of body hair (the corrugated surface of the limestone), and also provided with hands, relaxed and inactive at its sides. The pre-individual in its pre-historic context: a brutally primordial version of De Chirico's manikins.

That afternoon, the radio announced that Umbria had once again experienced a minor earthquake with its epicenter at Monte Cucco. It had caused no damage, and we had not felt it. "A burp," our friends remarked. Had the earth declared its satisfaction?

In 2003, my two companions—Pietro Livi and Toni Bellucci—after once again exploring the cavern, informed me that the cement egg had disappeared: it had probably been reabsorbed, enveloped within a limestone crust. Could that be possible, in less than twenty years?

Surely it could only be absurd to imagine that it might have been unbolted from its perch and carried away. Outside of its intended context, after all, it had no value. Removing it, moreover, couldn't have taken place without the use of heavy machinery, or without destroying it, and would surely have left conspicuous gashes in the limestone shelf into which it had been fixed.

I imagined that I could find the answer by making a third descent. Perhaps my friends from Gubbio had not returned to the exact spot at which it had been placed.

If I too were unable to find the egg, the final and only possible meaning of this complex operation, protracted throughout the years, would have to be that Gaia refuses to be understood in any anthropocentric way. And all my presumptuous discourse, with its interweaving of telluric movements and personal creative intentions, would find itself mocked and reduced to incoherent silence, sucked back up, like my cement egg, into Chaos and the great unknown.

But what about the other possibility, that I should find it all the same, in spite of its inevitable transformations among the constantly dripping waters of a limestone cavern?

A call to action came in the form of a number of esoteric texts that fell into my hands. I learned that the VITRIOL anagram of the seventeenth-century alchemists consisted of the initial letters of a Latin phrase that seemed to me to be prophetic, and a warning directed precisely at myself: *Visita Interiora Terrae Rectificando Invenies Occultam Lapidem*—"By rectifying the visit to the bowels of the earth, you will find the hidden stone."

But on requesting permission for a third descent, I was told that access to the cavern had been permanently suspended, owing to the risk of accidents. It was pointless, moreover, to hope that an exception might be made. To prevent all further descents, the dowels that had served as footholds had been removed. So, the confrontation between the cannibalism of the earth and the longed-for triumph of an old Ariadne in the limestone labyrinth remained undecided. Was there a third possibility, or had the alchemists taken me in?

I reread their texts. They counseled that their words be understood symbolically. So *Occultam Lapidem* might refer to the Philosopher's Stone, the final goal of the *opus*, of the ceaseless alchemical process: the gold of knowledge, concealed in the *Interiora Terrae* that lie within us, beyond the greed of reason. *Rectificando*, the last descent was into myself, into memory and already recorded images; the gift of a rediscovery lay in the restitution, already transpired, of a secrecy, of a Seal, of mystery, of a veto, which is always the final meaning of every form of poetry.

FIGURE 32 (facing and following two spreads)—
Operazione Orfeo (L'uovo nella caverna) (Operation Orpheus [The Egg in the Cavern]), 1982–85. Six photomechanical prints on paper, 10⅝ × 8⅛ in. (26.99 × 20.64 cm) each.

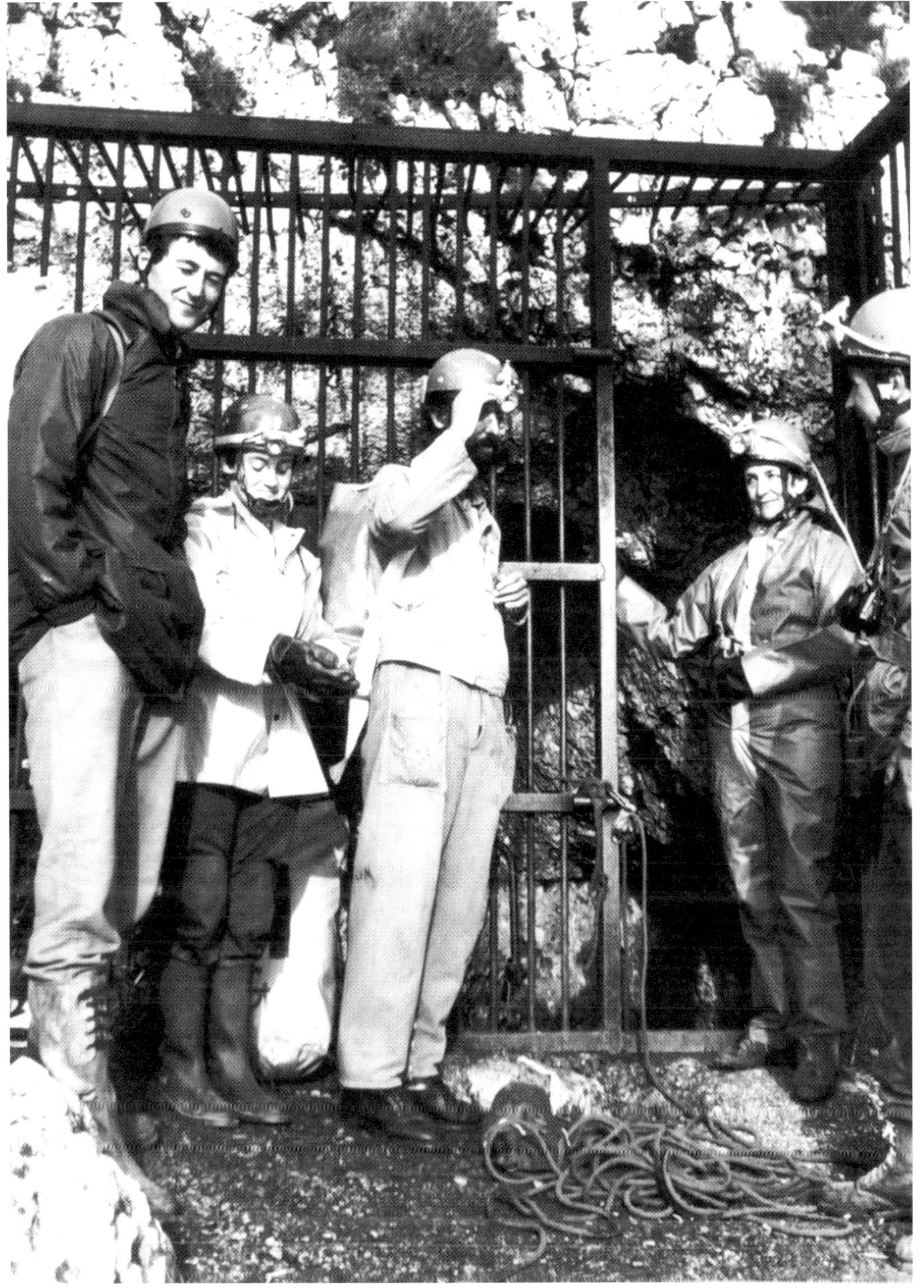

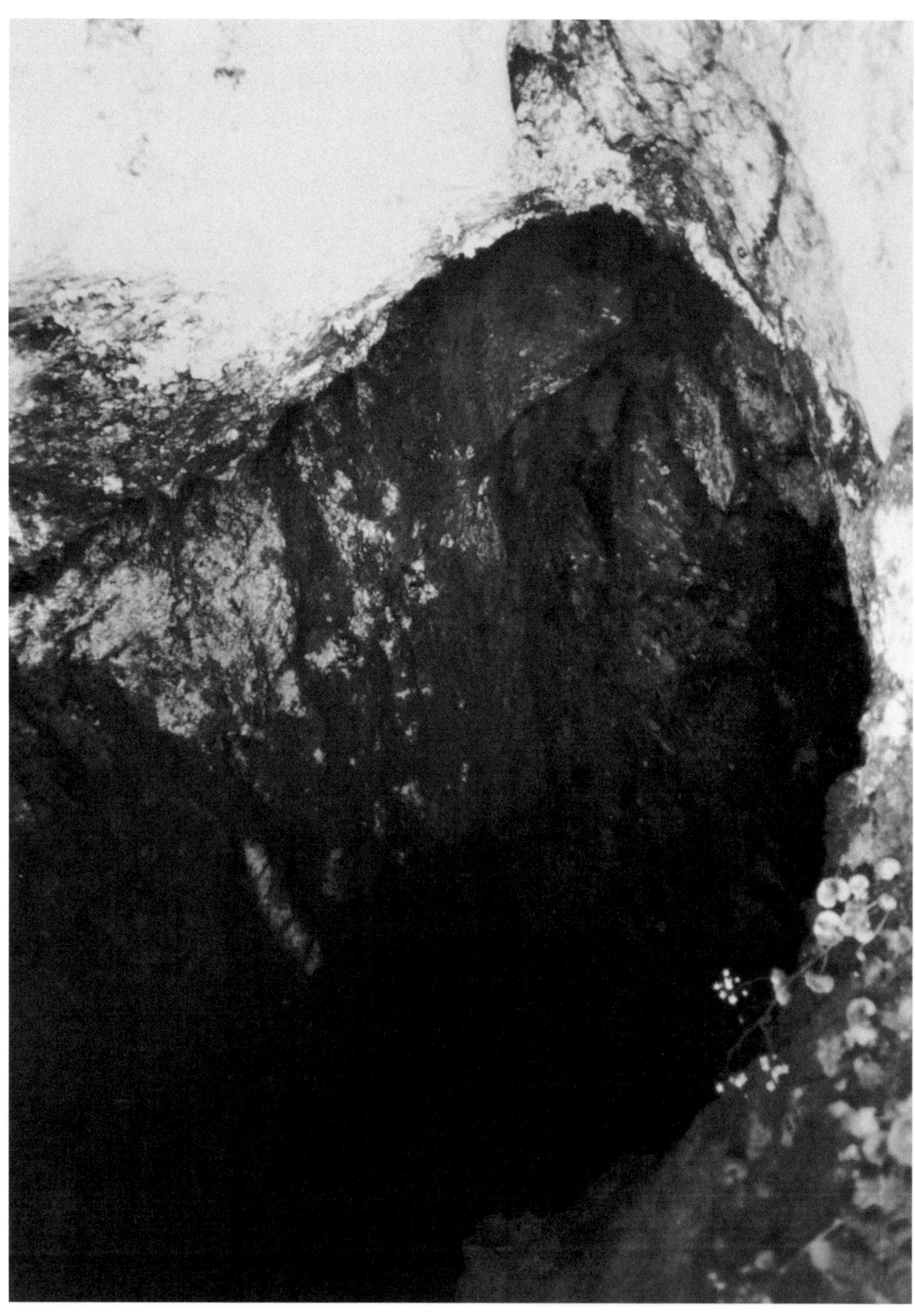

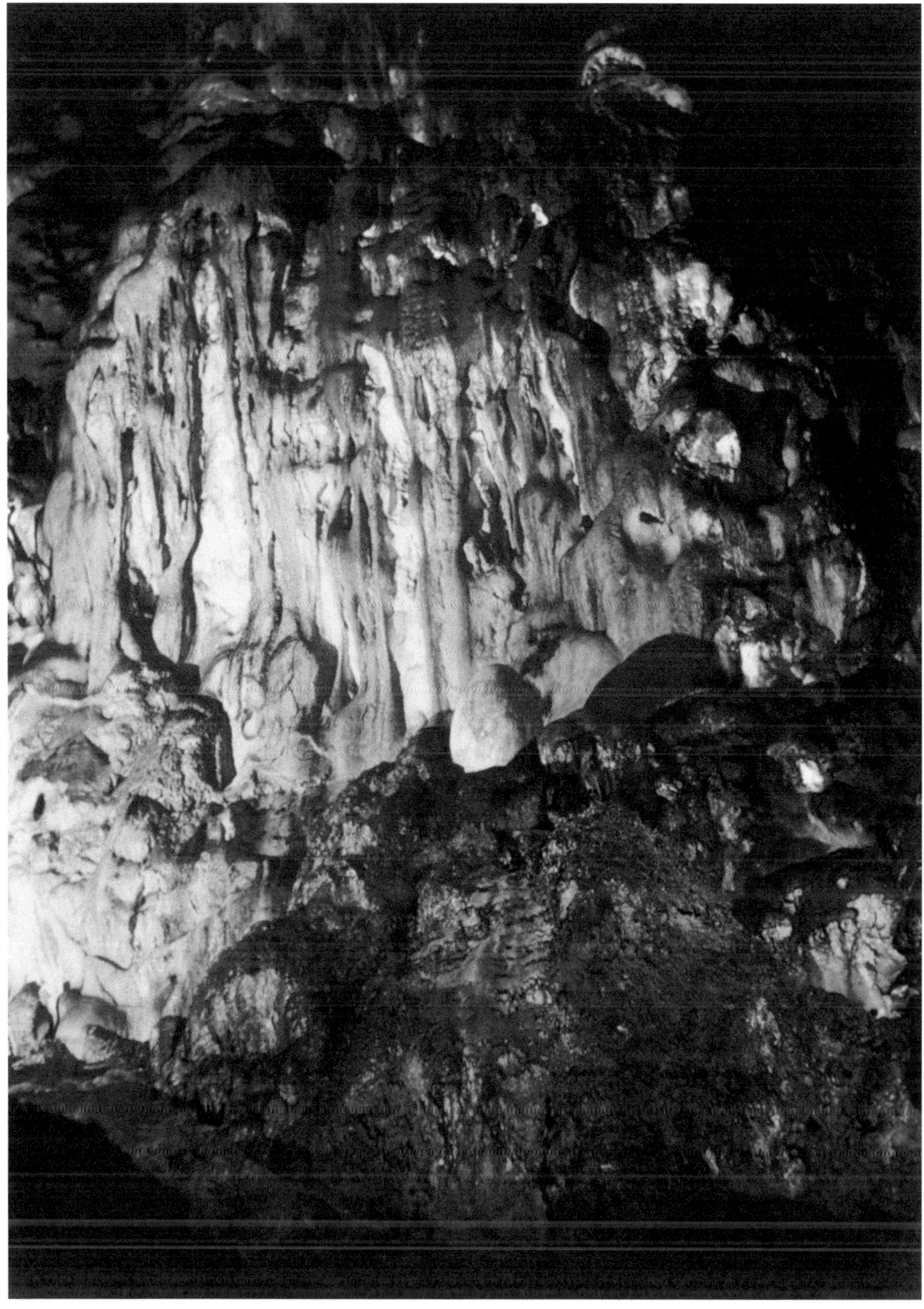

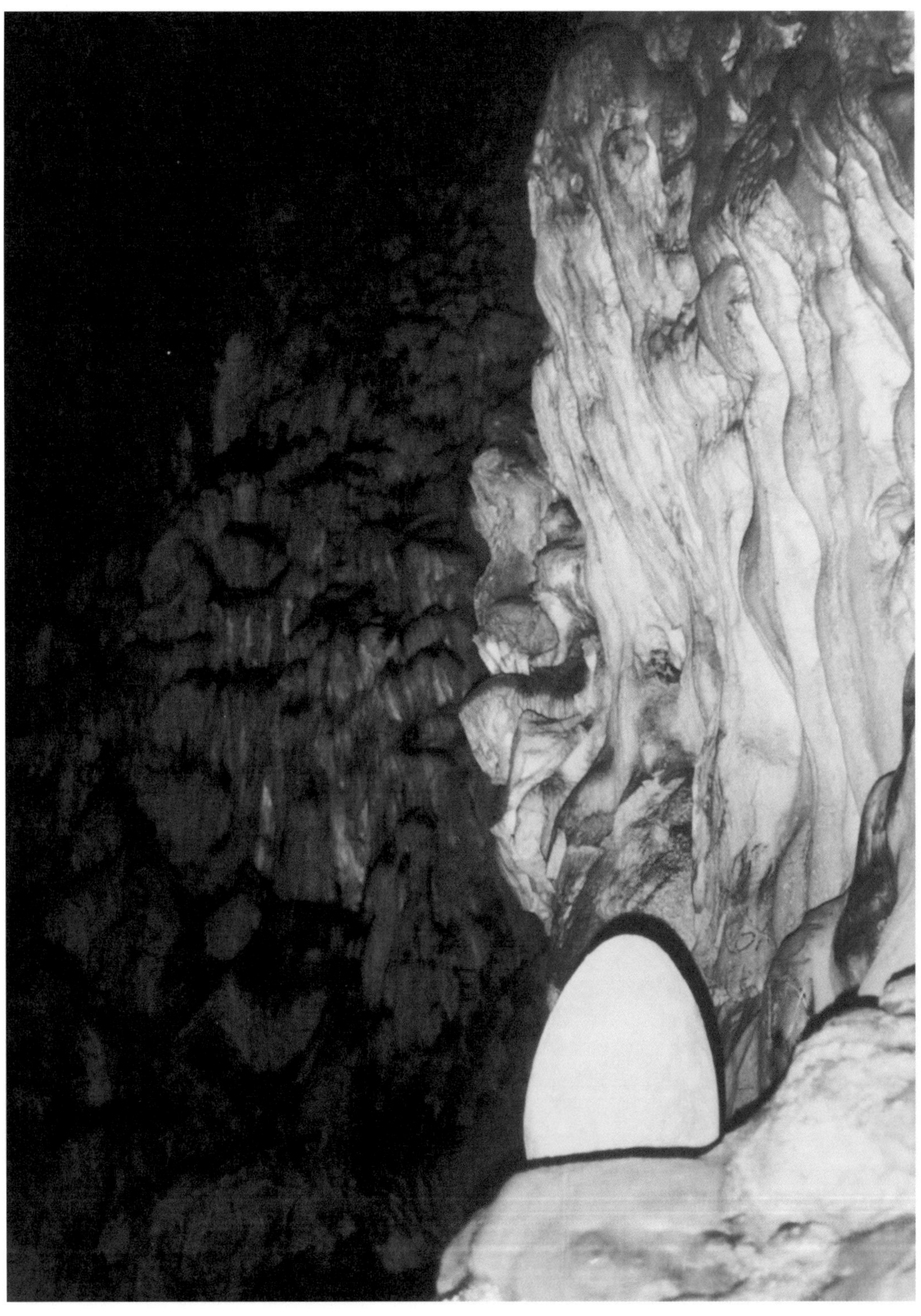

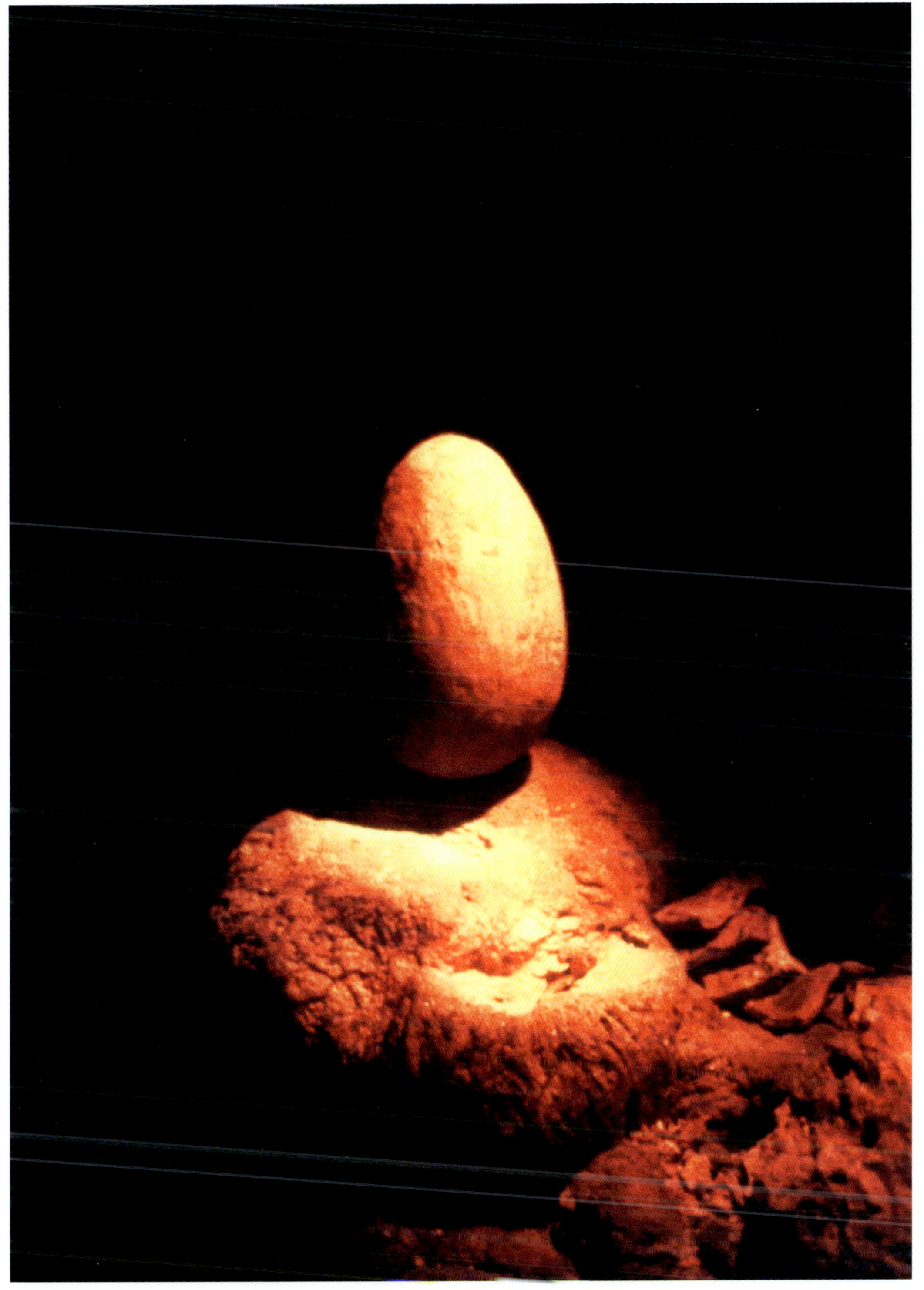

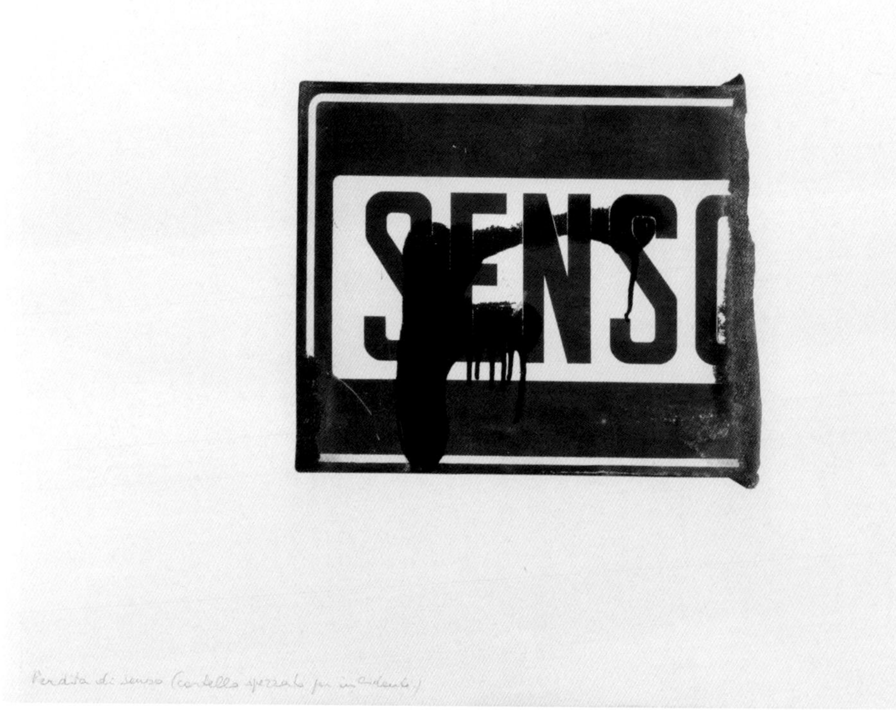

senso unico = one way (street sign)

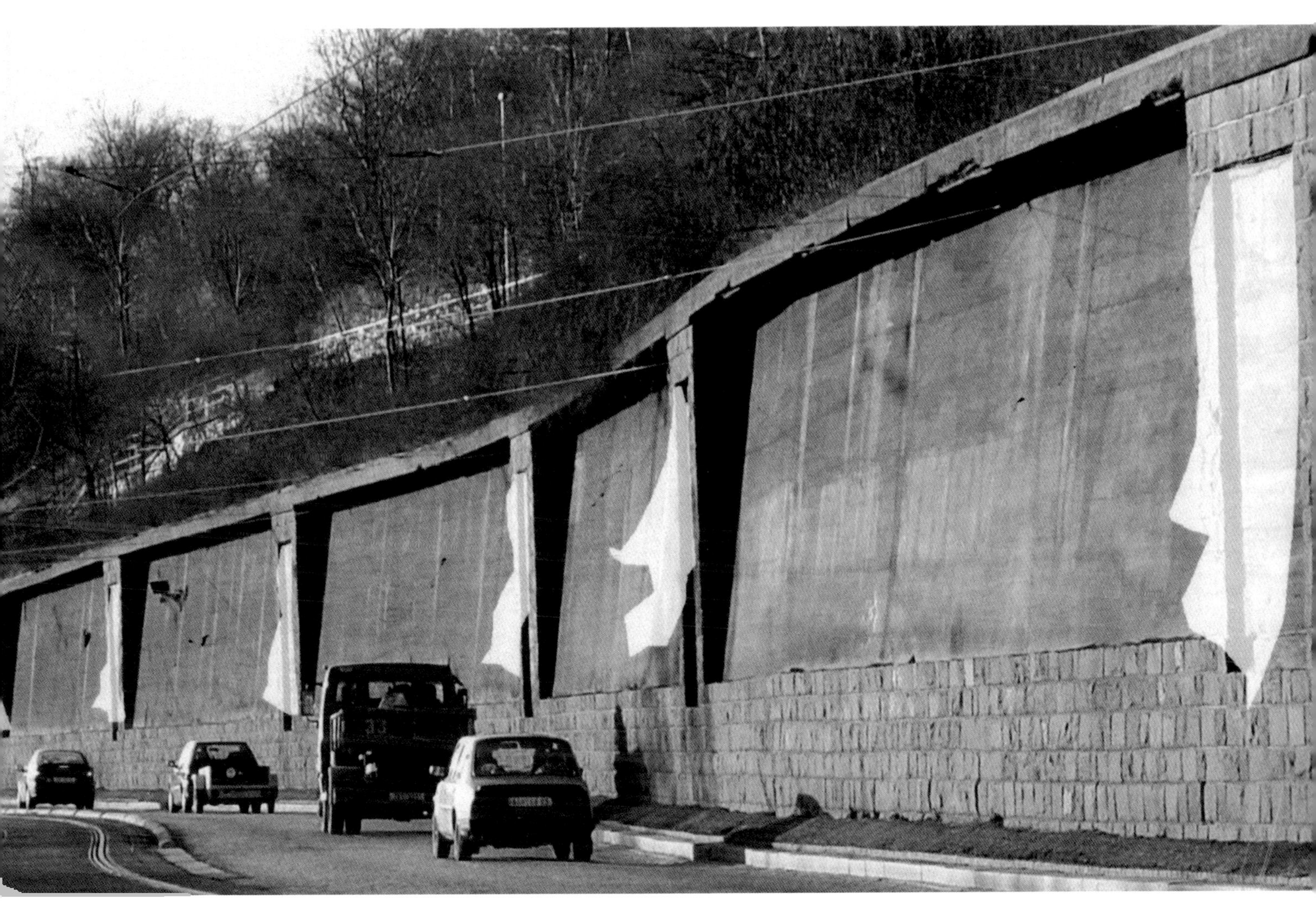

PLATE 22—
Wall along the Vltava River in Prague,
Czech Republic, location of installation
Facce Murate (Walled Faces), 2005.

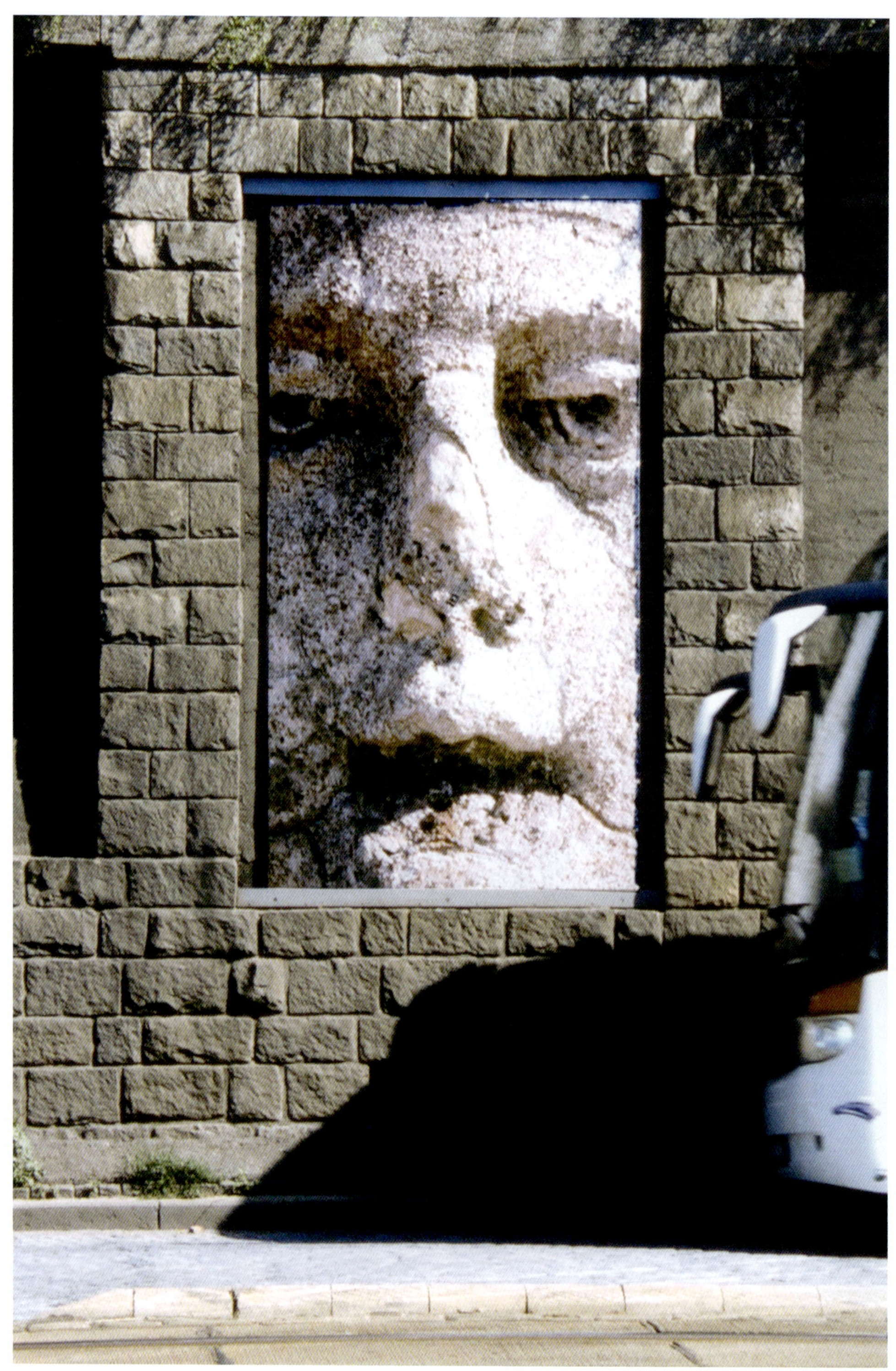

PLATE 23 (above and facing)—
Facce Murate (Walled Faces), with Alessandro
Alimonti, 2005. Details of public installation
in Prague, Czech Republic. Five photographs,
157½ × 86 in. (400 × 218.21 cm) each.

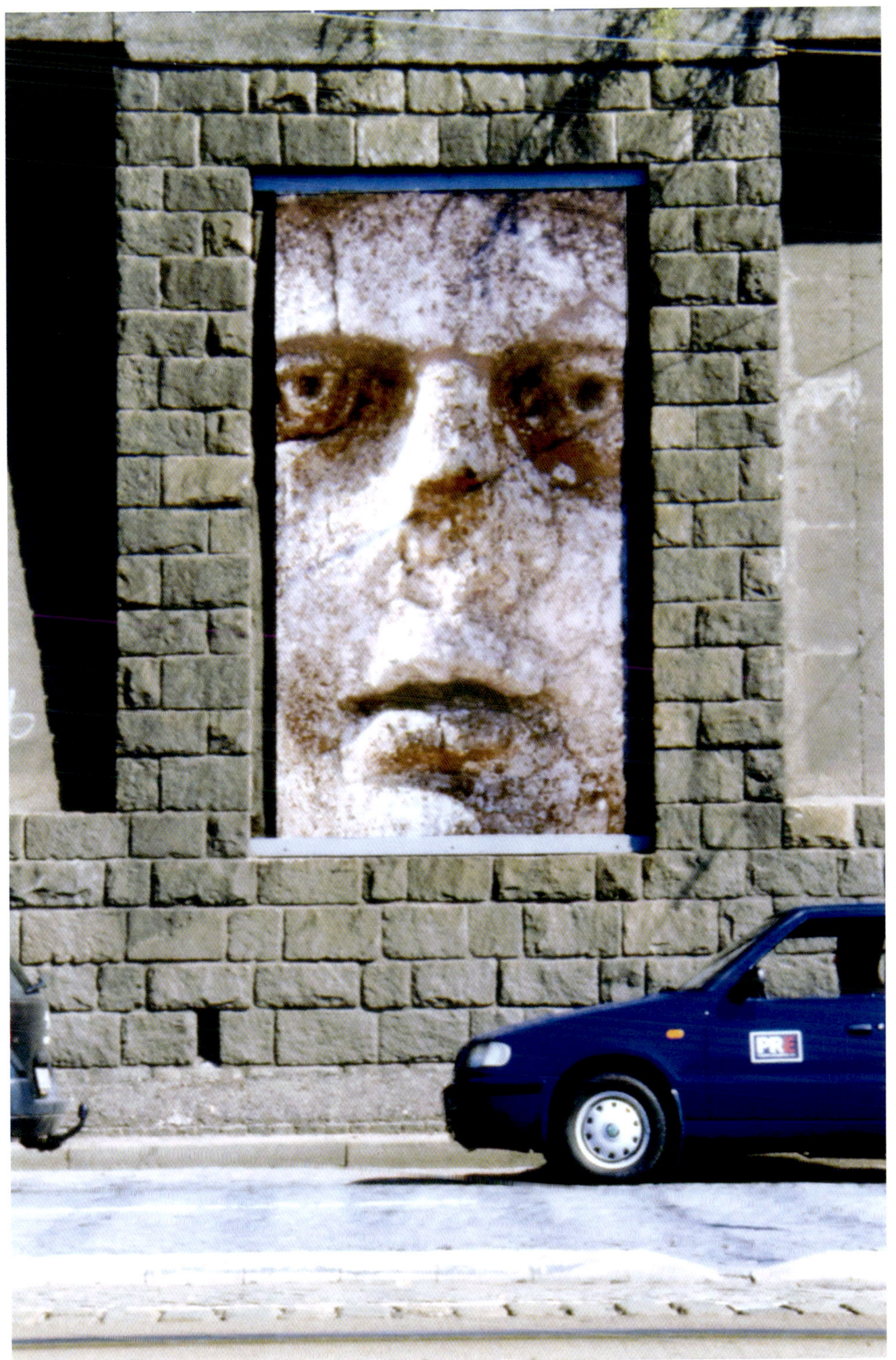

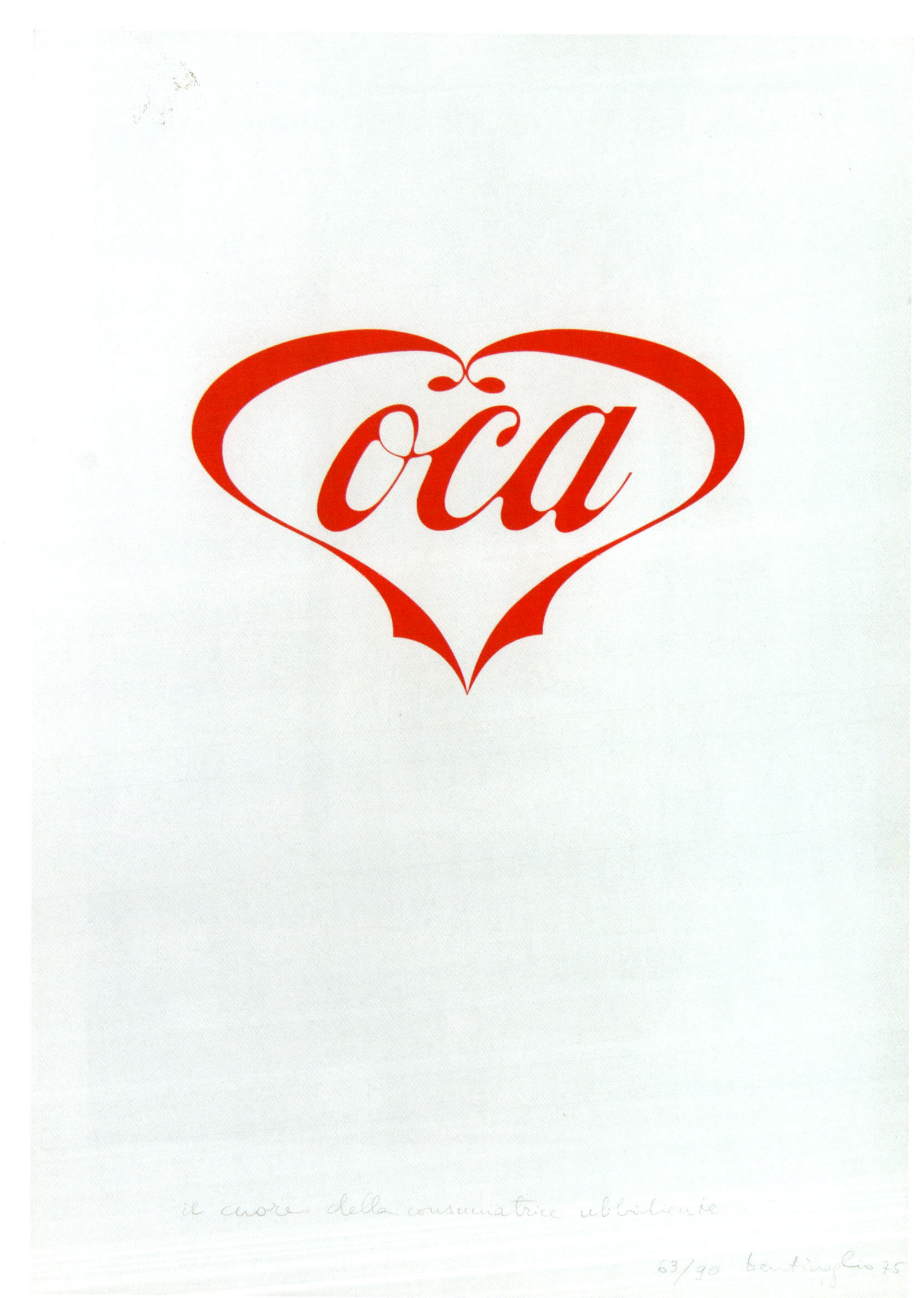

PLATE 24 ——
Il cuore della consumatrice ubbidiente (The Heart of the Obedient Consumer), 1975. Serigraph on paper, 27½ × 19⅝ in. (69.85 × 49.85 cm).

oca = silly goose, a feminine noun in Italian

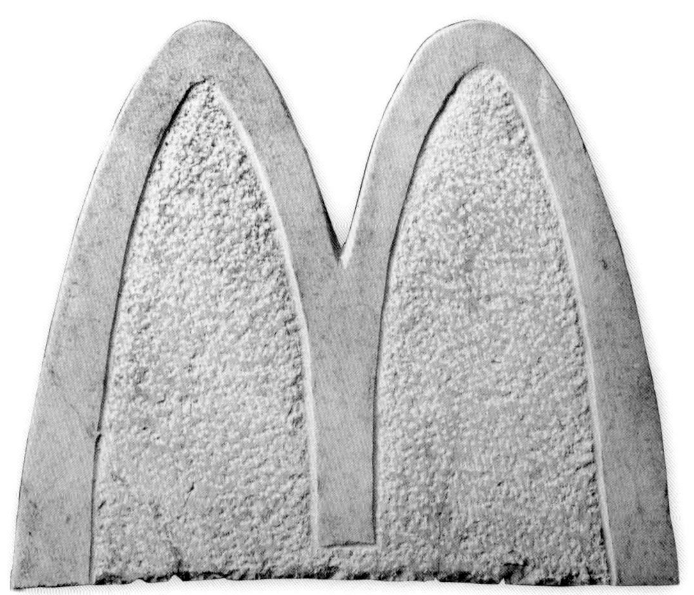

PLATE 25 —
*Tavole della legge del consumo (Tablets of the
Law of Consumerism),* 1992. Photomechanical
print on paper, 16⅜ × 19⅝ in. (41.59 × 49.85 cm).

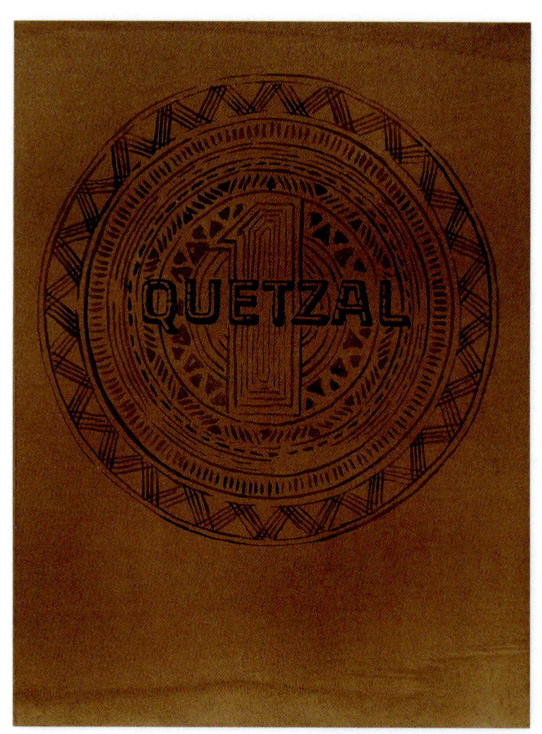

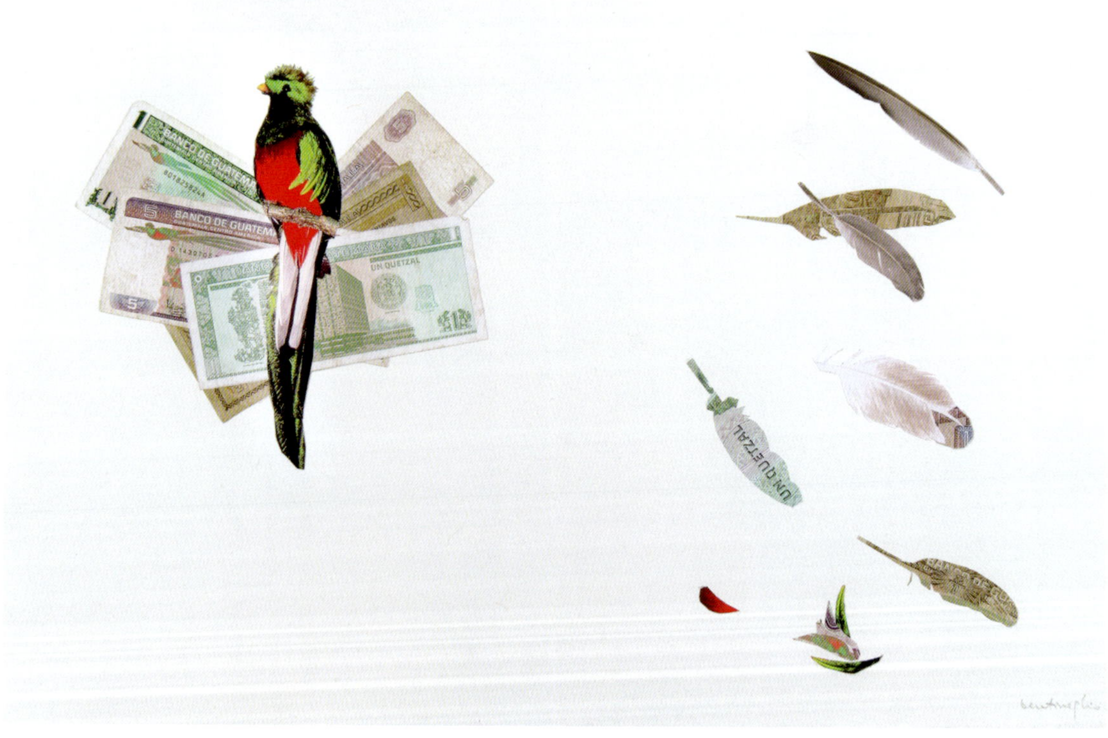

PLATE 26 —
Quetzal, with Marta Knobloch, 2001.
Artist's book with original collage.
13 × 9½ in. (24.13 × 24.13 cm).

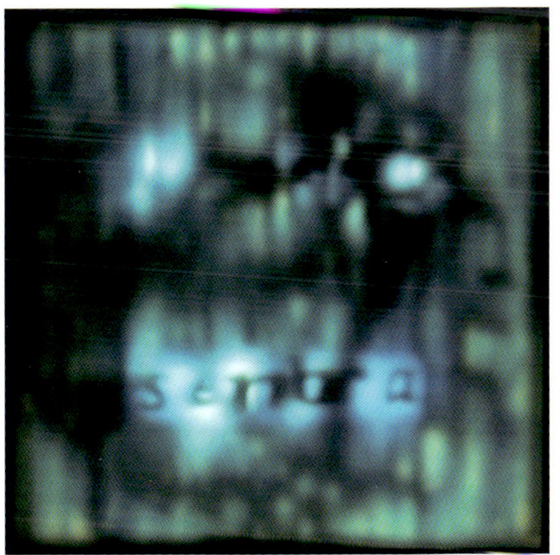

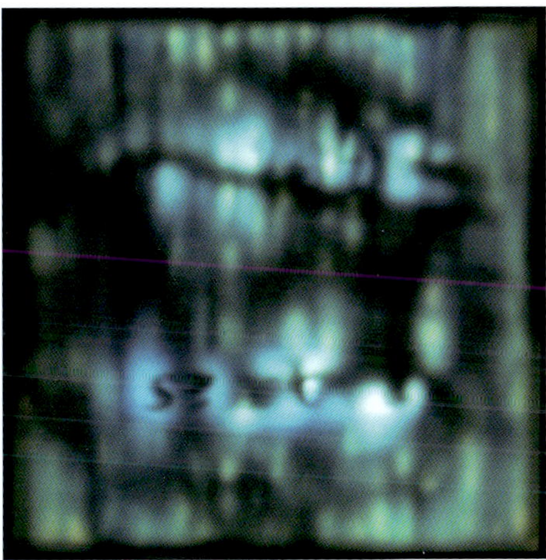

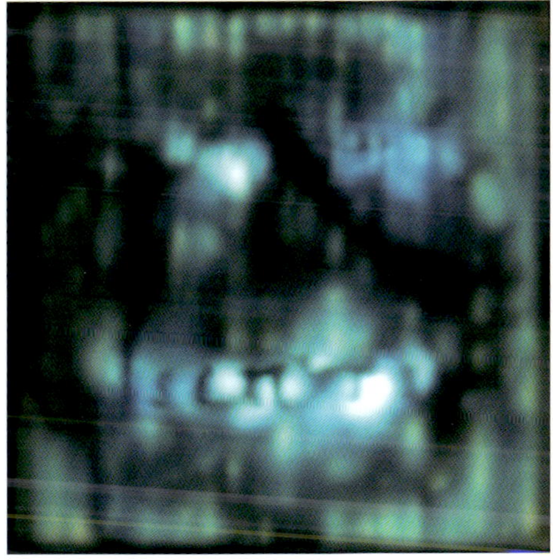

Sembra (It Seems), 1971/2013. Video documentation of kinetic object created with Nino Calos in 1971.

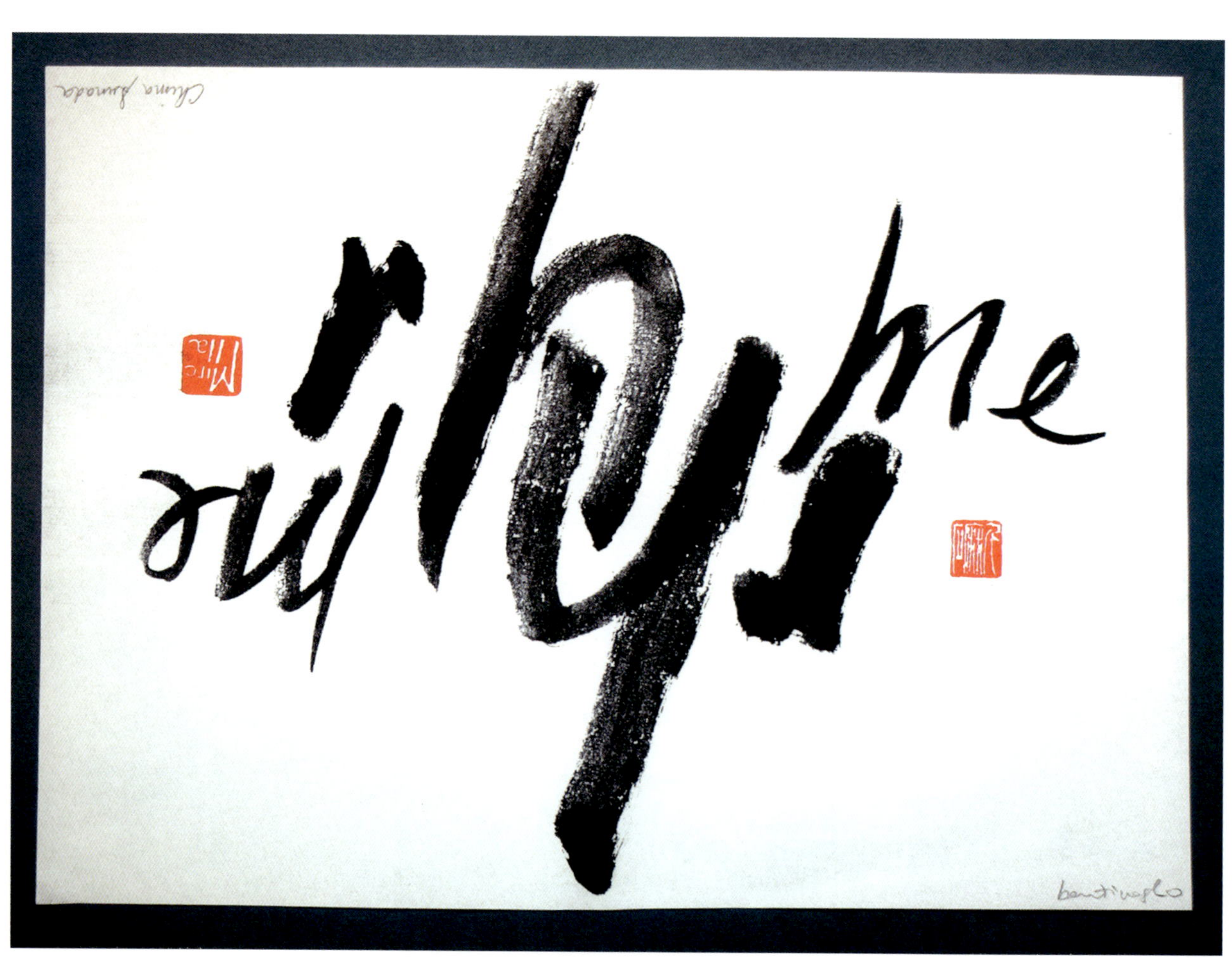

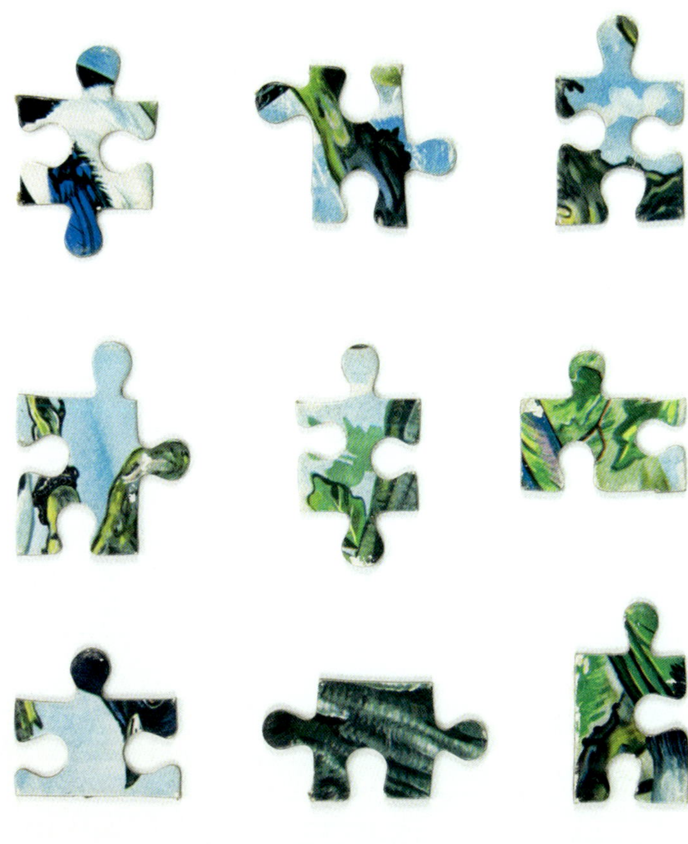

PLATE 29 —
Puzzle Poem, 1985. Collage and
Letraset on cardboard, 14⁵⁄₁₆ × 12 in.
(36.35 × 30.48 cm).

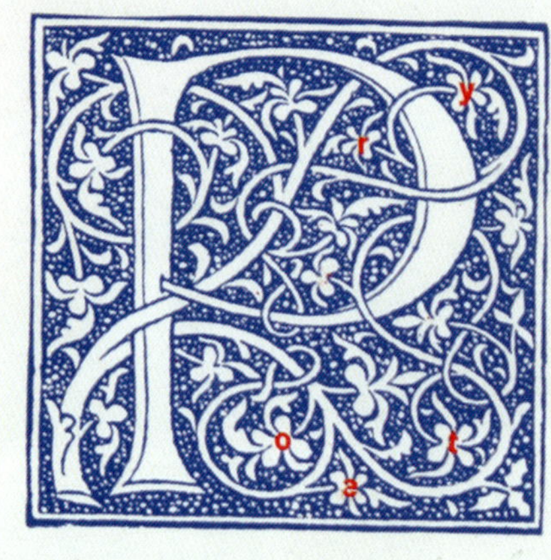

PLATE 30 ——
Flowers in the Tangle (Poetry), 1987.
Serigraph on paper with Letraset,
10¾ × 7¹³⁄₁₆ in. (27.31 × 19.84 cm).

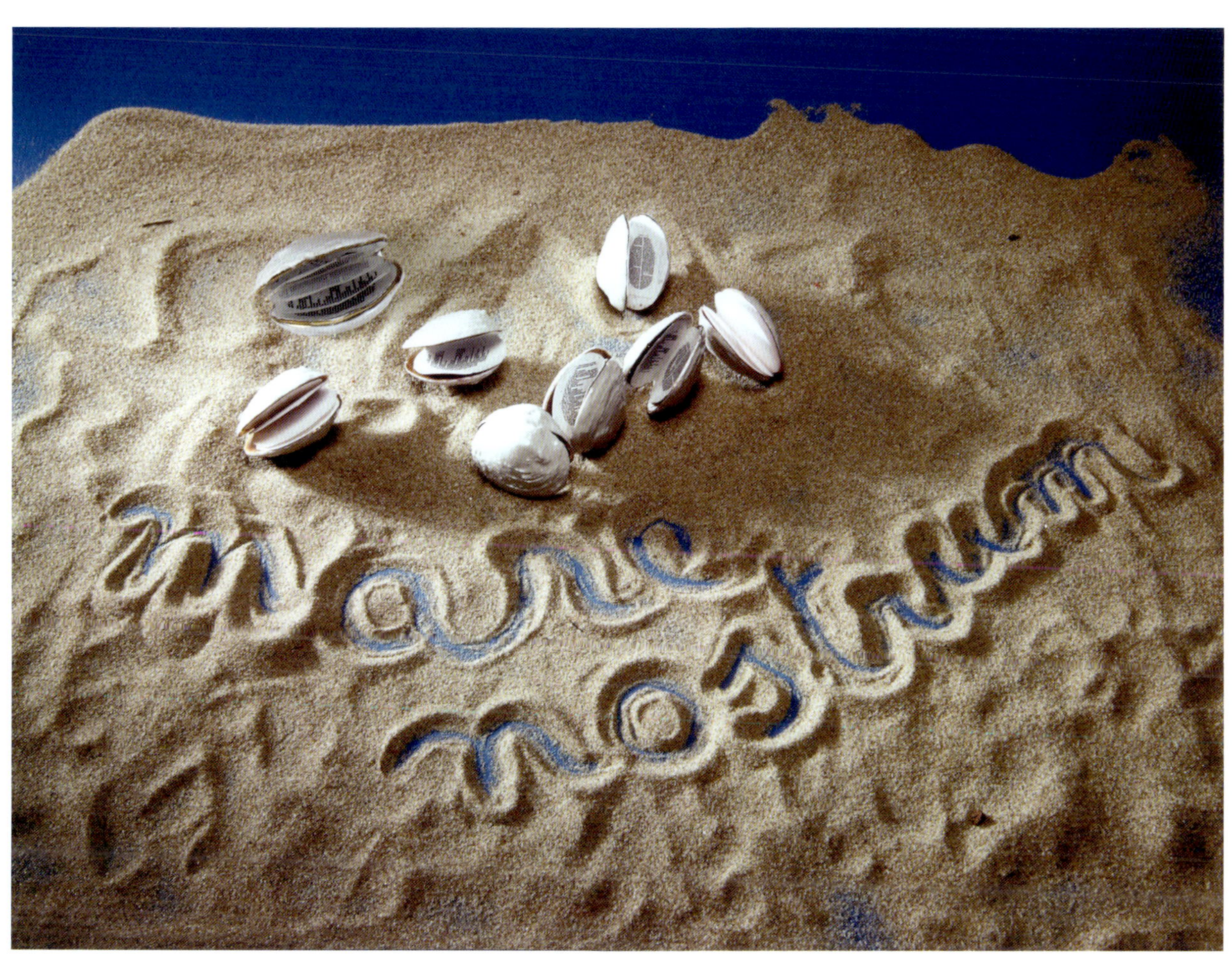

PLATE 31—
I frutti del nostro mare (The Fruits of Our Sea),
1986. Assemblage, photograph, and porcelain;
11⅜ × 15⅛ × 1½ in. (28.89 × 38.42 × 3.81 cm).

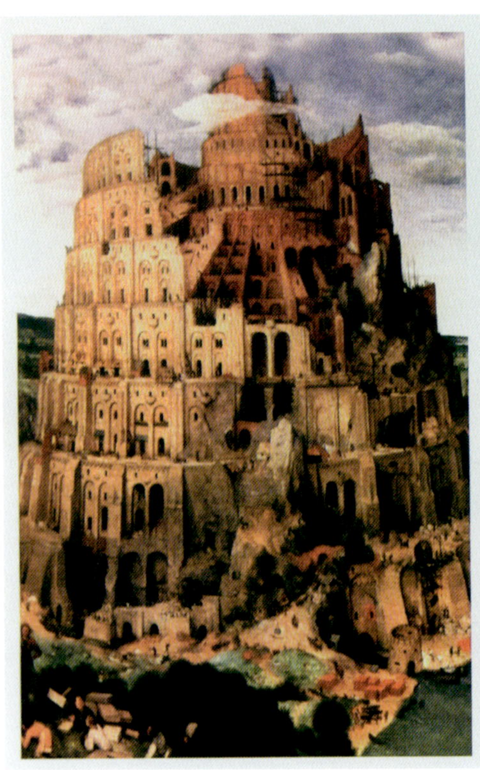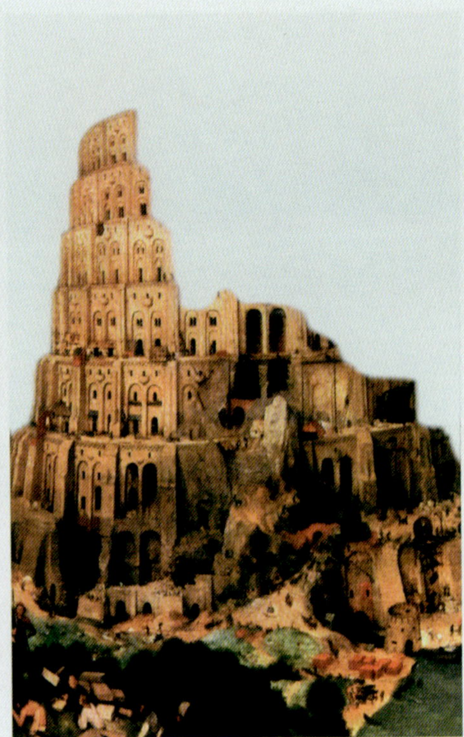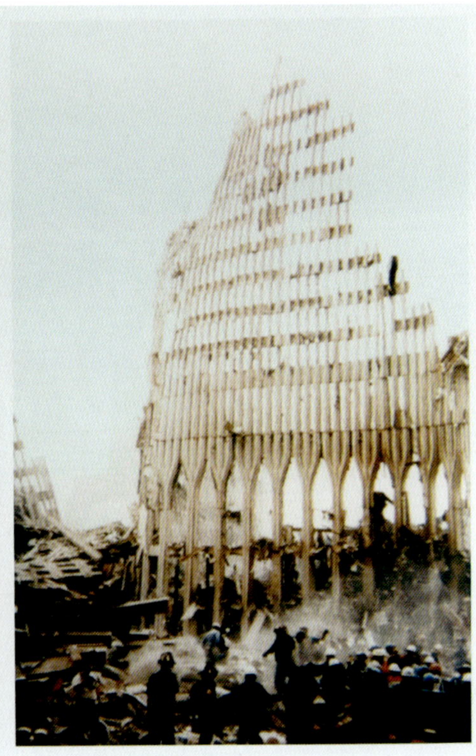

PLATE 32 —
La profezia (da Babele a Ground Zero) (The Prophecy [From Babel to Ground Zero]), 2001–2. Photomechanical print on paper, 12¼ × 23¼ in. (31.12 × 59.06 cm).

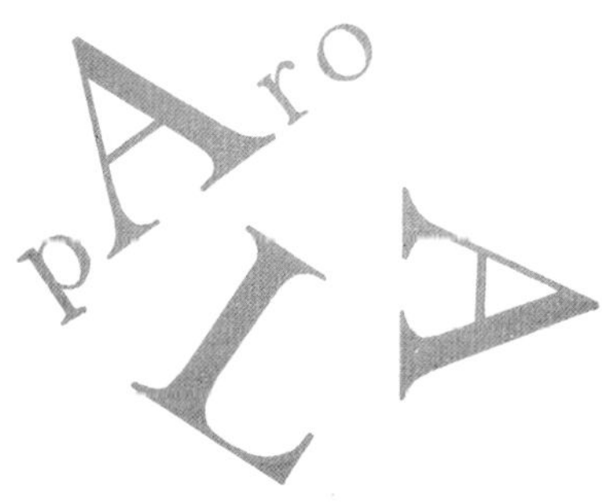

ala = wing

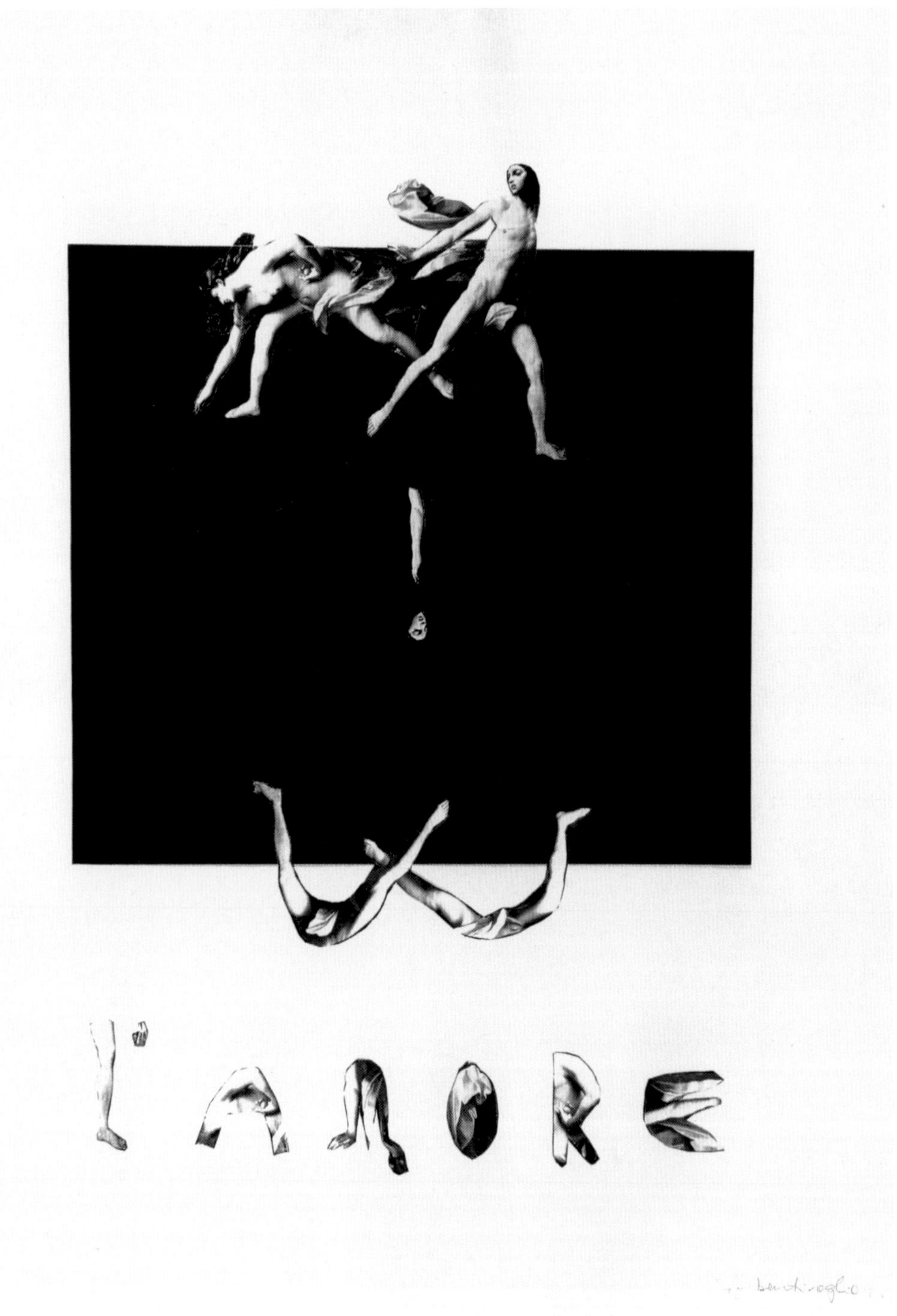

PLATE 34——
*Genesi della W (Viva l'amore! Abbasso l'amore!)
(Origin of the Letter W [Hurrah Love! Down with
Love!])*, 1995. Photomechanical print on paper,
24¼ × 17¹⁄₁₆ in. (61.6 × 43.34 cm).

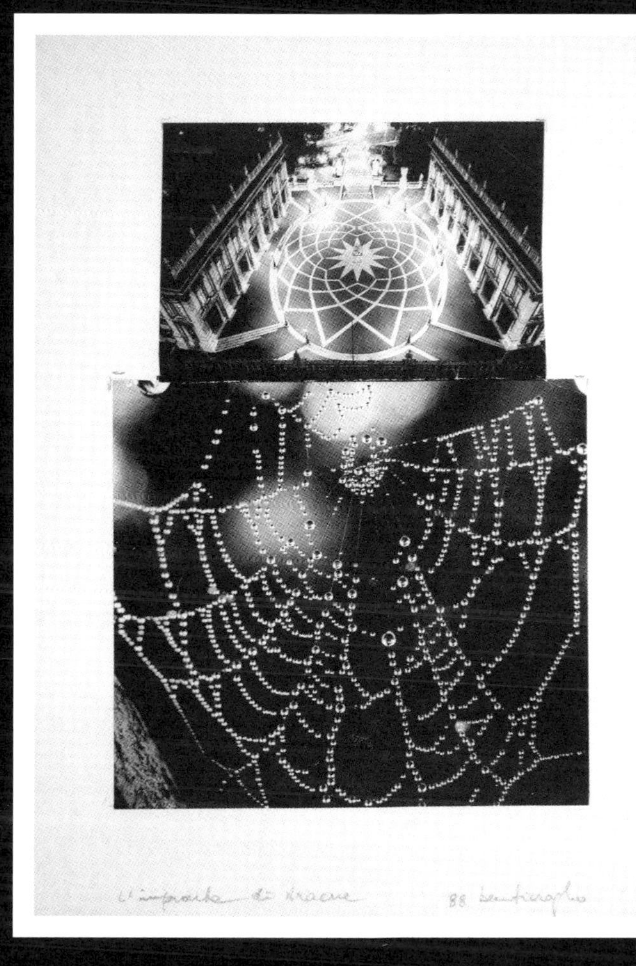

L'impronta di Aracne (Arachne's Imprint),
1978. Photomechanical print on paper,
14⅞ × 10¼ in. (34.93 × 25.08 cm).

ARACHNE'S IMPRINT: AN INTERVIEW WITH JOHN DAVID O'BRIEN ABOUT MIRELLA BENTIVOGLIO

Frances K. Pohl

ARACHNE'S IMPRINT: AN INTERVIEW WITH JOHN DAVID O'BRIEN ABOUT MIRELLA BENTIVOGLIO

Frances K. Pohl

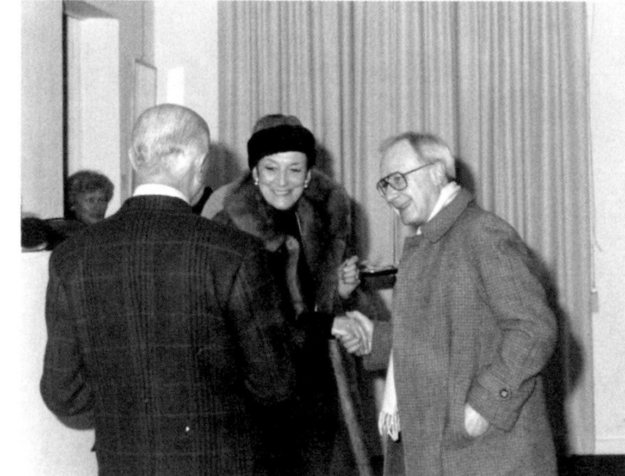

——————FRANCES K. POHL——————
How did you meet Mirella?

——————JOHN DAVID O'BRIEN——————
First of all you need to know that most of my memories are not analytical. I don't always mark things by dates or times; it's more the atmosphere and the general emotional and intellectual tenor of things that I can recall.

The Rome art world is quite small, and you kind of know everybody no matter where you are in it. So I knew of Mirella before we had our first significant exchange, which was at a place called Centro Luigi di Sarro, in 1982, during the exhibition "Mucha/O'Brien/Scarpelli," organized by Guido Strazza and Luisa Martina Colli, when the center was under the direction of Enrico Crispolti. Luigi di Sarro was a doctor and artist who was teaching *anatomia artistica*—artistic anatomy—at the Academy of Fine Arts and he was killed by mistake [on February 24, 1979] when they had the so-called *Legge Reale* in Italy, which meant that the police could shoot if they thought terrorist suspects were threatening politicians. Di Sarro was in a Porsche, with an American girlfriend, driving very fast somewhere in the vicinity of the home of Giulio Andreotti, Italy's Prime Minister at the time. Plainclothes police shot Di Sarro in the head, in what has been described as a tragic and fatal mistake. Because he was

committed to the arts, his mother and sister, who survived him, opened Centro di Sarro, in which they hosted a series of shows as homage to him. (It still exists.) And Enrico Crispolti, who is now mostly known as a historian of Futurism, was at that time a very active critic as well as historian and he was putting together exhibitions. He called me and some other artists to do a show about words and images. Mirella showed up and she had a lot to say about the relationship of the word to image in the exhibition. That was our first significant exchange. And we really enjoyed each other's company. She liked the fact that I could speak Italian so well. She liked the fact that I was working with poetry, because Mirella actually started as a verse poet even more than as a visual artist. We agreed to meet and have coffee. And that became the start of what is now a very deep and meaningful friendship in which we talk about everything. We talk about poetry, we talk about what's going on in the art world.

——————FP——————
Did you get a sense of her position in the Italian art world at that time?

——————JO——————
Yes. Mirella was an odd person then, because the Italian art world tended to be extraordinarily hierarchical. There were the artists who did art. There were the critics who assigned cultural value

to the arts, and there were the gallerists who made reference to the critics. It was extraordinarily linear. It was very, very difficult for someone to break ranks with that. Well, Mirella had been married to Ludovico Matteo (Teo) Bentivoglio, who was a university professor in the law faculty who specialized in space law. She also had three daughters, and she substantially and significantly withdrew from the art world to take care of them. Then she came back into the art world doing things that were not really allowed in Rome. She wrote about art, she promoted other artists, and she did her own work. For those times, she was quite an anomaly. It was also true—and is still (but less) true—that the Italian art world is pretty sexist. It tends to be dominated by men. I think that's changing, probably more so in the last five years, but in Italy it has always been a problem, and in Rome in particular.

So Mirella's position in the art world was very interesting. On the one hand, she was highly respected and liked, and she was an interesting and wonderful person. At the same time, she was a bit of an outsider because she did things that you weren't allowed to do. Also, she came out of a background where she was able to meet people at different social levels. For example, she knew Gillo Dorfles—a very important, powerful critic—personally (Figure 35). She knew quite a few people like Crispolti personally, and they allowed her to live a dual status. They let her be a theoretician, writer/ poet, and a visual artist. That was highly unusual at the time. As time has moved on and the art world has changed, it is much more common for artists to do what she does now, to organize exhibitions in which they place not only their own work, but the work of others. It is also much more common now for artists to give a written context to the work they are doing.

The other thing about Mirella that was entirely anomalous was that she went and sought out people in whom she was interested, and brought them either into her own archive or to the attention of others by writing about them. She had extensive contacts with South America and Japan. She really went out of her way to seek out artists and say, "Oh, I'm really interested in your work," which, within the Italian male-dominated psyche of the 1970s and 1980s, was not done. Most artists tried to get everyone to be attentive to their work, nothing about them going out towards others. If they did network with you, it's because they thought that maybe you were more powerful and could give them opportunities. They did not open many doors. They tended to stand back. That was the general trend. So that was what made her practice atypical.

Another thing that I've always maintained is that, in the United States, the term *conceptual art* in some ways is a misunderstanding of what in Italy was called *poesia visiva*, Visual Poetry. These poets weren't necessarily visual artists working with writing; they were sometimes the exact opposite. Americans tend to radicalize almost any practice, so they came back from Europe saying, "Wow, if we just use words we can do away with the object, we can just deal with the concept." Conceptual art appears, in many cases, to be very similar to *poesia visiva*, but its roots are different.

———FP———

Are you saying American artists went to Italy in the 1960s and saw this work as a new way to create, or were they already moving in this direction?

———JO———

I would never be so dogmatic as to say they went and took, but I would say that there were a lot of "transfusions" and transversal creativity going on. What was most important in transversal creativity was the way in which I believe the American artists understood what they considered a radical operation, which the Europeans did not think of as radical. They had examples of poets who had been manipulating typography for years, and so the idea that they would drag it even further toward the visual made perfect sense in a lineage that started with modified typographies and even, as

FIGURE 35 (facing)———
From left: Gillo Dorfles, art critic; Mirella Bentivoglio;
Luciano Marziano, art critic; Rome, 1990.

you well know from Mirella's history, with Futurism, with Marinetti.

——FP——

So that helps explain why Mirella insists that her work is different from conceptual art.

——JO——

Yes, she thinks that the Americans threw the baby out with the bathwater, that they really misunderstood what Italian artists were doing. The conceptual artists focused on paring away, the anti-object moment, the dematerialization of art. It was really about getting the object and the market out of their work. The visual poets never had this kind of a radical need. They didn't want to de-center the market. They couldn't care less. They were poets.

——FP——

Yes, she says visual poets are poets first, and then they bring to the visual their poetic sensibility. And conceptual artists began as visual artists and then brought words into their work.

——JO——

What is also funny is that, while conceptual artists were busy streamlining and paring away the visual in order to get to just the concept, the visual poets were doing the opposite: they were adding visual elements to the page so they could move up into meaning that went beyond the words. I also think that the visual poets by and large were attentive to meter. Mirella has done a lot of spoken performance in which she uses language and pronounces her texts and artworks in a very specific way. She was very interested in the way in which the phonetic pronunciation, the determined pronunciation of the work, has as much importance as the visual impact of it. She was remaining in the practice of poetry as a spoken practice, a read as well as a written practice.

——FP——

I remember the first years I went to visit her, in the mid-1980s, when we went to a lot of different galleries and events. She seemed so eclectic in her interests—in dance, in music, in different kinds of performance. She wasn't interested in painting or sculpture in the traditional sense of the words. I wonder if you could talk a little bit about the interdisciplinary nature of her interests—I mean not just poetry and the visual arts. She seemed to be connected to so many different kinds of art scenes.

——JO——

I've always characterized Mirella as having a restless imagination. She was not a world builder in the sense of one stylistic continuum. She was very interested in many stylistic continuums. She's always said, "I do this not because it is the only thing I am interested in, but because these are the means that I want to work with." She works with stone, primarily marble, and she works with writing on the page, but the truth of the matter is that she has a much broader set of interests. The anecdote that she usually tells people to give an idea of how restless she is, in terms of her imagination, is about her daughters. She says: "Look at my three daughters. One writes about dance. The other is a neuropsychiatrist. And the other works in the scientific section of the *camera* (the Chamber of Deputies or the Parliament), a political body. So you see, I never pushed them into one kind of thing." And that was typical of the way that she approached the world of the arts. She didn't think of it as just a sphere that was sectorally determined by the galleries and critics. And she also said, "You know, John, I've always been lucky. I did not have to live from these things. I could make my work, and my husband, who passed away young, left us enough money and homes so we could take care of ourselves, so I was very free, unfettered by the problems of the market."

The other thing about her was, because she was born in Klagenfurt, Austria, and from Milan, in northern Italy, she could break the rules. She was—and still is—a very striking person, so she would get up with her fairly northern accent and ask questions that were very pointed. In the Roman art world, that can be quite disconcerting. If you are not careful, it can cause problems with

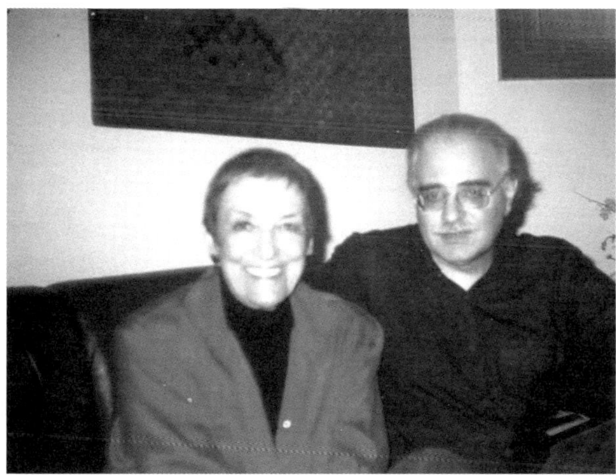

those who are in power. But in her case, she was independent, so they couldn't really do much about it, except accept that this rather brilliant person was asking a question that was to the point. And she wouldn't back down, she would continue to ask and to push forward until she got the answers she thought were important. She has said that in some cases that worked against her, and I'm sure that it did.

———FP———

Did you, in your stays in Rome, get a sense of what other people thought of her?

———JO———

I think that she is considered a venerable and important figure in the Rome art world. People in Rome tend to classify you. And when they can't, they say, "Oh, she's a great person." They'd say, "She's a little bit more of a poet than a visual artist," if you were talking to visual artists. Or they'd say, "She's more of a visual artist than a poet," if you were talking to poets. They would qualify that she is a little bit of an outsider of all fields. I think, on the one hand, that's really worked to her advantage. Everyone can say something positive about her because they are not part of her guild or she's not part of their guild. Vice versa, it also allowed her to enter many worlds where in some ways she would

have been excluded had she been a part of the guild. Does that make sense? I think, therefore, you are not going to find people speaking ill of Mirella. I can't think of a single instance. Occasionally, when she put her shows together as a curator, some artists would be miffed. They would think, "How come she got power, because she's not really a published critic. She doesn't have a magazine or a newspaper behind her, so why were people calling her?" Well, they were calling her because she's a clear authority. But if artists were excluded, they would often get quite miffed because, whether it was a show about fiber arts or Visual Poetry, they would want to be included. There were people who were constantly pushing her to make sure that she would include them in her group. Mirella was able to explain the qualification or the reason for that specific show that they weren't included in without dismissing their work. She didn't play the power game of the critic, who would basically say, "Your work is not good enough." She would say, "No, no, no, your work is amazing. However, this time I was really looking to do this, this, and this, so your work, although it would be perfect for another occasion, and I am going to work on that, it really wouldn't have worked for this occasion." So she was very good at not giving people any

Frances K. Pohl

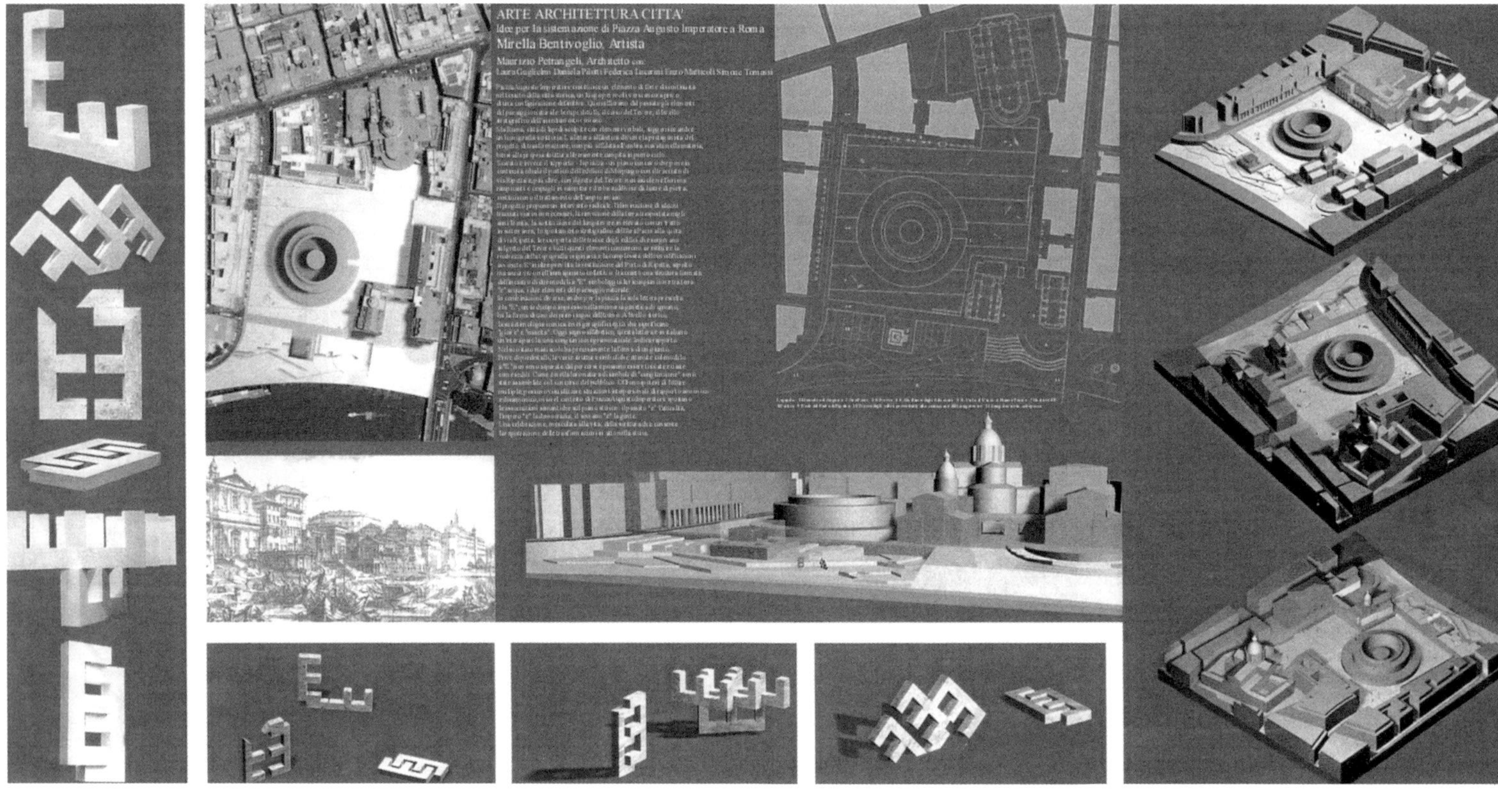

sense that she was excluding them, or dismissing their work.

I've also heard a lot of positive feedback about her work. For example, recently she was a part of a public art competition. The tomb of Augusto Imperatore, or the Emperor Augustus, is right behind the Ara Pacis, which was going to be developed (Figure 37). And a number of important artists were asked to make proposals, including her. She was kind of a dark horse in the sense that people didn't really figure that she had as much cachet in the art world as some of the other artists participating. But somehow Mirella ended up invited, and her project was extraordinarily well liked. It didn't receive any funding, but none of the other projects did either. She still thinks that this project of hers will be built after the economic crisis, presumably after her death.

——FP——

I have always gotten the sense that she is a very generous person, always wanting to set up opportunities for other people. I never felt that she was working solely for her own career.

——JO——

No, like I said, she was independent, she didn't really have to. Another thing I love about her is her view that the arts are greater than single individuals. She certainly feels that she is an important and necessary component of the art world and that she absolutely gave of herself to it. But she believes in the arts, and as a result, she is completely free in many ways to dedicate herself to other artists. And she was, without being particularly ferocious about it, an important proponent of women in the arts.

———FP———

Her interest in history is really fascinating too.

———JO———

In terms of?

———FP———

Borromini, alchemy. She's constantly mining historical records and ideas and seeing the germ of one of her ideas being manifested a hundred or a thousand years ago: the drawing by Leonardo that included what looked like her capital "E's" connected in a maze, or the fact that Borromini was an alchemist and that she did an installation in Prague (Plate 23) where alchemy was very popular So she makes these kinds of historical connections that inform her work in a way that is also quite different from a lot of other artists. I'm thinking back to the conceptual artists, the image/text group, who don't seem to have those rich historical allusions.

———JO———

I think that is typical of most Italian artists, truthfully. I think what is interesting about it, though, is that it allows Mirella to go "dredging history," as she used to call it, to find reminiscences of what she is looking for in the poetics of previous existences. One of the things, for example, that distinguishes "image plus text" work even from conceptual art and certainly from *poesia visiva* is the fact that the American artists would go to media. I don't think Mirella would go to media. I think she would find advertising, TV, and posters to be a little bit too strangely non-historical for her to do much with them. She'd be much more likely to find the manuscript of Da Vinci or Borromini that has an element that looks like an "I" that makes her suddenly say, "Ah, that's the 'I' I've been looking for." She would recognize that "I" much more readily

than if she saw it in a poster for a Fellini film from the 1960s. Yet one of the things about Mirella is that she transcends the problem of too much historical weight. She is able to go beyond it, because she is being very essential in what she is choosing. From my point of view, which is an Italian-American point of view, what's interesting about her is she didn't get too trapped in the historical underpinnings. Many Italian artists sink their roots into that history, but end up staying so bound by those conditions, by those considerations, that their work doesn't go toward the present; it stays rooted in the past.

———FP———

Would you agree that since Mirella emerged as an important figure in the late 1960s, she has managed to maintain a presence in the Italian art world, even as she has evolved and changed the way in which she works, for example, moving from primarily works on paper and smaller objects to larger sculptural works and public installations?

———JO———

I absolutely agree. I think one of the ways she kept herself in the art world was to go into the world of artists' books (Figure 13) and works on paper, which were considered less important parts of the market. So you could be there and nobody would try to kick you out and make space for whoever was the latest phenomenon of the day. She also established relationships with particular cities, for example Gubbio, and the artists who worked there. That relationship came through Crispolti, who for a long time took charge of the Gubbio Biennial. The Gubbio Biennial is not considered to be an especially significant event, but, in retrospect, it was a very important series of art in public places, and of large-scale sculpture. Mirella did her egg in Gubbio (Figure 12). She brought to Gubbio the strength of being a supporter of the arts and therefore of the artists from Gubbio, who felt a bit marginalized with respect to the artists of Rome, and who were supportive of her in turn. At the same time, they offered her opportunities

FIGURE 37 (facing)———
Project for Tomb of Augusto Imperatore,
Rome, with architect Maurizio Petrangeli, 2002.

Frances K. Pohl

that might not have existed otherwise to go and put things up in the park, to put public art in new places, which she was able to do with very little funding and with assistance from the artists and the city. So she did this funny game of dancing back and forth between the periphery and the center. Had she really tried to become a central figure of the market, it would have been a whole different situation for her. But her way of staying in the sphere of importance was to dance in and out of it and not try to bring all of the attention to herself. That's my opinion.

The other amazing thing about Gubbio is, as important a city as it is (being in the Umbria region right next to Assisi, Spoleto, and Todi, places that are incredibly important for tourists), it tended to be overlooked. So in some ways, the fact that it wasn't being showered with international attention—like the Festival of the Two Worlds in Spoleto—meant it did not become the place that people from the arts were vying to go to. At the same time, it presented an amazing architectural backdrop for contemporary art. In some ways, being secondary to the principal market ended up saving Gubbio, allowing for someone like Mirella to have a significant and long-term relationship with the city.

———FP———

I know many in the art worlds of cities such as London, São Paolo, Los Angeles, and Tokyo are familiar with Mirella's work. Do you think she should be known better internationally?

———JO———

Yes and no. I think her decision was to focus on the things that she cared about the most. Mirella and I have talked many times about the problems of fame. Mirella has served as a mentor for me, directly and indirectly. She hosted me as a Fulbright (I stayed at her little apartment down the hill) and we always talked back and forth about many things. One of the issues with people who become famous is that they have to relinquish their work, they have to become a stage director of their identity as other than themselves. So we

always talked about the difference between being famous and being renowned. If you have renown, it means your sphere is going to be connected, almost physically, to a community. I think Mirella would say, "I had three daughters, I lived in Rome, I couldn't get around that much." But I think in the end it was also her decision to not lean so far out of herself as to no longer be able to be in her work the way she feels like she is now, to be connected to the way that she does things in her community, and to be available for others. So, yes, she should be known internationally precisely for that reason, because we only know international figures who are celebrities, so we don't really know anything about them. We know these names, and they float around and the things they are now doing they don't even do themselves, they have other people do them. So it is interesting to have her as a counter-figure, to have her as a stand-in for another way of conceiving of being significant and important in an art world.

———FP———

But one wonders, if you make her better known, does she then become a celebrity, which works against the idea of being renowned?

———JO———

Well, now that she's old enough that she is no longer able to get out to those communities and lose herself in fame, there is really nothing to be lost. If she became famous now, it would be fine because it is not going to bother her. At a certain point, if one becomes famous and is in her eighties, who cares? She has already done what she wanted to do. Like the Los Angeles performance artist Rachel Rosenthal said, "I have done what I wanted to do. You can give me any awards you want. It's not going to destroy my identity. It's already done. It may alleviate the problem of finding money to get a hip replacement, that's about the end of it."

———FP———

What you've said reminds me of a work of Mirella's, *Arachne's Imprint* (1978) (Figure 34), which has a photograph of Michelangelo's

Piazza del Campidoglio on the Capitoline Hill in Rome at the top and a photo of a spider web underneath that replicates the design of the Campidoglio. That seems like a good image for Mirella. She's created this web of context, of ideas, and of institutions that is strong because of all of the various elements that she's established around the world, within Rome, across personal and professional communities.

——JO——

Absolutely. And the other thing is, in Rome they have something called *il salotto* or salon. The Roman salon can be very exclusionary. You get invited or not invited to tell you something about who you are. Mirella absolutely did not abide by those rules. She invited people who were wrong for this *salotto* to that *salotto*, people who were right for that *salotto* to this *salotto*. And she basically said, "Come if you'd like." So she cut across lines, and she did it so well and was so independent that nobody could really be angry with her about it. While some Romans thought, "Why is she bringing these other people to our *salotto*?" she didn't care. She was bringing interesting people. So her network, this web that you talk about, was also very intelligently constructed by being democratic, which was not the Roman way of doing things. The Roman way of doing things is very hierarchical. You know exactly who is in charge. Whether some person is organizing it down here or over there, it is set up to reiterate an existing hierarchy. Without going against those hierarchies, Mirella ignored them, and she actually ended up surrounding herself with a much stronger network, a much stronger group of people, because she didn't play by the rules as they were given.

——FP——

Do you think being a woman allowed her to do this more effectively than if she had been a man?

——JO——

Totally. You know, she'd say, "Oh, I'm not important anyway," when they would try to get her to tow the line. And she's an incredibly graceful person, as you know. She's very, very gracious. She deflects, and she'll occasionally stop before she answers, and come back with something. She lived in Taormina for a long time. In Sicily they say people tell you more about what they are thinking by what they don't say as opposed to what they say. Mirella likes the ambiguity of language. But it's not about keeping certain things secret or not exposing herself, it is about measuring and choosing responses for a clearer understanding.

——FP——

So she was diplomatic.

——JO——

I think so. I think she is a very good steward and ambassador for the arts in general. She was a great steward for women and for artists who are working with means that are drawn not from pictorial traditions but from literature and writing. And I think that she was a great ambassador in letting people know about these things and not making them so obtuse as not to be clear.

——FP——

And she has an incredible sense of humor. You see that in her work as well. Did that help her in these kinds of negotiations, do you think?

——JO——

I imagine so. With me it was never an issue because we met as peers and could laugh out loud about lots of things. There was never any reason to diffuse answers with me. But I assume that when dealing with power, her ability to be both diplomatic and use humor would be very useful to her so as to avoid conflicts.

——FP——

Can you briefly explain what the art market is like in Italy? I have the sense that it is not as organized or as extensive as it is in the United States.

——JO——

Well, I would have to preface this by saying that I don't know all of the ins and outs of the Italian art market because it is a fairly behind-the-scenes market, it is not as easy to trace as it is in the

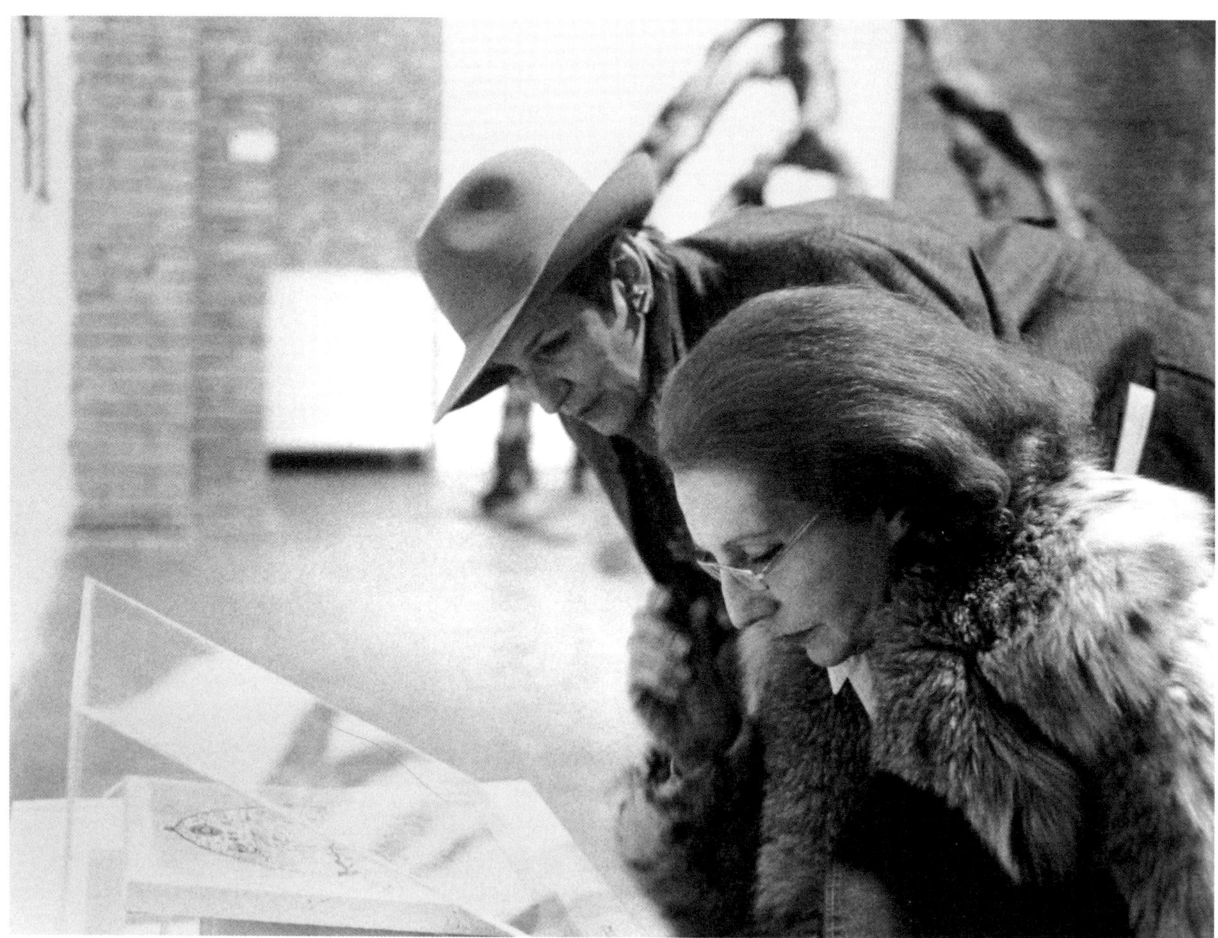

FIGURE 38——
Mirella Bentivoglio's one-person show, "Simbolo come struttura (Symbol as Structure)," Sala 1, Rome, 1984. Left: Mirella Bentivoglio; right: Palma Bucarelli, director, National Gallery.

United States. A number of people who are quite wealthy tend to support specific and different galleries. They tend to buy from the gallery in depth and profoundly to give it support. It is done through a network of people who know each other and often the artists themselves buy other artists' work. It is a relatively small market. So artists in Europe either have personal income that allows them to exist without selling their work, or they have another job, such as teaching, that keeps them busy two or three days a week and they are free to work in their studios the rest of the time. That's pretty much how it works. It is not a market in which you are going to find emerging collectors, although it appears to be changing some now. And oftentimes collectors contact critics and ask for help amassing a certain kind of collection. The independents are few and far between.

——FP——

Maybe in Rome, with its massive monuments to the past, it is difficult to draw people in to look at contemporary artwork. But I have a sense that there is civic, municipal, and state support for the arts.

——JO——

In Italy, unlike the United States, significant funds are available for cities, regions, and provinces to do exhibitions, and they are organized quite wonderfully in civic buildings that range from palaces to castles. Mirella is known in those circuits quite well. She is also appreciated because she will help them put together a really good show, not just of her work. She's not so self-centered that she'll bring only her things and fill the castle. She's also attentive to the importance of the territory in Italy. The Italians, and the Italian authorities who are putting these things on, don't want to perceive of themselves as being from a province, but they do need to represent their areas. And because Mirella knows so much about artists who are not just in the Milan-Turin market, which is the most important market, or the Rome market, she actually will be able to help them find really interesting artists who are connected to the area or to the territory. So she was often tapped not only to participate as an artist, but also to help jump-start a really interesting enterprise, and then because she's a writer herself, if she could, she would write about it, or she would call other writer friends and ask them to write about it. So she would also get coverage, which is what these municipalities are really looking for. At the end of the day, their justification for spending those monies was to do something in the context of the city, such as a city-wide festival, but also because the specialized press came and said, "Ah, what an amazing show." Mirella did a lot of work in those circuits. This is something in Italy that is dying now, because of the way the funding is changing. But for the longest time it was quite possible to imagine these extraordinarily intelligent and very versatile shows in places that were the provinces, basically.

You could argue that Mirella was not very strategic about her career, and I think she would argue that she never thought of her life as a career. So in a funny sort of way it is an absolutely logical outcome. I think that's something to be said in her favor. It was a way of imagining oneself as a mother and a woman and a person who has a community to make reference to, how you can continue to be a significant contributor to the arts without following some strange and abstract career model where you are constantly following the market and quantifying your work to fit that.

She didn't spend a whole lot of time treating her work as though it was a career, that's my point. That is something I took as a lesson, as opposed to considering it a mistake. I took it as being a way of thinking of oneself as a human being, in the context of creating a life of art, not just a series of works that get marketed. And it is certainly one of the answers to the question of why she didn't become so famous, because she wasn't seeking those places where that form of recognition during your lifetime is accorded you.

Frances K. Pohl

———FP———

You are right. Her renown is in so many different places, that web of being known as a critic, as a historian of women Futurists and other artists, as a visual poet and curator, and having an extensive archive and a record of assisting other women and men to gain some sense of community, if not visibility. She seems to be as interested in connecting people as in showing their work.

———JO———

This is something Mirella and I have been talking about this year, too. The conversation, as it is called—*la conversazione, il discorso sull'arte*—in Rome is not fundamentally that which shows up in print. It is that which comes up in conversation, literally, at the openings and afterwards.

And this is what most Roman artists really feel is the preeminent importance of exhibiting. Yes, it would be great to sell, and if you could, you would be very happy. But this is not really the reason why artists exhibit. They exhibit because they want to be a part of the *discorso*, they want that feedback, want that give and take, want even argumentation to take place. I think Mirella will tell you that this world of *discorso sull'arte* was absolutely a place in which she flourished. She was not only in it as a participant, she was orchestrating it, she was writing about it, she was even quantifying it. So that is the payback for all the work that one does, this sense of an incredibly vibrant community in Rome. Mirella really excelled at being a hub and being an active part of the discourse.

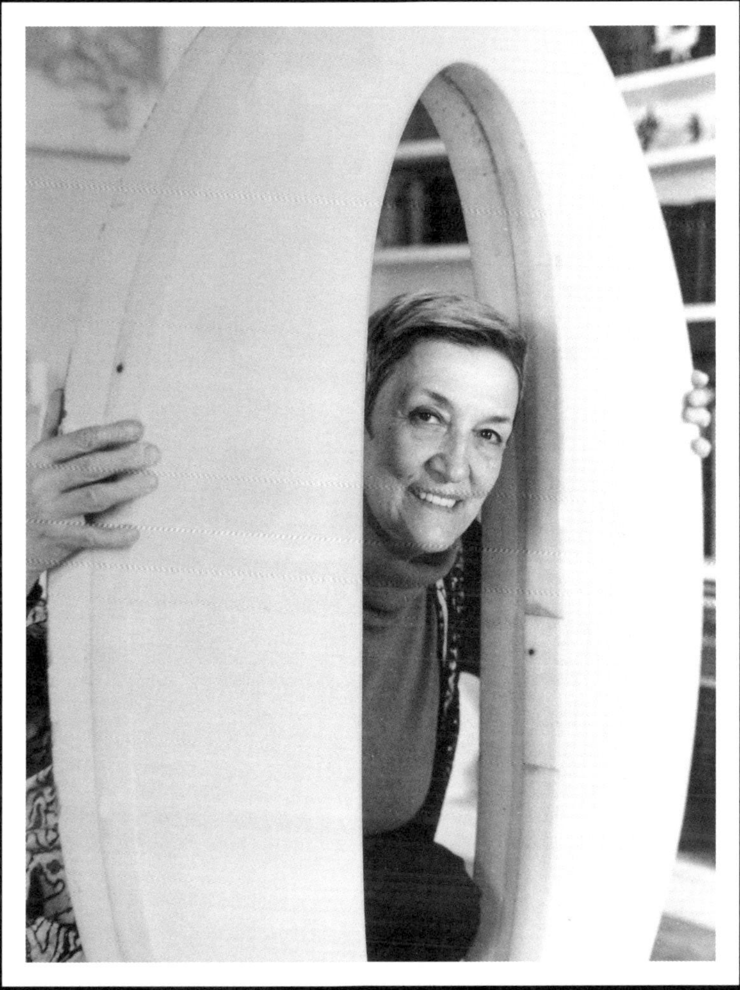

FIGURE 39—
Mirella Bentivoglio, late 1990s.

MIRELLA BENTIVOGLIO—
A BIOGRAPHICAL NOTE
Rosaria Abate

MIRELLA BENTIVOGLIO—
A BIOGRAPHICAL NOTE

Rosaria Abate

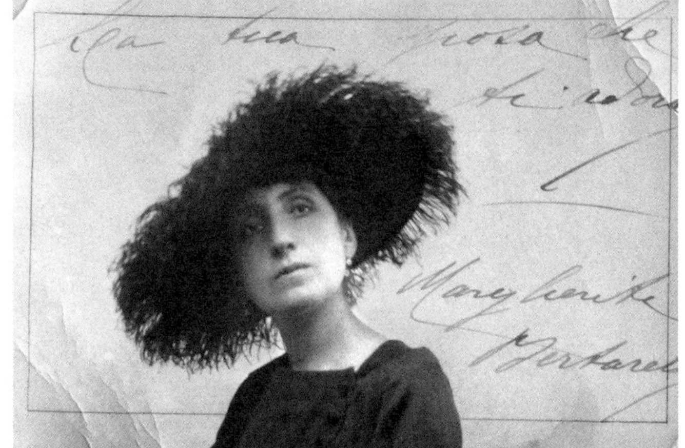

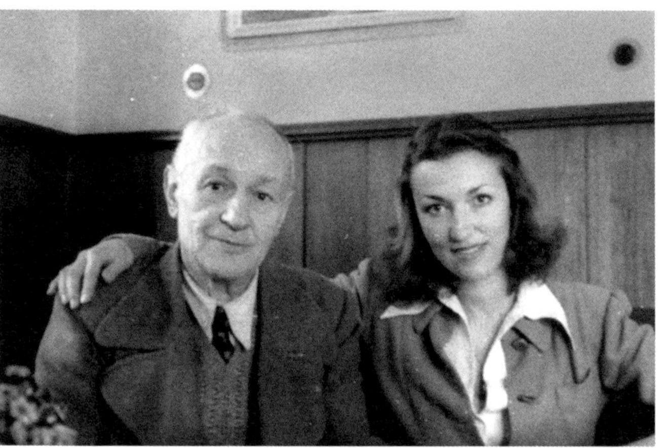

Mirella Bentivoglio was born in Klagenfurt, Austria, in 1922, of Italian parents, and her birth abroad seems to have predicted the international dimension that has typified the whole of her life. After a childhood spent in Milan, she was educated at Swiss and English boarding schools, and in 1939 was awarded certificates of proficiency in English by the University of Cambridge and University of Sheffield. In 1949, she married Ludovico Matteo (Teo) Bentivoglio and accompanied him to the United States, where they resided for a year. Their marriage gave birth to three daughters. Ludovico Bentivoglio, a university professor of aviation law as well as a United Nations expert on international problems relating to outer space, died prematurely in 1980 at the age of 55.

FIGURE 40 (top)——
Margherita Cavalli, c. 1910.

FIGURE 41 (bottom)——
Mirella Bentivoglio (Bertarelli) with
father, Ernesto Bertarelli, 1939.

The artist's father Ernesto Bertarelli—a scientist, a bibliophile and the president of the Hoepli publishing company—was particularly significant for the development of Mirella Bentivoglio's relationship with books. But, according to Bentivoglio, her husband, through their many conversations, exerted a more fundamental influence on the direction that her art was to take.

Her mother, Margherita Cavalli, was likewise a highly creative person, even though her artistic talents remained confined to the sphere of domestic life. Awareness of the ways in which her mother's gifts were held in check by her condition as a woman is likely to have played an important role in directing the artist's future activities toward the "liberation" of women artists. Toward the middle of the 1960s, Mirella Bentivoglio entered the ranks of the experimental avant-garde, first with Concrete Poetry, then with Visual Poetry, and finally with a kind of object poetry that makes metaphorical use of sculptural forms. All three types of visual expression were represented in her first one-person show, in 1971–72, at the Arturo Schwarz Gallery, in Milan. In the following years, she also turned to site-specific interventions in public spaces as well as to performance. Throughout her career, in fact, her work has always been distinguished by its lack of adherence to any one mode of expression and has been characterized most specifically by the fusion of words and images. This hybridization can also be seen as a comprehensive synthesis of the various areas of creativity in which she has been involved since early childhood. While still quite small, she engaged in theatrical activities; as an adolescent, she painted canvases of notable interest in the context of her involvement in Milanese cultural circles. During the war, in 1943, the well-known Milanese publisher Vanni Scheiwiller issued *Giardino*, her first collection of poetry. This book was followed in 1968 by *Calendario* (Vallecchi Publishers, Florence) and in 1976 by *Jet-P68* (Edikon Publishers, Rome), both of which were met with critical interest and nominated for important literary prizes (such as the Viareggio Prize).

Mirella Bentivoglio's subsequent advancement beyond painting and verse led to the experiments with images and words that put her in touch with similarly interested artists throughout the world. The exhibition of her work at highly prestigious institutions in Italy, Germany, England, Holland, Spain, the Czech Republic, the United States, Argentina, and Brazil came about as a result. Her most important recent retrospectives include those at the Palazzo delle Esposizioni, Rome (1996), the National Museum of Women in the Arts, Washington, D.C. (1999), the Pomona College Museum of Art, Claremont, California (2003, with the American artist Ben Shahn), and Oculus Gallery, Tokyo (2010). Her work has been shown on ten occasions, between 1969 and

2009, at the Venice Biennial; at the São Paolo Biennial in 1973, 1981, and 1994; at Centre Pompidou, in Paris, in 1978, 1981, and 1982; and at Documenta, in Kassel, in 1992. Her works and installations are found in the collections of the Museum of Contemporary Art of Rome (MACRO), Museum of Contemporary Art of Trento and Rovereto (MART), Uffizi Gallery Museum (Florence), Museo di Ca' Pesaro (Venice), the J. Paul Getty Museum (Los Angeles), Museum of Contemporary Art (MAC) (University of São Paolo), Museum of Modern Art (New York), Sackner Archive of Visual and Concrete Poetry (Miami), and many others. Her interventions in public spaces have appeared in various parts of Italy (Umbria, Matera, the Neapolitan countryside), as well as in Prague, in 2005, along the banks of the Vltava River. In Rome, the press has given particular attention to her project for the renewal of Piazza Augusto Imperatore in the center of the city, where she proposed a revitalization of this monumental historical site by way of an installation of the symbolic alphabetical structures (the letter "E") that she first constructed in 2003 (Figure 37).

Mirella Bentivoglio's activity as an artist has been flanked by her commitments as a critic and as a curator and organizer of specialized group exhibitions —often inclusive of her own work—that hinge on the conjunction of language and image.

Her efforts as a critic first began with studies of the work of the American painter Ben Shahn, who was the subject of a research project she conducted during a seminar in American Studies in Salzburg in 1958. This project was later amplified in the monograph that she published with De Luca Publishers in 1963. In 1968, thanks to her publications, she was officially promoted in Italy to Professor of Art History and Aesthetics (*idoneità all'insegnamento*). She has authored articles for the daily press and magazines, as well as essays for catalogs and books. She has also chaired conferences and debates and conducted lessons and seminars at a range of educational institutions. She has curated approximately one hundred exhibitions for, among others, the Institutes of Italian Culture in Tokyo, Los Angeles, Helsinki, and New York; the Perth Festival in Australia; New York's Museum of Modern Art; and the Biennials of Venice, Italy; São Paolo, Brazil; and Medellin, Colombia.

Mirella Bentivoglio's organizational activities in the field of creative expression that lies between word and image have also been distinguished by her promotion of the work of women artists. She was the first curator, as early as the 1970s, to champion the inclusion of women in the international exhibitions that have become fundamental reference points for artists working in this field. Such exhibitions include, among others, the "Esposizione

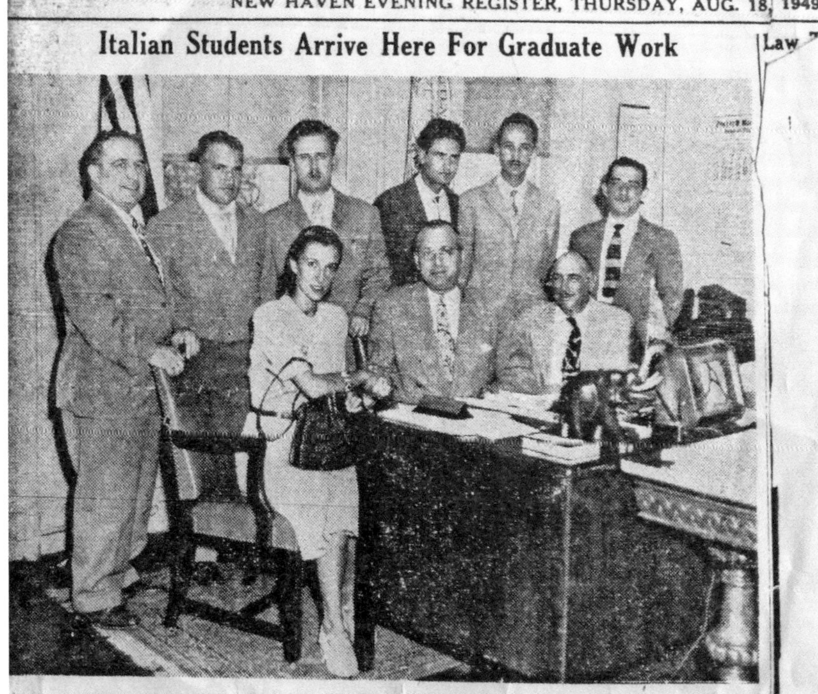

NEW HAVEN EVENING REGISTER, THURSDAY, AUG. 18, 1949

Italian Students Arrive Here For Graduate Work

Mayor William C. Celentano greets Mrs. Mirella Bentivoglio, wife of one of three Italian students who have arrived here to do graduate work at American universities. On Mayor Cenentano's right is Police Comsr. Daniel J. Adley. Standing, left to right, Dr. Frank Mongillo, Albert Cupelli, Italian Consul at New Haven; Ludovico M. Bentivoglio, studying at the Yale Law School; Francesco Mei, studying literature at University of Notre Dame, South Bend, Ind.; Virginio Rognoni, studying international relations at Yale University; and Dr. Frank M. Anastasio.

internazionale di operatrici visuali" at Milan's Centro Tool (1971), "Materializzazione del linguaggio" at the Venice Biennial (1978); "O quadrato do dizer" at the São Paolo Biennial (1981); and "Volùmina" at Rocca Roveresca at Senigallia, Ancona (1988). Her interest in women's art that explores the relationship between word and image extends beyond the area of contemporary art to include the work of the early twentieth-century Italian Futurist avant-garde. Her research in the archives of the Getty Research Institute has helped generate a greater focus on the work of these women artists and has led to university seminars and exhibitions, as well as two monographic publications co-authored by Bentivoglio and Franca Zoccoli, the first published in the United States (Midmarch, 1997) and the second in Italy (De Luca Publishers, 2008). In 2010, the latter was awarded the first *Il paese delle donne* prize in the visual arts category.

FIGURE 42—
"Italian Students Arrive Here for Graduate Work," *New Haven Evening Register* (New Haven, Connecticut), August 18, 1949. Seated, far left: Mirella Bentivoglio; standing, third from left: Ludovico Matteo (Teo) Bentivoglio.

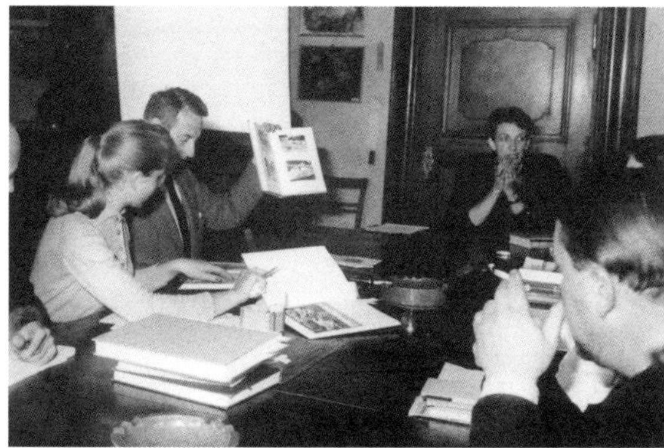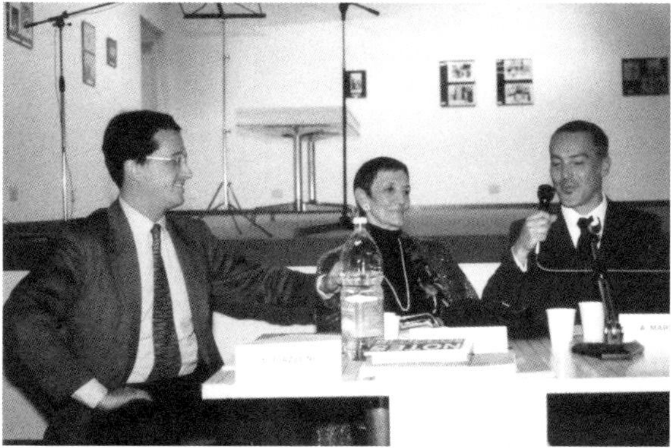

Mirella Bentivoglio's correspondence with an extensive network of women artists who work with word and image resulted in the accumulation of a substantial archive of works and documents. She donated the bulk of this collection to Rovereto's MART, in 2011. This act of generosity was celebrated with a large show of the donated works at MART, accompanied by a richly illustrated catalog.

In addition to her own creative work, Mirella Bentivoglio's critical and theoretical contribution to the field of "the new poetry" has been fundamental for the understanding and appreciation of this form of artistic expression. For example, her article "*Poesia Visiva* (Visual Poetry)," written at the invitation of Giulio Carlo Argan for the supplement to the *Enciclopedia Universale dell'Arte* (Unedi Publishers, 1978), presents an exhaustive analysis of all the various directions that work moving along the horizon between word and image has taken. She also coined the term *librismo* to describe that specific dimension of aesthetic research that concerns itself with the notion of the book (artists' books, book-objects, book-installations, and so forth).

At ninety-two years of age, and still active as both an artist and critic, Mirella Bentivoglio now also has turned her attention to the organization of the extensive body of creative work that she herself has authored over her numerous decades of intense cultural activity.

FIGURE 43 (left)——
Mirella Bentivoglio, seated at center right, Salzburg, Austria, 1958.

FIGURE 44 (right)——
Da pagina a spazio (From Page to Space) seminar, La Spezia, 1998. Center: Mirella Bentivoglio; left: Filippo Marinetti Piazzoni, grandson of F.T. Marinetti.

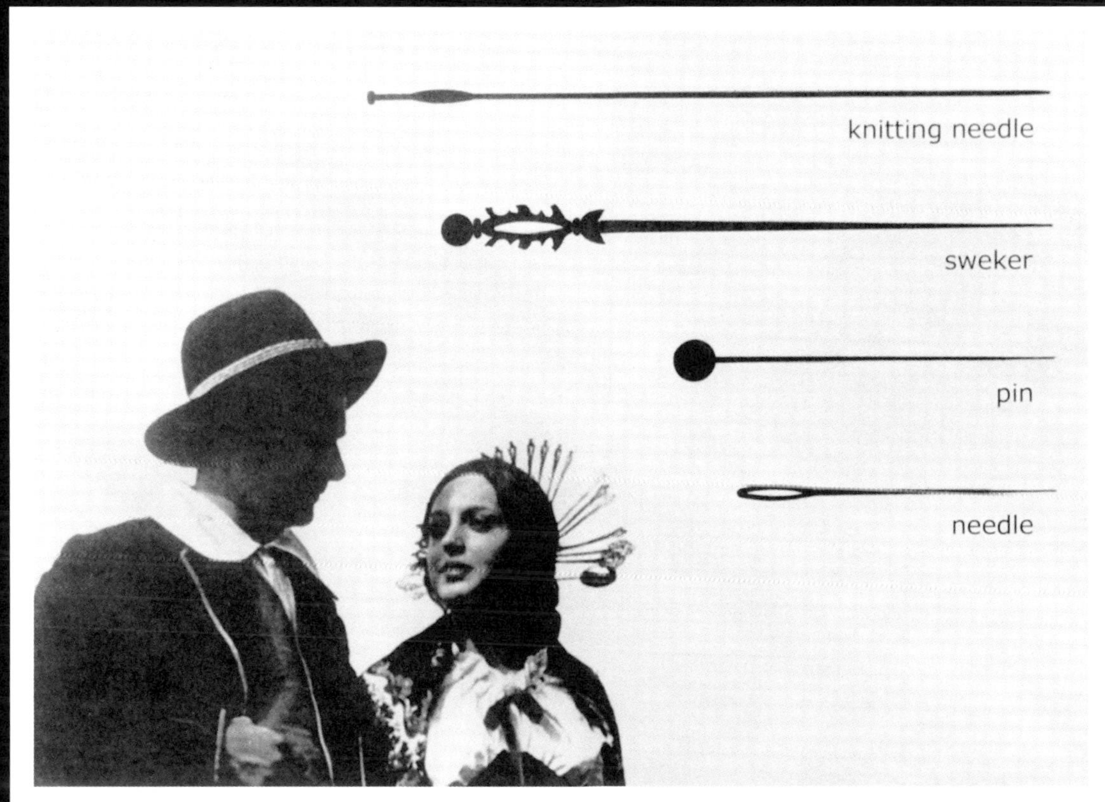

SELECTED EXHIBITION HISTORY

BIBLIOGRAPHY

EXHIBITION CHECKLIST

FIGURE 45 —
Analisi semiotica—la fattura per non pensare (la raggiera della donna é la sua condanna) (Semiotic Analysis— The Spell for Not Thinking [The Halo of the Woman Is Her Condemnation]), 1978. Offset lithograph on paper, 13¹⁵⁄₁₆ × 16⁹⁄₁₆ in. (35.4 × 42.07 cm).

SELECTED EXHIBITION HISTORY

SOLO EXHIBITIONS

"Bentivoglio," Galleria Schwarz, Milan, 1971

"Mirella Bentivoglio. Poesia visiva," Galleria Pictogramma, Rome, 1973

"XII São Paulo Biennial," São Paulo, 1973

"Mirella Bentivoglio. Typographische Poesie," Klingspor Museum der Buch-und-Schriftkunst, Offenbach-am-Main, 1974

"Mirella Bentivoglio," Studio Santandrea, Milan, 1975

"Mirella Bentivoglio," Galleria Il Brandale, Savona, 1976

"Bentivoglio-Display," Poetry Collection, State University of New York at Buffalo, Buffalo, 1977

"Distratti dall'ambiente," Galleria d'Arte Moderna, Bologna, 1978

"Mirella Bentivoglio: Poegraphy," Other Books and So Gallery, Amsterdam, 1978

"Poesia-azione," Spazio Alternativo, Rome, 1978

"Ab Eva," Spazio Alternativo, Rome, 1979

"Mirella Bentivoglio," Casa Italiana, Nazareth College, Rochester, 1979

"The Egg," Italian Cultural Institute, New York, 1980

"Scritture di pietra," Galleria Arte Duchamp, Cagliari, 1982

"Pietra filosofale," Galleria Il Segno, Turin, 1983

"La Poesia fatta pietra," Pinacoteca Comunale, Chiesa di San Paolo, Macerata, 1984

"Simbolo come struttura," Sala 1, Rome, 1984

"Percorso," Club Il Centro, Rome, 1985

"Hyper Ovum," Torre del Lebbroso, Aosta, 1987

"Mirella Bentivoglio," Banco di Santo Spirito, Rome, 1987

"Histoire d'E," Writers' Forum, London, 1988

"Mirella Bentivoglio," Palazzo dei Consoli, Gubbio, 1988

"Fotoalchimia," Comune de La Spezia, Centro Culturale Il Gabbiano, La Spezia, 1990

"Mirella Bentivoglio a Gubbio," Artefiera, Bologna, 1991

"Mirella Bentivoglio," Micro Hall Art Center, Edewecht-Klein Scharrel, 1991

"Eidos," Galleria Quantica, Turin, 1993

"Silenziario," Studio Bocchi, Rome, 1993

"Un albero di pagine," Galleria Mercato del Pesce, Milan-Sesto, 1993

"Controlapide," Biblioteca Ariostea, Ferrera, 1994

"Palio d'autore," Palazzo Ducale, Gubbio, 1994

"Un albero di pagine," Palazzo dell'Archiginnasio, Bologna, 1994

"Un albero di pagine," Associazione Culturale Eralov, Rome, 1995

"Dalla parola al simbolo," Palazzo delle Esposizioni, Rome, 1996

"The Visual Poetry of Mirella Bentivoglio," National Museum of Women in the Arts, Washington, D.C., 1999

"L'itinerario di Mirella Bentivoglio," Senigallia (Ancona), Museo Comunale d'Arte Moderna e dell'Informazione (Musinf) / Palazzo del Duca, 2005; Quaderni del Musinf, Senigallia, 2006

GROUP EXHIBITIONS: CONCRETE AND VISUAL POETRY

"Poesia Concreta," Club Turati, Milan, 1967

"Mostra di poesia concreta / indirizzi concreti, visuali e fonetici," Venice: Ca' Giustinian, Sala delle Colonne, 1969

"Mostra di poesia concreta," Biennale di Venezia, Venice, 1969

"Novisima Poesia," Instituto Torcuato Di Tella, Buenos Aires, 1969

"Konkrete Poezie," Stedelijk Museum, Amsterdam, 1970

"La Poesia degli anni '70," Museo del Castello, Brescia, 1970

"Archivio Denza di poesia visiva—selezione internazionale 1969–71," Studio Santandrea, Milan, 1972

"Il libro come luogo di ricerca," Biennale di Venezia, Venice, 1971

"Italian Visual Poetry, 1912–1972," Finch College Museum of Art, New York and Galleria Civica d'Arte Moderna, Turin, 1972

"Poesia visiva internazionale 74," Galleria Il Canale, Venice, 1974

"Visuele Poezie," Van Gogh Museum, Amsterdam, 1975

"La scrittura," Galleria Seconda Scala, Rome; Studio Santandrea, Milan; Galleria Unimedia, Genoa, 1976

"Parola Immagine Oggetto" (curated by Mirella Bentivoglio), Lamberto Pignotti and Tokihisho Shimizu, Istituto Italiano di Cultura, Tokyo, 1976

"La forma della Scrittura," Galleria d'Arte Moderna, Bologna, 1977

"Concreto e Visuale," University of Sydney and National Gallery, Melbourne, 1978

"Materializzazione del linguaggio" (curated by Mirella Bentivoglio), Biennale di Venezia, Venice, 1978

"Photopoetry," Polytechnic of Central London, London, 1978

"Segnoepoesia," Centro Culturale d'Arte Bellora, Milan, 1978

"Utopia e crisi dell'antinatura-Intenzioni architettoniche in Italia," Biennale di Venezia, Venice, 1978

"From Page to Space" (curated by Mirella Bentivoglio), Columbia University, New York, 1979

"La poesia visiva," Palazzo Vecchio, Florence, 1979

"Sprachen jenseits von Dichtung," Westfälischer Kunstverein, Műnster, 1979

"Testuale," Rotonda della Besana, Milan, 1979

"Il tempo del Museo Venezia," Biennale di Venezia, Venice, 1980

"Ecritures," Fondation Nationale des Arts Graphiques et Plastiques, Paris, 1980

"De la pagina al espacio" (curated by Mirella Bentivoglio), I Bienal de Arte, Medellin, Colombia, 1981

"Linee della ricerca artistica in Italia, 1960–1980," Palazzo delle Esposizione, Rome, 1981

"Nucleus I," São Paulo Biennial, São Paulo, 1981

"O quadrato do dizer" (curated by Mirella Bentivoglio), São Paulo Biennial, São Paulo, 1981

"Arte italiana 1960–1982," Hayward Gallery, London, 1982

"Documenta Urbana," Documenta, Kassel, 1982

"Raffaello Cinquecento anni dopo," Galleria Bonaparte, Milan, 1983

"Arte e Alchimia," Biennale di Venezia, Venice, 1986

"Arte come scrittura," XI Quadriennale Nazionale d'Arte, Palazzo dei Congressi, Rome, 1986

"Triennale europea d'arte sacra," Celano (L'Aquila), Castello Piccolomini, 1986

"Parola come immagine" (curated by Mirella Bentivoglio), Comune di Senigallia, 1987

"Mare & mare—biennale internazionale del mare," Castel dell'Ovo, Naples, 1988

"Terza Biennale d'Arte Sacra 'la Croce,'" Archivio di Stato, Pescara, 1988

"Textilia—interpretazioni tessili e trame nell'arte," Basilica Palladiana, Vicenza, 1988

"Traccia corporea," Palazzo dei Consoli, Gubbio (Perugia), 1988

"Crossing the Line: Word and Image in Art, 1960–1990," Montgomery Gallery, Pomona College, Claremont, California, 1990

"Le muse inquietanti, aspetti attuali della ricerca artistica femminile," Museo Civico, Rende (Cosenza), 1990

"Nuova scrittura nella Collezione della Banca Commerciale Italiana," Banca Commerciale Italiana, Milan, 1990

"Un itinerario sul filo della scultura," Centro Saint-Bénin, Aosta, 1990

"Visual Poetry," Otis-Parsons Instituto, Los Angeles, 1990

"Blank Page 5," Three Tyers Gate, London, 1991

"Le arti in carta," ex Chiesa di San Giovanni Battista, Riolo Terme (Bologna), 1991

"Parola immagine. Per l'aggiornamento di un museo," Civica Galleria d'Arte Moderna, Gallarate (Varese), 1991

"The Second International Exhibiton of Visual Poetry, Melbourne," Linden Gallery, St. Kilda, 1991

"Fotoidea" (curated by Mirella Bentivoglio and Alessandro Allmonti), São Paulo Biennial, São Paulo, 1994

"Palio d'autore," Palazzo Ducale, Gubbio, 1994

"Identità e differenza," Biennale di Venezia, Venice, 1995

"Sedicesima biennale internazionale del bronzetto—piccola scultura Padova '95. Scultura e oltre," Palazzo della Ragione and Giardini dell'Arena, Padua, 1995

"V Bienal Internacional de Poesia Visual/Experimental," Museo Universitario del Chopo, Mexico City, 1996

"Sintonle—Omaggio a Martini," Galleria Dieda, Bassano del Grappa (Vicenza), 1996

"Arte Contemporanea 'lavori in corso n. 5,'" Galleria Comunale d'Arte Moderna e Contemporanea, ex stabilimento Peroni, Rome, 1998

"Poesia totale," Palazzo della Ragione, Mantova, 1998

"Post Scriptum," Biennale Donna, Palazzo Massari, Ferrara, 1998

"Immaginazione aurea—artisti-orafi e orafi-artisti in Italia nel secondo Novecento," Mole Vanvitelliana, Ancona, 2001

"Carthusia 2002—Territori," Certosa di Pontignano, Siena, 2002

"Figurare la parola—editoria e avanguardie artistiche dal Novecento nel fondo Bertini," Biblioteca Nazionale Centrale, Florence, 2003

"Il non gruppo—testi-immagine a Roma negli anni Sessanta" (curated by Mirella Bentivoglio), Biblioteca Angelica, Rome; Galleria Miralli—Palazzo Chigi, Viterbo, 2004–5

"Il libro come tema, il libro come opera," Galleria Nazionale d'Arte Moderna, Rome, 2006

"Pagine immagine—Mirella Bentivoglio, Bruno Conte, Emilio Villa," Galleria Cortese & Lisanti, Rome, 2007

"La parola nell'arte: Ricerche d'avanguardia del '900 dal Futurismo a oggi attraverso le collezioni del MART," MART, Rovereto (Trento), 2007–8

"Poesia visiva—what to do with poetry," MART, Rovereto (Trento), 2010

"Autoritratte: Artiste di capriccioso e destrissimo ingegno," Galleria degli Uffizi, Sala delle Poste Reali, Florence, 2011

"Poesia visiva—la donazione Bentivoglio," MART, Rovereto (Trento), 2011

"Di-segni poetici 2," Palazzo Marchesale del Tufo, Matino (Lecce), 2013

GROUP EXHIBITIONS: BOOK-OBJECTS AND ARTIST'S BOOKS

"Cinquantenaire des Editions Scheiwiller," Centre Georges Pompidou, Paris, 1978

"Formato Lib&ro," Fortezza da Basso, Florence, 1978

"Two Centuries of Art Magazine," Victoria and Albert Museum, London, 1976

"Buchobjekte," University of Fribourg, Fribourg, 1980

"Livres d'Art et d'Artistes," Galerie NRA, Paris, 1980

"Artists Books," Stedelijk Museum, Amsterdam, 1981

"Il Manifeste du Livre d'Artiste," Centre Georges Pompidou, Paris, 1981

"Il Manifeste du Livre d'Artiste," Centre Georges Pompidou, Paris, 1982

"Not(e) Books" (curated by Mirella Bentivoglio), Quentin Gallery, Perth; City Art Institute, Sydney; University of Melbourne, Melbourne, 1982

"Artists Books," Centro de Arte y Comunicación, Buenos Aires, 1984

"The Book as a Container of Ideas," University of Oldenburg, Oldenburg, 1985

"Il non libro" (curated by Mirella Bentovogio), Biblioteca Centrale della Regione Siciliana, Palermo, 1985

"Arcana Scheiwiller," Accademia dei Lincei, Rome, 1987

"International Artists Books," Musée Roi Saint Etienne, Szekasfehervar, Hungary, 1987

"Volúmina" (curated by Mirella Bentivoglio), Rocca Roveresca, Senigallia, 1988

"Book as Art II," The National Museum of Women in the Arts, Washington, D.C., 1989

"Far libro 1955–1988," Casermetta del Forte Belvedere, Florence, 1989

"Book as Art III," The National Museum of Women in the Arts, Washington, D.C., 1990

"Il librismo," Regione Autonoma Sardegna, Fiera di Cagliari, 1990

"Book as Art IV," The National Museum of Women in the Arts, Washington, D.C., 1991

"The Artist and the Book in XXth Century Italy," The Museum of Modern Art, New York, 1992

"Book as Art V," The National Museum of Women in the Arts, Washington, D.C., 1992

"Der Buchismus," Gutenberg Museum, Minipressen Messe, Mainz, 1993

"Book as Art VI," The National Museum of Women in the Arts, Washington, D.C., 1993

"Libri d'artista italiani del novecento," Collezione Peggy Guggenheim, Palazzo Venier dei Leoni, Venice, 1994

"Il seme del libro," Palazzo Massari, Ferrara, 1994

"Lapus libri d'artista," National Central Library, Rome, 1995

"13th Mainzer Minipressen Messe," Gutenberg Museum, Mainz, 1995

"Buchobjecte aus Italien," Buchgalerie Mergemeier, Düsseldorf, 1996

"I Biennale del libro-oggetto d'artista," City Library, Monte Cassino, 1997

"Testo e contesto: il libro-ambiente" (curated by Mirella Bentivoglio), Palazzo Falconieri, Rome, 1998

"Book as Art XIII," The National Museum of Women in the Arts, Library and Research Center, Washington, D.C., 2001

SELECTED BIBLIOGRAPHY

Compiled by
Rosaria Abate

PUBLICATIONS BY MIRELLA BENTIVOGLIO

Books:

Mirella Bertarelli, *Giardino* (poetry). Milan: Edizioni Scheiwiller, 1943.

Ben Shahn. Rome: De Luca, 1963.

Calendario (poetry). Florence: Nuovedizioni Vallecchi, 1968.

La Collezione Astaldi (art criticism). Rome: De Luca, 1971.

Monumento (experimental poetry). Rome: De Luca, 1971.

Jet-P68 (poetry). Rome: Edikon, 1976.

Un albero di pagine (artist's book). Mirano (Venice): Eidos, 1992.

Da pagina a spazio: Futuriste italiane tra linguaggio e immagine. Bassano del Grappa (Vicenza): Galleria Dieda, 1997.

Women Artists of Italian Futurism—Almost Lost to History (with Franca Zoccoli). New York: Midmarch Arts Press, 1997.

Mezzo secolo fa (short stories with etchings by Gillo Dorfles). Rome: Il Bulino, 1998.

Le futuriste italiane nelle arti visive (with Franca Zoccoli). Rome: De Luca, 2008.

Exhibition Catalogs:

Arti visive / Poesia visiva. Rome: Studio d'Arte Contemporanea Artivisive, 1974.

Poesia visiva. Rome: Galleria Artivisive, 1975.

Tra linguaggio e immagine. Venice: Galleria Il Canale, 1976.

Poesia concreta (with Italo Mussa). Milan: Studio Santandrea, 1977.

Materializzazione del linguaggio. Venice: Biennale di Venezia, 1978.

Filo, genesi, filogenesi. Cagliari: Galleria Arte Duchamp, 1980.

De la pagina al espacio. Medellin, Colombia: IV Bienal de Arte, 1981.

Filo-logìa. Rome: Galleria Il Luogo delle Immagini del Segno e della Scrittura, 1981.

The Square of Saying. São Paulo: XVI Biennale di São Paulo, 1981.

Fil-Sophia: El concepte del fil en la dona-artista. Valencia: Sala Parpalló, 1982.

Not(e)books: An Exhibition of Object Books. Perth: Quentin Gallery, 1982.

Effetto donna (with Elverio Maurizi). Macerata: Coopedit Macerata, 1984.

Ideogramma come poesia (with Carla Vasio). Turin: Galleria Il Segno; Cagliari: Galleria Arte Duchamp, 1984.

Il non libro: Bibliofollia ieri e oggi in Italia. Palermo: Biblioteca Centrale della Regione Sicilia; Rome: De Luca, 1985.

L'ideogramma universale. Turin: Galleria Il Segno, 1986.

Volúmina. Senigallia: Museo dell'Informazione, 1988.

Il Librismo 1896–1990: Dalla cornice alla copertina, dal piedestallo allo scaffale. Cagliari: Arte Duchamp, 1990.

Fotoidea, São Paulo: São Paulo Biennale, 1994.

Profilo d'artista (with Floriano de Santi and Carlo Melloni). Ascoli Piceno: Palazzo Malaspina, 1995.

Ascoltare l'immagine. Pisa: Maschietto e Musolino, 1996.

Post Scriptum: Artiste in Italia tra linguaggio e imagine negli anni '60 e '70. Ferrara: VIII Biennale Donna, 1998.

Testo e contesto: Il libro-ambiente. Rome: Accademia d'Ungheria, Palazzo Falconieri, 1998.

Fotoalchimie: La fotografia in Italia: sperimentazioni e innesti. Prato: Centro per l'Arte Contemporanea Luigi Pecci, 2000.

(S)cripturae: Le scritture segrete: artiste tra scrittura e immagine. Padua: Galleria Civica, 2001.

Il non gruppo: Testi-immagine a Roma negli anni Sessanta. Rome: Biblioteca Angelica; Viterbo: Galleria Miralli / Palazzo Chigi, 2004–5.

Essays:

"La XII Biennale di San Paolo del Brasile." *Nuova Antologia* (Rome) 109, no. 2077 (January 1974), pp. 140–45.

"Poesia visiva." In *Nuovo conoscenze e prospettive del Mondo dell'Arte: aggiornamento dell'Enciclopedia Universale dell'Arte*. Rome: Unione Editoriale, 1978, pp. 462–69.

"Anmerkumgen sur Konkreten Dicktun." In *Sprachen jenseits von Dichtung*, edited by Thomas Deecke, pp. 185–87. Münster: Westfälischer Kunstverein, 1979.

"Una Testimonianza di Mirella Bentivoglio: Dieci Collettive al Femminile." *Informazioni Arti Visive* (December 1980), pp. 20–21.

"Materializzazione del linguaggio." In *Linee della ricerca artistica in Italia*, vol. II, pp. 91–92. Rome: Palazzo delle Esposizioni/De Luca, 1981.

"La poesia concreta brasiliana." In *Immagini del Brasile*, pp. 411–13. Rome: Bulzoni, 1986.

"Des livres muets, livres en langue européenne / I bri muti, libri in lingua europea." *Europa I*, no. 4 (October 1987): 35–44.

"Scritture del Silenzio." In *Donne e scrittura*, edited by Daniela Corona, pp. 377–87. Palermo: La Luna, 1990.

"La carta e il libro." *Le arti in carta: Il libro sperimentale in Italia*, pp. 4–5. Riolo Terme: Assessorati alla Cultura e al Turismo, 1991.

"La poesia concreta giapponese." In *Scrittura e immagine*, edited by Elisa Debenedetti and Jolanda Nigro Covre, pp. 99–107. Rome: Università La Sapienza/Bagatto-Libri, 1992.

"The Reinvention of the Book in Italy." *The Print Collector's Newsletter* 24, no. 3 (July–August 1993): 93–96.

"Modello o feticcio? La poesia concreta." In *Il Brasile in Italia, 1500–1995*. Rome: Presidenza del Consiglio dei Ministri, Dipartimento Informazione, 1995.

"Il libro-oggetto come fusion di tecniche e codici diversi." *Nuova Meta: Parole & immagini* 10, no. 7 (1996): 54–55.

"Percorso." In *Mirella Bentivoglio: dalla parola al simbolo*, pp. 49–51. Rome: De Luca, 1996.

"Trasposizioni da sonoro a visivo e scritture para-musicali." In *Le immagini della musica*. Rome: Istituto dell'Enciclopedia Italiana, Palombi, 1996.

"Dictatorial Relations: a Face for all Seasons." *American Journal of Graphic Art* 16, no. 3 (1998).

"Post-scriptum." In Anna Maria Fioravanti Beraldi, *Post-scriptum: Artiste in Italia tra linguaggio e imagine negli anni '60 e '70*, pp. 3–9. Cento (FE): Siaca Arti Grafiche, 1998.

"Innovative Artist's Books of Italian Futurism." In *International Futurism in Arts and Literature*, pp. 473–86. Berlin/New York: De Gruyter, 1999.

"(S)cripturae." In *(S)cripturae: Le scritture segrete: Artiste tra scrittura e immagine*, pp. 9–15. Padua: Galleria Civica, 2001.

"Meeting Ben Shahn." In Pomona College Museum of Art, *Love and Joy about Letters: The Work of Ben Shahn and Mirella Bentivoglio*, pp. 36–38. Claremont: Pomona College Museum of Art, 2003.

"Biennale di Venezia 78: Una precisazione a proposito della rassegna *Materializzazione del linguaggio. La donna tra parola e immagine*." *Terzo Occhio* 115 (June 2005): 45.

"Introduction." In *Futurismo ex novo*. Bassano del Grappa (Vicenza): Art Bug, 2009.

"I segni del femminile." In *Poesia visiva: La donazione di Mirella Bentivoglio al MART*, pp. 15–25. Milan: Sivana Editoriale, 2011.

"Ponti sull'Atlantico." In *Crossings: Ponti sull'Atlantico: Testi in ricordo di Regina Soria*, edited by Frederick Mario Fales, pp. 45–48. Naples: Liguori, 2011.

"La poesia verbovisiva: Lezione all'università Ca' Foscari, 2004." In *Di-segni poetici 2*, pp. 11–19. Lecce: Palazzo Marchesale del Tufo/Edizioini Grifo, 2013.

CRITICAL WRITINGS ON BENTIVOGLIO'S WORK

Books, Exhibition Catalogs, Book Chapters, Journal Essays, Dictionary Entries:
Accame, Vincenzo. "La poesia concreta in Italia." In *Uomini e Idee* 9 (May 1967): 61–65.

Apollonio, Umbro. "Rigore e fantasia nell'opera di Mirella Bentivogio." In *Bentivoglio*. Milan: Schwarz, 1971.

Barilli, Renato. "La parola materializzata di Mirella Bentivoglio." In *Bentivoglio*. Milan: Schwarz, 1971.

Venturoli, Marcello. "Bentivoglio." Catalogo nazionale Bolaffi della grafica, no. 3 (1972), p. 18.

Dorfles, Gillo. *Ultime tendenze nell'arte d'oggi: Dall'informale al concettuale*, pp. 143, 159, 202. Milan: Feltrinelli, 1973.

Apollonio, Umbro. "Mirella Bentivoglio." In *Eco della critica*, p. 23. Rome: Donati Editore, 1974.

Lubich, Roberta. "Intervista a Mirella Bentivoglio." In *Mass-media, pubblicità, esperienze artistiche in atto*. Graduation Thesis, Università degli Studi di Bologna, Facoltà di Lettere e Filosofia, 1976.

Menna, Filiberto. "Fotografia analitica, narrative art, nuova scrittura." In *L'Arte moderna* 14 (1975), pp. 193–224.

Bierther, Ursula. "Mirella Bentivoglio." In *Künstlerinnen International 1877–1977*, p. 295. Berlin/Frankfurt: Orangerie of the Charlottenburg Palace/Frankfurter Kunsteverein, 1977.

Menna, Filiberto. *Arte in Italia 1960–1977*. Turin: Galleria Civica d'Arte Moderna, 1977.

Accame, Vincenzo. *Il segno poetico*, pp. 72–73. Samedan: Munt Press, 1977.

Zatti, Susanna. "Mirella Bentivoglio." In *Dizionario degli artisti italiani del XX secolo*, vol. I, p. 36. Turin: Giulio Bolaffi Editore, 1978.

"Mirella Bentivoglio." In Luciano Caramel and Flavio Caroli, *Testuale: Le parole e le immagini*, p. 122. Milan: Rotonda della Besana, 1979.

Rescio, Bruno. *Mirella Bentivoglio, una poetica del significante*. Rome: Edikon, 1979.

Peignot, Jérome, and Marc Dachy. *Ecritures: Graphies notations typographies*. Paris: Fondation Nationale des Arts Graphiques et Plastiques, 1980.

Pignotti, Lamberto, and Stefania Stefanelli. *La scrittura verbo-visiva*. Rome: Editoriale L'Espresso, 1980.

Rosenberg, Judy. "Visual Poetry: The Avant-Garde in Italy." *Women Artists News* 6, no. 2–3 (Summer 1980): 8.

Di Genova, Giorgio. *Generazione anni Venti*, pp. 156–57, 179, 187–89. Bologna: Edizioni Bora, 1981.

Sacerdote, Franca. "Mirella Bentivoglio." In *Dizionario-guida dei pittori e scultori moderni e contemporanei*, p. 20. Milan: Rizzoli, 1981.

Crispolti, Enrico, and Agnes Denes. *Les estructures simboliques de Mirella Bentivoglio*. Barcelona: Galleria Metrònom, 1982.

"Mirella Bentivoglio." In *Bolaffi: Catalogo dell'Arte Moderna Italiana*, no. 19, p. 171. Milan: Giorgio Mondadori, 1983.

Mirella Bentivoglio: La poesia fatta pietra. (Excerpts from critical essays by Umbro Apollonio, Renato Barilli, Piero Berengo Gardin, Giorgio Brizio, Luciano Cherchi, Enrico Crispolti, Agnes Denes, Giorgio Di Genova, Gillo Dorfles, Emilio Isgrò, Carlo Laurenzi, Romana Loda, Henry Martin, Sandra Orienti, Piero Pacini, Michele Perfetti, Bruno Rescio, Stelio Rescio, Enzo Spera, Lorenza Trucchi, Miklos N. Varga, Marcello Venturoli, and Franca Zoccoli.) Macerata:

Coopedit Macerata/ Pinacoteca e Musei Comunali, 1984.

Spera, Enzo. *Le referenze bivalenti di Mirella Bentivoglio.* Bari: Centrosei, 1984.

Pohl, Frances K. "Language/ Image/Object: The Work of Mirella Bentivoglio." *Woman's Art Journal* 6, no. 1 (1985): 17–22.

Lacava, Elena. "Futurismo e libri d'artista." In *Italics 1925–1985: Sessant'anni di vita culturale in Italia,* pp. 205–15. Rome: Edizioni Treccani, 1986.

Brall, Artur. *Künstlerbücher Artist's Books—Book as Art.* Frankfurt am Main: Verlag Kretschmer & Großmann, 1986.

Crispolti, Enrico. "Un'architettura di sculture." In Manuela Crescentini, Enrico Crispolti, Danilo Fruscoloni, Cristina Piersimoni, and Ilaria Vanni, *Campo del sole,* pp. 9–30. Milan: Edizioni Mazzotta, 1986.

Brall, Artur. "Buchobjekts." In *Lexikon des gesamten Buchwesens,* vol. I, pp. 629–30. Stuttgart: Verlag Anton Hiersemann, 1987.

Pohl, Frances K. "Introduction." In *Histoire d'E.* London: Writers Forum, 1988. Artist's book.

Di Genova, Giorgio. *Storia dell'arte italiana del '900 per generazioni: Generazione anni Venti.* Bologna: Edizioni Bora, 1991.

Dorfles, Gillo. "Nove libri di nove artisti." In Francesca Cataldi, *Libri-oggetto,* pp. 5–9. Naples: Liguori, 1992.

Liccardo, Stefania. "Mirella Bentivoglio." Graduation thesis, Naples, Accademia di Belle Arti, 1992.

Crescentini, Manuela. "L'ambiente romano." In *La pittura in Italia: Il Novecento/2,* pp. 505–35. Milan: Edizioni Electa, 1993.

De Marco, Gabriella. "Il disegno tra utopia e progetto nell'arte povera e concettuale." In *Disegno italiano del Novecento,* pp. 302–17. Milan: Edizioni Electa, 1993.

Crispolti, Enrico "'Multimedialità' ed 'extramedialità.'" In *La pittura in Italia: Il Novecento/3.* Milan: Edizioni Electa, 1994.

Saur, K.G. "Mirella Bentivoglio." In *Allgemeines Künstler-Lexikon,* vol. VI, pp. 166–67. München: Leipzig, 1994.

Cerritelli, Claudio, and Luisa Somaini, *Gioielli d'artista in Italia 1945–95.* Milan: Edizioni Electa, 1995.

Sterling, Susan Fischer. *Women Artists: The National Museum of Women in the Arts,* p. 267. New York/ London/Paris: Abbeville Press, 1995.

Giulivi, Ariella, and Raffaella Trani. *Arturo Schwarz: La Galleria 1954–75.* Milan: Edizioni Mudima, 1995.

Pohl, Frances K. "Mirella Bentovoglio: Dismantling Images of Power in Italy." *Women's Studies* 25, no. 3 (1996): 239–68.

Barilli, Renato. "Alla ricerca del simbolo perduto." In *Mirella Bentivoglio: dalla parola al simbolo,* pp. 11–14. Rome: De Luca, 1996.

Johnson, Deborah. "Mirella Bentivoglio and Franca Zoccoli: Women Artists of Italian Futurism." *College Art Journal* (Providence [Rhode Island]) (Autumn 1998), p. 98.

Pohl, Frances K. "An Art of Alternatives: The Work of Mirella Bentivoglio." In National Museum of Women in the Arts, *The Visual Poetry of Mirella Bentivoglio,* pp. 11–14. Washington, D.C.: The National Museum of Women in the Arts and Rome: Edizioni De Luca, 1999.

Wasserman, Krystyna. "An Interview with Mirella Bentivoglio." In National Museum of Women in the Arts, *The Visual Poetry of Mirella Bentivoglio,* pp. 37–41. Washington, D.C.: The National Museum of Women in the Arts and Rome: Edizioni De Luca, 1999.

Berghaus, Günter. *International Futurism in Arts and Literature.* Berlin/New York: Walter de Gruyter, Berlin-New York, 2000.

Di Genova, Giorgio. *Generazione anni Trenta.* Bologna: Edizioni Bora, 2000.

Heller, Nancy G. "Artist's Book." *Women Artists: Works from the National Museum of Women in the Arts,* New York: Rizzoli International Publications, 2000.

Wasserman, Krystyna. "Mirella Bentivoglio." *Women Artists: Works from the National Museum of Women in the Arts,* pp. 210–11. New York: Rizzoli International Publications, 2000.

Iamurri, Laura, and Sabrina Spinazzè. *L'arte delle donne nell'Italia del Novecento.* Rome: Meltemi, 2001.

Pohl, Frances K. "Love and Joy About Letters: Ben Shahn and Mirella Bentivoglio," and "Mirella

Bentivoglio: Between Image and Word." In Pomona College Museum of Art, *Love and Joy about Letters: The Work of Ben Shahn and Mirella Bentivoglio.* Claremont: Pomona College Museum of Art, 2003.

Guglielmi, Laura, and Maurizio Petrangeli. "Un intervento radicale." In *Arte architettura città: 38 proposte per la sistemazione di Piazza Augusto Imperatore a Roma,* edited by Manuela Crescentini, Enrico Crispolti, and Paola Rossi, pp. 56-57. Rome: Prospettive Edizioni, 2003.

Abate, Rosaria. "L'attività artistica di Mirella Bentivoglio." Graduation thesis, Rome, Università degli Studi La Sapienza, Facoltà di Scienze Umanistiche, Corso di Laurea in Lettere, 2004.

Cogliani, Solveig. "Futurismi al femminile." Graduation thesis, Rome, University of Fine Arts, 2007.

Larkins, Zoe. "Antimonumentale monumentalità: 'Antimonumental Monumentality' in the Work of Mirella Bentivoglio." Graduation thesis, Claremont, CA, Scripps College, 2009.

Boglione, Riccardo. *I colpi di dado di Mirella Bentivoglio.* Senigallia (Ancona): Quaderni del Musinf, Senigallia, 2011.

Dencker, Klaus Peter. *Optische Poesie.* Berlin/New York: De Gruyter, 2011.

Ferrari, Daniela. "'Bussate (ai sogni) e vi sarà aperto': Mirella Bentivoglio, tessitrice di trame tra simboli, linguaggi e poesia." In *Poesia visiva, La donazione di Mirella Bentivoglio al MART*, pp. 27–33. Milan: Editoriale Silvana, 2011.

Newspapers and Magazines:

Caproni, Giorgio. "Due volumi di poesia." *La Fiera Letteraria* (Rome) 2, no. 36, September 1, 1947, p. 6.

De Feo, Italo. "Un fiore nel deserto." *Radiocorriere TV* (Turin) 46, no. 32, August 37, 1969, p. 37.

Laurenzi, Carlo. "Il piccolo paradosso." *Corriere della Sera* (Milan), August 12, 1969.

Isgrò, Emilio. "Libri in vetrina. Calendario di Mirella Bentivoglio." *Oggi Illustrato* (Milan) 25, no. 39, September 24, 1969, p. 114.

Perfetti, Michele. "Nuovo spazio poetico." *Corriere del Giorno* (Taranto), October 15, 1969.

Perfetti, Michele. "Una poesia in 'Calendario' e oltre." *Arte e Poesia* (Rome) 2, nos. 9–10 (July–December 1970), pp. 88–91.

Perfetti, Michele. "Poesia visiva da tutto il mondo ad Amsterdam." *Corriere del Giorno* (Taranto), January 19, 1971.

Perfetti, Michele. "La poesia visiva in Italia." *Arte e Poesia* (Rome) 3, nos. 11–14 (January–December 1971), pp. 185–99.

Perfetti, Michele. "Poesia visiva internazionale." *Corriere del Giorno* (Taranto), February 18, 1971.

Praz, Mario. "Il 'Calendario' di Mirella Bentivoglio." *Ausonia* (Siena) 26, nos. 1–2 (January–April 1971), pp. 101–2.

Perfetti, Michele. "Mirella Bentivoglio. La parola all'attacco." *Corriere del Giorno* (Taranto), December 23, 1971.

Finizio, Luigi Paolo. "Mirella Bentivoglio." *Il Pensiero Nazionale* (Rome) 26, no. 2, January 16, 1972, p. 30.

Zanchi, Pino. "Bentivoglio alla Schwarz." *L'Ottagono* (Milan), January 5, 1972, p. 5.

Carrega, Ugo. "Cronistoria della poesia grafica in Italia." *Il Bimestre* (Florence) 4, nos. 1–2 (January–April 1972), insert, pp. VII–XVII.

Perfetti, Michele. "Archivio Denza di poesia visiva." *Corriere del Giorno* (Taranto), February 18, 1972.

Martin, Henry. "Milan–December." *Art International* (Lugano) 26, no. 2, February 20, 1972, pp. 41–42, 61–62.

Brizio, Giorgio. "Mirella Bentivoglio o della poesia visiva." *Graphicus* (Turin) 53, no. 5 (May 1972), p. 31.

Brizio, Giorgio. "Problemi del linguaggio. Poesia visiva e arte concettuale: labili confini." *Graphicus* (Turin) 53, no. 9 (September 1972), pp. 25–26.

Barilli, Renato. "Il libro come luogo di ricerca." *Le Arti* (Milan) 23, no. 11 (November 1972), pp. 72–74.

Brizio, Giorgio. "Parallelismo di linguaggi nelle odierne comunicazioni visive." *Quinta Parete* (Turin) 3, no. 5 (Winter 1972–73), pp. 48–51.

Barilli, Renato. "Le due anime del concettuale." *Op. Cit.* (Naples) 10, no. 26 (January 1973), pp. 63–88.

Perfetti, Michele. "Poesia visiva internazionale al centro Tool di Milano: Una mostra di operatrici." *Prospetti* (Rome) 8, no. 29 (March 1973), p. 78.

Venturoli, Marcello. "La poesia visiva di Mirella Bentivoglio." *Il Globo* (Rome), June 17, 1973.

Hart, John. "Bentivoglio's Mischievous Mix of Words and Visuals." *Daily American* (Rome), June 21, 1973.

Trucchi, Lorenza. "Bentivoglio al Pictogramma." *Momento Sera* (Rome), June 22–23, 1973.

Niccolai, Giulia. "Mirella Bentivoglio—And." *Tam Tam* (Mulino di Bazzano [Parma]) 2, no. 5 (Fourth Quarter, 1973), p. 60.

Halbey, Hans A. "Sommer-Ausstellungen des Klingspor Museum." *Offenbach-Post* (Offenbach), May 6, 1974.

Hoffmann, Dieter. "Geist-Zeichen in Schrift-Zeichen." *Frankfurter Neue Presse* (Frankfurt), May 6, 1974.

Perfetti, Michele. "Poesia visiva internazionale alla Galleria Il Canale di Venezia." *Prospetti* (Rome) 9, nos. 35–36 (September–December 1974), pp. 81–82.

Varga, Miklos N. "Bentivoglio: la 'ri-crea-zione' delle cose." *Gala International* (Milan) 12, no. 70 (February 1975), p. 97.

Niccolai, Giulia. "Mirella Bentivoglio: Punto ambig-uo." *Tam Tam* (Mulino di Bazzano [Parma]) 4, nos. 10–12 (October 1975), pp. 146–47.

Oberto, Anna. "Poesia al femminile." *Le Arti* (Milan) 26, nos. 10–12 (October–December 1975), pp. 43–44.

Miccini, Eugenio. "La poesia visiva." Monographic issue of *Iterarte* (Bologna) 2, no. 6 (November 1975), p. 19.

Orienti, Sandra. "Italiani in Giappone." *Il Popolo* (Rome), January 15, 1976.

Dorfles, Gillo. "Le lettere dell'alfabeto." *Corriere della Sera* (Milan), April 12, 1976.

Conti, Viana. "Mirella Bentivoglio." *Corriere Mercantile* (Genoa), July 2, 1976.

Pacini, Piero. "Apollinaire e la Bentivoglio visualizza-no la pioggia." *Il Cristallo* (Bolzano) 28, no. 2 (August 1976), pp. 122–28.

Brizio, Giorgio "Poesia visiva a Tokyo." *Graphicus* (Turin) 57, nos. 11–12 (November–December 1976), p. 14.

Dorfles, Gillo. "Poesia e non poesia dopo i Novissimi." *Quinta Generazione* (Forli) 5, nos. 31–32 (January–February 1977), pp. 14–18.

Bissert, Ellen Marie. "International Exibition of Visual Writing." *13th Moon* (New York) 3, no. 2 (1977), p. 68.

Vergine, Lea. "Artista fa rima con femminista." *Il Manifesto* (Rome), March 8, 1977.

Rasy, Elisabetta. "Quando l'arte è vissuta al femmi-nile." *Paese Sera* (Rome), April 25, 1977.

Paloscia, Tommaso. "Il volume-oggetto." *La Nazione* (Florence), January 12, 1978.

Bissert, Ellen Marie. "Mirella Bentivoglio—all'adultera lapidata: A Symbolic Structure." *13th Moon* (New York) 4, no. 1 (1978), p. 34.

Berenice, "Bentivoglio visuale e fonetica." *Paese Sera* (Milan), February 10, 1978.

Barilli, Renato. "Un libro fatto a mano." *L'Espresso* (Roma) 24, no. 8, February 26, 1978, pp. 78–81.

Gardin, Pietro Berengo. "Mirella Bentivoglio." *Il Messaggero* (Rome), March 22, 1978.

Eletti, Valerio. "L'arte di fare l'uovo." *La Repubblica* (Rome), March 24, 1978.

Zoccoli, Franca. "La favola dell'albero morto." *Il Resto del Carlino* (Bologna), March 24, 1978.

Hart, John. "Poetic Leaves Grew on Tree in Gubbio '76." *Daily American* (Rome), March 28, 1978.

Boccacci, Paolo. "Albero umbro da esposizione." *Paese Sera* (Rome), March 29, 1978.

Dorfles, Gillo. "La poesia visiva e lotta poetica." *Il Cristallo* (Bolzano) 20, no. 1 (April 1978), pp. 92–95.

D'Amore, Bruno. "Bentivoglio lapidaria." *Gala International* (Milan) 20, no. 87 (May 1978), p. 76.

Cherchi, Luciano. "Carte nuove. *Jet-P68* di Mirella Bentivoglio." *Arte-Stampa Liguria* (Genoa) 28, nos. 5–6 (May–June 1978), p. 5.

Venturoli, Marcello. "Artiste a Venezia." *Questarte* (Pescara) 2, no. 11 (November 1978), p. 8.

Hart, John. "Women Have Last and First Word Too." *Daily American* (Rome), October 4, 1978.

Pouchard, Ennio. "La materializzazione del linguaggio." *La Voce Repubblicana* (Rome), October 10, 1978.

Varga, Miklos N. "Critica e autocritica: Bentivoglio, Fagone, Sanesi." *Gala International* (Milan) 15, no. 90 (December 1978), pp. 20–24.

Hart, John. "Eggs, Women and Mirella Bentivoglio." *Daily American* (Rome), March 11, 1979.

Brizio, Giorgio. "La Biennale 1978." *Graphicus* (Turin) 60, no. 3 (March 1979), p. 43.

Niccolai, Giulia. "Feminism and Italian Avant-garde Art." *Invisibile City* (San Francisco), nos. 23–25 (March 1979), pp. 14-15

Obenhaus, M. "Jenseits der Dichtung." *Münsterische Zeitung* (Münster), May 4, 1979.

Jh., Bp. "Sprachen jenseits von Dichtung." *Westfälische Nachrichten* (Münster), May 11, 1979.

Vincitorio, Francesco. "Dice Bentivoglio," *L'Espresso* (Rome), 25, no. 42 (October 21, 1979).

Accame, Vincenzo. "L'arte delle donne non è femminista." *Il Secolo XIX* (Genoa), November 22, 1979.

Hart, John. "Textilia Pages." *Daily American* (Rome), November 27, 1979.

Crispolti, Enrico. "Mirella Bentivoglio: Gubbio: l'uovo di sassi." *Iterarte* (Bologna) 6, no. 18 (December 1979–January 1980), pp. 60–61.

Paparoni, Demetrio. "Artiste italiane a New York." *Il Diario di Siracusa* (Siracusa), January 27, 1980.

De Flora, Alberta. "La donna nell'arte." *Gala International* (Milan) 17, no. 95 (March 1980), pp. 32–34.

Binder-Hagelstange, Ursula. "Das Ei auf dem Marmor-Folianten." *Frankfurter Allgemeine Zeitung* (Frankfurt), July 8, 1980.

Spatz, Christa. "Wider die Zerstörung des Buchs." *Frankfurter Rundschau* (Frankfurt), July 16, 1980.

Venturoli, Marcello. "Anche la donna protagonista alla biennale dell'arte." *Messaggero del Lunedì* (Udine), June 23, 1980.

Brizio, Giorgio Sebastiano. "Poesia tutta e sempre poesia." *Graphicus* (Turin) 61, no. 743 (June 1980), p. 28.

Kleiß, Mariette. "Schrift als Lebenselixier." *Börsenblatt* (Frankfurt), 36, no. 67 (August 12, 1980), pp. 1927-28.

Rosenberg, Judy. "A Feminist Sculpture for an Italian Town." *Women Artists News* (New York) 10, nos. 2-3 (Summer 1980), p. 8.

Rosenberg, Judy. "Visual Poetry: The Avant-garde in Italy." *Women Artists News* (New York) 10, nos. 2–3 (Summer 1980), p. 8.

Restany, Pierre. "Il tempo del Museo Venezia." *Domus* (Milan) 54, no. 614 (February 1981), p. 33.

Di Gioia, Bartolomeo. "Mirella Bentivoglio: Oxford, Friburgo, Parigi, Cagliari, San Paolo, Rieti, Venezia." *Iterarte* (Bologna) 7, no. 20 (May 1981), pp. 68–69.

Niccolai, Giulia. "Italian Poetry 1960–1980: From Neo to Post Avant-garde." *Invisible City* (San Francisco), no. 28 (December 1981), p. 15.

Vescovo, Marisa "1er Manifeste du livre d'artiste." *Art Press* (Paris), no. 54 (December 1981), pp. 26–27.

Accame, Vincenzo. "De la poésie visuelle a la 'Nouvelle Ecriture.'" *Cimaise, Art et Architécture Actuelles* (Paris), nos. 156–157 (February–April 1982), pp. 49–54.

Sales, Enric. "Mirella Bentivoglio o la poesia feta pedra." *El Mon* (Barcelona), March 26, 1982.

Restany, Pierre. "16° San Paolo." *D'Ars* (Milan) 23, no. 98 (April 1982), pp. 72–73.

Dell'Acqua, Salvatore "Strutture simboliche di una femminista." *Art Magazine* (Milan) 1, May 1982, pp. 62–63.

Morse, Gareth. "Watch this Cultural Space." *The Australian* (Perth), October 29, 1982.

Mason, Murray. "A Stylish Exhibition to Tease and Intrigue." *The Western Australian* (Perth), October 30, 1982.

Snell, Ted. "Books as Things of Great Beauty." *The Western Australian* (Perth), October 30, 1982.

Zoccoli, Franca. "Mirella Bentivoglio: Arte Duchamp." *Flash Art* (Milan), 16, no. 110 (November 1982), p. 69.

Crispolti, Enrico. "Mirella Bentivoglio." *D'Ars* (Milan) 23, no. 100 (December 1982), pp. 148–51.

Panfili, Stefania. "E la pietra 'racconta' la storia di Gubbio." *L'Unità* (Rome), February 10, 1983.

Blanch, M. Teresa. "Los viajes de los artistas." *El Pais* (Barcelona), March 19, 1983.

Dragone, Angelo. "Il simbolo nell'uovo di Mirella." *La Stampa* (Turin), April 13, 1983.

Mastrolonardo, Enotrio. "Libri di pietra." *Arte Rama* (Milan) 15, nos. 5–6 (May–June 1983), p. 8.

Zoccoli, Franca. "Pietra filosofale di Mirella Bentivoglio." *Terzo Occhio* (Bologna) 9, no. 3 (28) (September 1983), p. 66.

Snell, Ted. "It's time to think of the Festival." *The Western Mail Newspaper* (Perth), January 1, 1984.

Conti, Viana. "Le uova di pietra di Mirella Bentivoglio." *Il Buongiorno* (Genoa) 6, no. 8 (February 25, 1984), pp. 64-65.

Barbero, Giovanna. "La poesia fatta pietra di Mirella Bentivoglio." *Bergamo Oggi* (Bergamo), March 5, 1984.

Serafini, Giuliano. "Mirella Bentivoglio: La poesia fatta pietra." *Terzo Occhio* (Bologna) 10, no. 2 (31) (June 1984), p. 91.

Rescio, Stelio. "La poesia oggettuale di Mirella Bentivoglio." *Spirali* (Milan) 7, no. 65 (July–August 1984), p. 37.

Di Stefano, Eva. "Pagine trabocchetto." *Giornale di Sicilia* (Palermo), January 24, 1985.

Paterna, Claudio. "Bibliofollia." *L'Ora* (Palermo), January 24, 1985.

Rebulla, Eduardo. "Pagine buie." *L'Ora* (Palermo), January 26, 1985.

Quatriglio, Giuseppe. "E dal libro di preghiere spunta la pistola." *Il Messaggero* (Rome), January 27, 1985.

Zoccoli, Franca. "Alla Biblioteca Centrale di Palermo 'Il non libro' mostra sul volume oggetto." *Il Cristallo* (Bolzano) 27, no. 1 (April 1985), pp. 93–94.

Di Stefano, Eva. "Palermo—Il non libro—bibliofollia ieri ed oggi in Italia." *Terzo Occhio* (Bologna) 11, no. 2 (35) (June 1985), p. 57.

Borrini, Sergio. "Le scelte della grafica: incontro con Mirella Bentivoglio." *Arte & Cornice* (Milan), 3, no. 2 (June 1986), pp. 40–44.

Vincitorio, Francesco. "Scrivere con le immagini." *La Stampa* (Turin), August 29, 1987.

"Difference in Italy." *Women Artists News* (New York) 12, no. 4 (Autumn–Winter 1987), p. 62.

Frazzetto, Giuseppe. "Mirella Bentivoglio." *La Sicilia* (Catania), November 13, 1987.

Ugliano, Anna. "Torre del Lebbroso: Mirella Bentivoglio." *Quaderni d'Arte della Valle d'Aosta* (Aosta) 1, no. 4 (November 1987).

Lagnier, Emanuela "Alchimia: tra medioevo e nostro tempo." *Corriere della Valle d'Aosta* (Aosta), December 10, 1987.

"L'Hyper Ovum di Mirella Bentivoglio." *Arte & Cornice* (Milan) 4, no. 4 (December 1987), p. 22.

Sermonti, Giuseppe. "In un ciottolo l'immaginario collettivo." *Il Tempo* (Rome), January 6, 1988.

Sermonti, Giuseppe "Davanti alla silenziosa suggestione dell'uovo primordiale." *Messaggero Veneto* (Udine), January 7, 1988.

Bossaglia, Rossana. "Se l'uovo contiene solo un uovo." *Corriere della Sera* (Milan), January 17, 1988.

Re Fiorentin, Maria Luisa. "Vive nella torre l'iperuovo della Bentivoglio." *Arte* (Milan) 18, no. 181 (January 1988), p. 20.

Bortolon, Liana. "Con il filo di Arianna le nuove trame dell'arte." *Grazia* (Milan) 61, no. 2492 (November 27, 1988), pp. 37–38.

Fedi, Fernanda. "Intervista a Mirella Bentivoglio." *Panorama Lombardia* (Milan) 4, no. 53 (November 1988), pp. 8–9.

Rescio, Stelio. "Festa grande a Gubbio." *Arte & Cornice* (Milan) 5, no. 4 (December 1988), p. 26.

Pohl, Frances K. "Feminist Forum." *Women's Studies International Forum* (Oxford) 12, no. 1 (1989), pp. I–II.

Conti, Carlo M. "La sillaba sonora." *Zeta* (Pasian di Prato [Udine]) 9, nos. 11–13 (February 1989), pp. 46–47, 196.

Rescio, Stelio. "Londra: Mirella Bentivoglio." *Terzo Occhio* (Bologna) 15, no. 1 (50) (March 1989), p. 63.

Rescio, Stelio. "Mirella Bentivoglio: Histoire d'E." *Flash Art News* (Milan) 3, no. 151 (Summer 1989), p. 13.

Vincitorio, Francesco. "Poesia visiva." *La Stampa* (Turin), January 13, 1990.

Cremolini, Valerio P. "Mirella Bentivoglio ha una 'Fotoidea.'" *Il Secolo XIX* (Genoa), April 15, 1990.

Mistrangelo, Angelo. "Come orchestrare un'idea con la macchina fotografica, esperimenti di Bentivoglio." *Stampa Sera* (Turin), May 22, 1990.

Salvagni, Giulia "Ma la storia è donna? Intervista a Mirella Bentivoglio." *Avvenimenti* (Rome) 3, no. 28 (June 18, 1990), pp. 58–59.

Rescio, Stelio. "Cagliari: Il Librismo." *Terzo Occhio* (Bologna) 16, no. 3 (56) (September 1990), p. 53.

O' Brien, John. "Los Angeles: Visual Poetry." *Contemporanea* (Los Angeles), no. 22 (November 1990), pp. 93–94.

Forbice, Aldo. "Ma perché non emergono pittrici e scultrici? Colloquio con Mirella Bentivoglio." *Lavorosocietà* (Rome) 4, no. 1 (January 1991), pp. 86–92.

Crescentini, Manuela. "Cos'è il Librismo? Incontro con Mirella Bentivoglio." *La Gazzetta delle Arti* (Venice-Mestre) 23, nos. 1–2 (January–February 1991), p. 24.

Lieser, Stefan. "Der Mensch als Frühstücksei." *Nordwest Zeitung* (Edewecht), April 29, 1991.

Serafini, Giuliano. "Mirella Bentivoglio." *Segno* (Pescara) 15, no. 104 (May 1991), p. 47.

Vitiello, Maurizio. "Mirella Bentivoglio e Gubbio." *Politica Meridionalista* (Naples) 19, no. 12 (December 1991), p. 18.

"Il librismo." *Zeta News* (Pasian di Prato [Udine]) 13, nos. 17–18 (January 1992), p. 22.

Pouchard, Ennio. "Mirella Bentivoglio: La sintesi di una ricerca 'Erga Ovum.'" *Il Cristallo* (Bolzano) 34, no. 1 (April 1992), pp. 101–4.

Di Genova, Arianna. "In mostra al MoMA libri-oggetto italiani." *Il Manifesto* (Rome), November 1, 1992.

Zoccoli, Franca. "Questi volumi non si leggono. Sono solo da guardare." *Il Resto del Carlino* (Bologna), November 6, 1992.

Mingozzi, Paola. "Mirella Bentivoglio: Un albero di pagine." *Leggere Donna* (Ferrara) 13, no. 42 (January–February 1993), p. 18.

Gismondi, Federico. "Parola di critico stuzzicato da artista, intervista a Mirella Bentivoglio." *Qnst* (Venice) 1, no. 2 (January–April 1993), p. 3.

Rescio, Stelio. "Un albero di pagine." *Terzo Occhio* (Bologna) 19, no. 1 (66) (March 1993), p. 50.

Trucchi, Lorenza. "Ecco l'arte all'età della pietra." *Il Giornale* (Milan), April 4, 1993.

Baradel, Virginia. "L'albero di pagine allevato dalla gente." *La Nuova Venezia* (Venice), April 16, 1993.

Lezziero, Paolo. "L'albero di pagine della Bentivoglio." *Nuova Sesto* (Sesto San Giovanni [Milan]), May 1, 1993.

Saviantoni, Vinicio. "Silenziari e il perspex." *Paese Sera* (Rome), May 22, 1993.

Lev., Pa. "Mirella Bentivoglio e Paola Levi Montalcini." *La Repubblica* (Turin), May 30, 1993.

Sermonti, Giuseppe. "Le radici dell'eterno albero." *Il Giornale* (Milan), June 20, 1993.

Torrente, Maria. "Mirella Bentivoglio." *Terzo Occhio* (Bologna) 19, no. 3 (68) (September 1993), p. 65.

Bossaglia, Rossana, and Gillo Dorfles. "Un albero a San Leonardo." *Nexus* (Venice) 1, no. 3 (September–October 1993), p. 5.

Phillpot, Clive. "Twentysix Gasoline Stations that Shook the World: The Rise and Fall of Cheap Booklets as Art." *Art Libraries Journal* (London) 3, no. 1, 1993, p. 13.

Evangelisti, Silvia. "Sotto l'albero dell'avanguardia. Le opere di Mirella Bentivoglio esposte a Bologna." *Il Resto del Carlino* (Bologna), January 5, 1994.

De Marco, Gabriella. "Una madre d'arte." *L'Unità* (Rome), August 29, 1994.

De Candia, Mario. "Lo strano albero della Bentivoglio." *Trovaroma* (Rome), February 23, 1995.

Padovan, Mario. "Mirella Bentivoglio: Galleria Eralov." *Momento Sera* (Rome), February 28, 1995.

Gigliotti, Guglielmo. "Mirella Bentivoglio." *Terzo Occhio* (Bologna) 21, no. 2 (75) (June 1995), p. 62.

Brizio, Giorgio Sebastiano. "Libri d'artista nell'ambito della Biennale del centenario." *Graphicus* (Turin) 76, no. 10 (923) (December 1995), p. 46.

Bentivoglio, Mirella. "Das Buch-object." *Bücher-Markt Hannover*, no. 4 (April 1996), pp. 32–33.

Di Genova, Arianna. "Il paese degli artisti 'sonori.'" *Il Manifesto* (Rome), April 12, 1996.

Rescio, Stelio. "Buchobjekte aus Italien." *Terzo Occhio* (Bologna) 22, no. 2 (79) (June 1996), p. 69.

Pouchard, Ennio. "Ascoltare l'immagine." *Flash Art* (Milan) 29, no. 199 (Summer 1996), p. 34.

De Candia, Mario. "E il linguaggio poetico si materializza." *Trovaroma* (Rome), October 10, 1996.

Malara, Giuseppe. "Bentivoglio, 'Dalla parola al simbolo.'" *Il Tempo* (Rome), October 10, 1996.

Ferroni, Gianfranco. "Bentivoglio, o 'della comunicazione.'" *Corriere Laziale del Martedì* (Rome), October 15, 1996.

De Candia, Mario. "Mirella Bentivoglio." *Trovaroma* (Rome), October 17, 1996.

Di Genova, Arianna. "Il mondo degli archetipi: Tra parole che odorano di miele e misteriose uova." *Il Manifesto* (Rome), October 25, 1996.

Padovan, Mario. "Dalla parola al simbolo." *Momento Sera* (Rome), October 27, 1996.

Raponi, Mauro. "Mirella Bentivoglio." *Terzo Occhio* (Bologna) 22, no. 4 (81) (December 1996), p. 37.

Gaché, Sherry. "Mirella Bentivoglio." *Sculpture* (Washington) 16, no. 2 (February 1997), p. 68.

Rescio, Stelio. "Da Pagina a spazio: Futuriste italiane tra linguaggio e immagine." *Terzo Occhio* (Bologna) 23, no. 4 (85) (December 1997), p. 71.

Simongini, Gabriele. "'Il riscatto della lattina,' l'alluminio riciclato va in mostra." *Il Tempo* (Rome), January 16, 1998.

Talpo, Bruno. "Il riscatto della lattina: Recycling Art." *Terzo Occhio* (Bologna) 24, no. 1 (85) (March 1998), p. 53.

Di Genova, Arianna. "'Post Scriptum,' quando la poesia si fa tattile." *Il Manifesto* (Rome), June 2, 1998.

Crocella, Nicoletta. "Il Libro-campo, un capolavoro di Mirella Bentivoglio." *Corriere di Viterbo* (Viterbo), August 14, 1998.

Kivirinta, Marja-Tertuu. "Naisfuturistien asianajaja." *Helsingin Sanomat* (Helsinki), September 19, 1998.

Rescio, Stelio. "Post scriptum." *Terzo Occhio* (Bologna) 24, n. 4 (89) (December 1998), p. 68.

Di Genova, Arianna. "Se il museo è donna." *Amica* (Milan), 38, no. 13 (March 26, 1999), p. 12.

Zoccoli, Franca. "Dalla parola all'oggetto trovato." *Terzo Occhio* (Bologna), 25, no. 1 (90) (March 1999), p. 50.

Talpo, Bruno. "Mirella Bentivoglio al 'The National Museum of Women in the Arts Washington.'" *Il Cristallo* (Bolzano) 41, no. 1 (April 1999), pp. 126–27.

Wasserman, Krystyna. "An Interview with 'Visual Poetry' Mirella Bentivoglio." *Signature* (Washington) 19, no. 6 (April 1999).

Lewis, Nicole. "Italian Artist Mirella Bentivoglio." *The Washington Post* (Washington, D.C.), May 23, 1999.

Battilana, Marilla. "Mirella Bentivoglio artista internazionale." *La Nuova Tribuna Letteraria* (Montemerlo [Padua]) 10, no. 57 (First Quarter 2000), p. 55.

Di Genova, Arianna. "Alchimie fra polaroid." *Il Manifesto* (Rome), November 2000.

Gerosa, Ida. "Mirella Bentivoglio: Fotoalchimie." *MC–Microcomputer*, November 2000, pp. 74–77.

Conte, Gisella. "Roma: Mirella Bentivoglio Transitorio/Durevole." *Terzo Occhio* (Bologna) 26, no. 4 (97) (December 2000), p. 64.

Zoccoli, Franca. "Washington: The National Museum of Women in the Arts." *Terzo Occhio* (Bologna) 26, no. 4 (97) (December 2000), pp. 13–17.

Rescio, Stelio. "Materiale futurista a sorpresa." *Il Manifesto* (Rome), April 21, 2001.

Talpo, Bruno. "(S)cripturae: le scritture segrete tra linguaggio e immagine. Galleria Civica di Padova." *Il Cristallo* (Bolzano) 43, no. 2 (August 2001), pp. 116–21.

Stringa, Nico. "Padova. (S)cripturae. Le scritture segrete: Artiste tra linguaggio e immagine." *Terzo Occhio* (Bologna) 27, no. 3 (100) (September 2001), p. 68.

Zoccoli, Franca. "La materia, il libro e l'ombra." *Il Manifesto* (Rome), May 8, 2002.

Dorfles, Gillo. "Histoire d'E." *Territori* (Frosinone) 8, no. 1 (13) (March 2003), pp. 9–11.

Bordini, Valter. "Ara Pacis, lettera aperta di docenti di architettura." *La Stampa* (Rome), April 1, 2003.

Montanucci, Daniela. "The Ben Ben Show: Ben Shahn e Mirella Bentivoglio." *Terzo Occhio* (Bologna) 29, no. 4 (109) (December 2003), p. 48.

Shaw-Eagle, Joanna. "Pages of tragedy. Female artists use books as art." *The Washington Times* (Washington, D.C.), April 17, 2004.

Tischler, Gary. "Reading Between the Lines." *The Washington Diplomat* (Washington, D.C.) 10, no. 8 (August 2004), p. 14.

Liveri, Laura Turco. "Roma, ben ti voglio…." *Terzo Occhio* (Bologna) 31, no. 1 (114) (March 2005), pp. 38–39.

Talpo, Bruno. "Il Non Gruppo: Testi-immagine a Roma negli anni Sessanta a cura di Mirella Bentivoglio." *Rivista di Equipèco* (San Cesareo [Rome]) 2, no. 4 (Summer 2005), pp. 53–56.

Abate, Rosaria. "Facce Murate." *Terzo Occhio* (Bologna) 31, no. 3 (116) (September 2005), pp. 38–39.

Abate, Rosaria. "I libri di latta per il mondo." *Resine* (Savona) 27, nos. 106–107 (Fourth Quarter 2005–First Quarter 2006), pp. 74–78.

Zoccoli, Franca. "Installazione e mostra di Mirella Bentivoglio a Praga." *Rivista di Equipèco* (San Cesareo [Rome]) 3, no. 7 (Spring 2006), p. 50.

Venuti, Silvia. "Mirella Bentivoglio: La realtà dentro la parola." *D'Ars* (Milan) 47, no. 195 (September 2008), pp. 56–59.

Mori, Gioia. "Tutte le donne di Marinetti." *Corriere della Sera* (Milan), January 4, 2009.

Mendia, Fabiana. "Artiste vere, non solo mogli." *Il Messaggero* (Rome), January 20, 2009.

Encolpio, Natalia. "Velocità più donna uguale Futurismo. Alla riscoperta delle artiste del movimento." *Il Resto del Carlino* (Bologna), *La Nazione* (Florence), *Il Giorno* (Milan), January 22, 2009.

Mendia, Fabiana. "Appuntamento alla GNAM con le donne futuriste." *Il Messaggero* (Rome), January 29, 2009.

Duranti, Massimo. "Mirella Bentivoglio, Franca Zoccoli: Le futuriste italiane nelle arti visive (Rome: De Luca, 2008)," *Contemporart—arte e cultura* (Modena) 19, no. 58 (March 2009), p. 52.

Tornatore-Long, Maria Connie. "Poesia Visiva: Italian Concrete & Visual Poetry of the 1960s & 1970s." *News* (Sydney), no. 18 (June 2009).

Mattarella, Lea. "Quelle artiste da collezione." *La Repubblica* (Rome), January 12, 2012.

Brunetti, Carmelita. "La donazione Bentivoglio al MART di Rovereto." *Arte Contemporanea* (Grottaferrata [Rome]) 7, no. 30 (January–February 2012), pp. 46–47.

Gazzotti, Melania. "La donazione Bentivoglio." *Contemporart* (Modena), no. 69 (January–February 2012).

Pouchard, Ennio. "La parola si fece immagine e fu donna." *Colophon* (Belluno) 14, no. 36 (June 2012), pp. 24–31.

Bentivoglio, Mirella. "Poesia concreta: Parole lunari d'artista." *Il Manifesto* (Rome), March 21, 2013.

Bucci, Carlo Alberto. "L'arte di Mirella Bentivoglio: Ode alla luna in forma di libro." *La Repubblica* (Rome), March 21, 2013.

EXHIBITION CHECKLIST

Ab ovo, ab Eva, Ave Eva, ea, 1979–86
Four serigraph prints on paper
13⅝ × 9⅝ in. (34.61 × 24.45 cm) each
FIGURE 3 ———————————— p2003.12.5

A las cinco de la tarde (Ladies Afternoon Tea) (At Five in the Afternoon [Ladies Afternoon Tea]), 1973
Ink on stitched cloth
6½ × 6½ in. (16.51 × 16.51 cm)
FIGURE 2 ———————————— p2013.3.25a–c

All'adultera lapidata—L'ovo di Gubbio (To the Stoned Adulteress—The Egg of Gubbio), 1995
Three photomechanical prints on paper
14¾ × 16⅛ in. (50.17 × 69.53 cm) each
FIGURE 11 ———————————— p2013.3.17a–c

Amputazione (Amputation), 1971
Serigraph on paper
5⅝ × 5⅝ in. (14.29 × 14.29 cm)
PLATE 8 ———————————— p2012.15.7

An Anthology of Essays on Swift's Gulliver, 1995
Mixed media
13⅝ × 13⅛ × 2⅛ in. (34.61 × 33.34 × 5.4 cm)
PLATE 16 ———————————— p2013.3.44

Analisi semiotica—la fattura per non pensare (la raggiera della donna é la sua condanna) (Semiotic Analysis—The Spell for Not Thinking [The Halo of the Woman Is Her Condemnation]), 1978
Offset lithograph on paper
13¹⁵⁄₁₆ × 16⁹⁄₁₆ in. (35.4 × 42.07 cm)
FIGURE 45 ———————————— p2013.3.10

Analisi semiotica—la fattura per non pensare (la raggiera della donna é la sua condanna) (Semiotic Analysis—The Spell for Not Thinking [The Halo of the Woman Is Her Condemnation]), 1978
Postcard
5⅞ × 4⅛ in. (14.92 × 10.48 cm)
———————————— p2011.1.19

Anatomia del braccio sinistro della Statua della Libertà (Anatomy of the Left Arm of the Statue of Liberty), 1992
Photomechanical print on paper
8½ × 17 in. (21.59 × 43.18 cm)
FIGURE 10 ———————————— p2013.3.22

Correzione (Correction), 1985
Photomechanical print on paper
17 × 16 in. (43.18 × 40.64 cm)
PLATE 10 ———————————— p2011.1.37

Da 'H' a 'E', da lettora muta a parola-congiunzione (From H to E, from Silent Letter to Word Conjunction), 1979
Four photomechanical prints on paper
7 × 9⅜ in. (17.78 × 23.81 cm) each
FIGURE 15 ———————————— p2013.3.41a–d

Da punto a nota (diminuendo musicale) (From Point to Note [Musical Diminuendo]), 1971
Lithograph on paper
12⅝ in. × 9 in. (32.07 cm × 22.86 cm)
PLATE 20 ———————————— p2011.1.26

Davide e Golia (David and Goliath), 1989
Collage
10¾ × 7¾ in. (27.31 × 19.69 cm)
PLATE 4 ———————————— p2013.3.26

E = congiunzione (And = Conjunction), 1973
Serigraph on paper
16½ × 18⅛ in. (20.96 × 29.85 cm)
FIGURE 20 ———————————— p2011.1.36

Eclissi alchemica (Alchemic Eclipse), 1995
Photomechanical print on paper
14⅞ × 10¼ in. (37.78 × 26.04 cm)
FIGURE 19 ———————————— p2013.3.31

Egemonia op (Hegemony Op), with Francesco Balladore, 1977
Two panels of photomechanical prints
26 × 36 in. (66.04 × 91.44 cm) each
FIGURE 9 ———————————— p2013.3.35a–h

Facce Murate (Walled Faces), with Alessandro Alimonti, 2005
Six photographs of public installation in Prague, Czech Republic
11⅛ × 7⅜ in. (28.26 × 18.73 cm) each
PLATE 23 ———————————— p2013.3.39a–f

Facce Murate (Walled Faces), with Alessandro Alimonti, 2005
Mural-sized photographic documentation of detail of public installation in Prague, Czech Republic
Digital print
PLATE 23 ————————————

Flowers in the Tangle (Poetry), 1987
Serigraph on paper with Letraset
10¾ × 7¹³⁄₁₆ in. (27.31 × 19.84 cm)
PLATE 30 ———————————— p2012.15.2

Gabbia (Ho) (Cage [I Have]), 1966/1969
Serigraph on paper
13 × 9 in. (33.02 × 22.86 cm)
PLATE 7 ———————————— p2003.12.8

Genesi della W (Viva l'amore! Abbasso l'amore!) (Origin of the Letter W [Hurrah Love! Down with Love!]), 1995
Photomechanical print on paper
24¼ × 17¹⁄₁₆ in. (61.6 × 43.34 cm)
PLATE 34 ———————————— p2013.3.18

Histoire d'O (Story of O), 1985
Ink on stone
3¼ × 3⅝ × 1¼ in. (8.26 × 9.21 × 3.18 cm)
PLATE 17 ———————— p2008.14.14

I frutti del nostro mare (The Fruits of Our Sea), 1986
Assemblage, photograph, and porcelain
11⅜ × 15⅛ × 1½ in. (28.89 × 38.42 × 3.81 cm)
PLATE 31 ———————— p2013.3.48a–b

Il cuore della consumatrice ubbidiente (The Heart of the Obedient Consumer), 1975
Serigraph on paper
27½ × 19⅝ in. (69.85 × 49.85 cm)
PLATE 24 ———————— p2003.12.10

Il volto e il nome: la maschera e i suoi lacci (The Face and the Name: The Mask and Its Strings), 1995
Mixed media on paper and board
17¾ × 13¼ in. (45.09 × 33.66 cm)
PLATE 3 ———————— p2011.1.35

I muri di Singapore (Walls of Singapore), 1978
Six photographs on wood panels
6⅝ × 4⅝ in. (16.8 × 11.7 cm) each
On loan from the artist
PLATE 11 ————————

Io (Me), 1979
Photomechanical print on paper
23⅝ × 15¾ in. (60.01 × 40.01 cm)
FIGURE 30 ———————— p2013.3.4

JeruSalem, 2012
Five photomechanical prints
10¾ × 7¹¹⁄₁₆ in. (27.31 × 19.53 cm) each
FIGURE 24 ———————— p2013.3.29a–e

L'altra Veronica (Ecce Mulier) (The Other Veronica [Behold the Woman]), 1992
Photomechanical print on canvas
13⅝ × 10⅜ in. (34.61 × 26.35 cm)
FIGURE 7 ———————— p2013.3.19

La macchina da scrivere di Dio (God's Typewriter), 1988
Photomechanical print on paper
15⅝ × 15⅝ in. (39.69 × 39.69 cm)
PLATE 18 ———————— p2013.3.7

La profezia (da Babele a Ground Zero) (The Prophecy [From Babel to Ground Zero]), 2001–2
Photomechanical print on paper
12¼ × 23¼ in. (31.12 × 59.06 cm)
PLATE 32 ———————— p2013.3.11

La realtà e il libro (Reality and the Book), 1986
Mica and Letraset
9 × 5½ × 3 in. (22.86 × 13.97 × 7.62 cm)
PLATE 12 ———————— p2008.14.1

L'(assente), positivo/negativo, segno/figura (The Absent One, Positive/Negative, Sign/Figure), 1971
Serigraph on paper
24⅝ × 19 in. (62.55 × 48.26 cm)
FIGURE 26 ———————— p2011.1.38

Leggere l'albero (Read the Tree), 1990
Xylography on paper
16½ × 24¾ in. (41.91 × 62.87 cm)
PLATE 14 ———————— p2013.3.45

Libro campo (Field Book), 1998
Photographic reproduction of land-poetry installation, Bassano in Teverina, Italy
Digital print
15¾ × 21⅝ in. (40 × 54.9 cm)
FIGURE 1 ———————— p2013.3.5

L'impronta di Aracne (Arachne's Imprint), 1978
Photomechanical print on paper
14⅛ × 10¼ in. (34.93 × 25.08 cm)
FIGURE 34 ———————— p2011.1.7

Lina e il cavaliere (Lina and the Knight), 1978/2012
Eight photomechanical prints on paper
15½ × 11⅝ in. (39.37 × 29.53 cm) each
FIGURE 23 ———————— p2013.3.23a–h

Litolattine (Tin Book), 1995
Tin, aluminum
5⅝ × 3⅞ × 2⅛ in. (14.29 × 9.84 × 5.4 cm)
PLATE 13 ———————— p2008.14.15

Moduli a E (E Combinations), 1977/2014
Obliquitá stabilizzate (Stabilized Obliquities)
Mutilazione per accentuazione (la porta dell'essere) (Mutilation for Accentuation [The Door of Being])
Predominio sull'altro (Predominance Over the Other)
Three works reconstructed in 2014 according to the specifications of the artist
Wood
Each individual "E" is 60 in. (152.40 cm) high
PLATE 6 and FIGURE 21 ————————

Monumento (Monument), with Annalisa Alloatti, 1968
Original large panels, 1966
Six pages of offset lithographs on paper
13⅝ × 9½ in. (34.61 × 24.13 cm) each
FIGURE 6 ———————— p2003.12.6

Monumento Memento (Memento Monument), 1978
Photograph of collage
9½ × 7 in. (24.13 × 17.78 cm)
FIGURE 5 ———————— p2011.1.20b

Moon/ument, 2011
Photomechanical print on paper
17¾ × 8½ in. (45.09 × 21.59 cm)
PLATE 19 ———————— p2013.3.20

Nascita seconda (Second Birth),
2009
Book (paper, stone)
11¾ × 11¾ × ¼ in. (29.85 × 29.85 × .64 cm)
FIGURE 13 ——————— p2013.3.40

*Operazione Orfeo (L'uovo nella
caverna) (Operation Orpheus [The
Egg in the Cavern])*, 1982–85
Six photomechanical prints on paper
10⅝ × 8⅛ in. (26.99 × 20.64 cm) each
FIGURE 32 ——————— p2013.3.27a–f

Pagina/finestra (Window/Page), 1971
Serigraph on plexiglass
14 × 7³⁄₁₆ × ¹⁄₁₆ in. (35.56 × 18.29 × .21 cm)
PLATE 5 ——————— p2003.12.2

Parola (Word), 1969
Serigraph on paper
10½ × 14⅝ in. (26.67 × 37.15 cm)
PLATE 33 ——————— p2011.1.12

Perdita di senso (Loss of Sense),
1997
Offset lithography on paper
19¾ × 27⅜ in. (50.17 × 69.53 cm)
PLATE 21 ——————— p2003.12.3

*Piante in pianta in pianta in pianta
(Plants in Plan in a Plant in Plan)*, 1979
Offset lithograph on paper
16⁷⁄₁₆ × 11⅝ in. (41.75 × 29.53 cm)
PLATE 35 ——————— p2013.3.13

Puzzle Poem, 1985
Collage and Letraset on cardboard
14⁵⁄₁₆ × 12 in. (36.35 × 30.48 cm)
PLATE 29 ——————— p2013.3.36

Quetzal, with Marta Knobloch, 2001
Artist's book with original collage
13 × 9½ in. (24.13 × 24.13 cm)
PLATE 26 ——————— p2011.1.13

*Rapporto come gabbia (Relationship
as Cage)*, 1977
Wood
Based on drawing by Leonardo da
Vinci from *Codex Atlanticus*, Folio 263,
1478–1519
27 × 27 × 27 in. (68.6 × 68.6 × 68.6 cm)

Riaprire (Open Up Again), 1989
Mixed media installation (wood,
photographs, Styrofoam)
13¾ × 19⅜ × 8½ in. (34.93 × 49.21 ×
21.59 cm)
FIGURE 8 ——————— p2013.3.1a–f

*Rima: oriente e occidente (Rhyme:
East and West)*, with Chima Sunada,
2003
Photograph on paper
17¾ × 24 in. (45.09 × 60.96 cm)
PLATE 28 ——————— p2011.1.34

Sembra (It Seems), 1971/2013
Video documentation of earlier kinetic
object created with Nino Calos
PLATE 27 ——————— p2013.3.50

Sinonimi (Synonyms), 1971
Etching on paper
13¼ × 9½ in. (33.66 × 24.13 cm)
PLATE 2 ——————— p2011.1.11

*Soggettivismo oggettivato
(Objectified Subjectivism)*, 1972
Lithograph on paper
9 × 10¾ in. (22.86 × 27.31 cm)
FIGURE 4 ——————— p2011.1.10

*Tavole della legge del consumo
(Tablets of the Law of Consumerism)*,
1992
Photomechanical print on paper
16⅜ × 19⅝ in. (41.59 × 49.85 cm)
PLATE 25 ——————— p2013.3.14

*Transitorio/durevole (Transitory/
Durable)*, with Regina Silveira, 2002
Installation, heavy plastic, wood
65 × 168 × 80 in. (165.1 × 426.72 ×
203.2 cm)
FIGURE 18 ——————— P2013.21.1

*Un albero di pagine (A Tree of
Pages)*, 1992
Book
12 × 12 in. (30.48 × 30.48 cm)
FIGURE 14 ——————— p2013.3.2

Un arco di tempo (An Arch of Time),
1980
Xerography collage on board
13⅞ × 9⅞ in. (35.24 × 25.08 cm)
PLATE 1 ——————— p2011.1.29

Vuoto al centro (Void in the Center),
1966
Serigraph on paper
16½ × 17¹⁄₁₆ in. (41.91 × 43.34 cm)
PLATE 9 ——————— p2013.3.16

Writ in Water, 2005
Accordion book
8 × 12 × ½ in. (20.32 × 30.48 × 1.27 cm)
closed; 141¼ in. (358.77 cm) in length
open
FIGURE 46 ——————— p2008.14.18a

Writ in Water, 2005
Photomechanical print on paper
17⅞ × 13 in. (45.40 × 33.02 cm)
FIGURE 46 ——————— p2008.14.18b

ACKNOWLEDGMENTS

Frances K. Pohl

This exhibition has been several years in the making and would have not come about without the talents and generosity of Mirella Bentivoglio. Her experience as a curator and author, as well as a visual poet, has informed our many conversations and was crucial in shaping the form and content of this exhibition. My student Benjamin Kersten, who accompanied me on a trip to Rome, not only provided much needed logistical assistance, but also helped me see Bentivoglio's work in new ways. I am also grateful to those who contributed essays and who were willing to be interviewed. Their multiple perspectives have helped enrich our understanding of Bentivoglio's complex work. The expert editing of Elizabeth Pulsinelli ensured that these perspectives were conveyed clearly and accurately, and Kimberly Varella has created a fine layout and design for this publication that is in keeping with Bentivoglio's aesthetic sensibilities. I would like to thank the staff of the Pomona College Museum of Art—senior curator Rebecca McGrew, associate director and registrar Steve Comba, and senior preparator Gary Murphy—whose hard work and organization resulted in such a finely crafted exhibition. Finally, I would like to thank Pomona College for financially supporting my research on Mirella Bentivoglio, and museum director Dr. Kathleen Howe for providing me the opportunity to share with a wider audience the work of an artist I have come to know so well and admire over the past three decades.

—

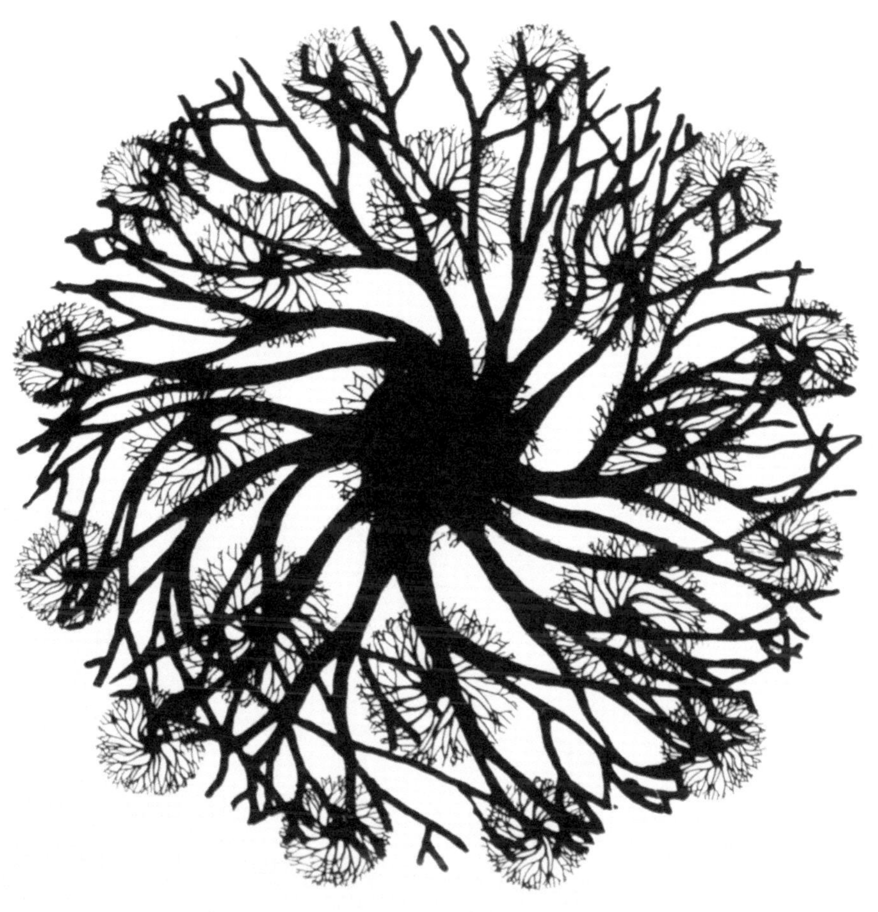

PLATE 35—
Piante in pianta in pianta in pianta (Plants in Plan in a Plant in Plan), 1979. Offset lithograph on paper,
16⁷⁄₁₆ × 11⅝ in. (41.75 × 29.53 cm).

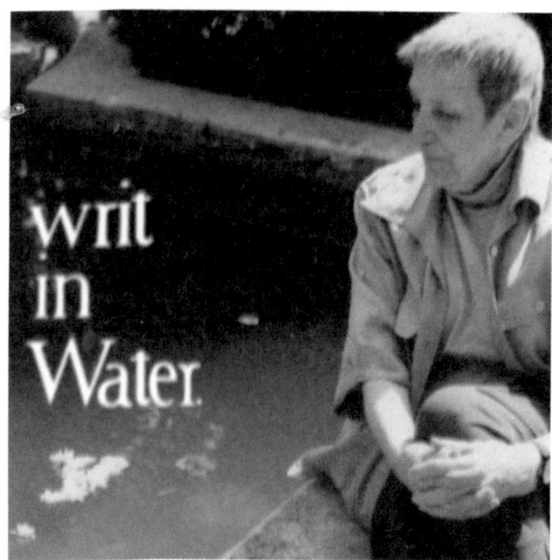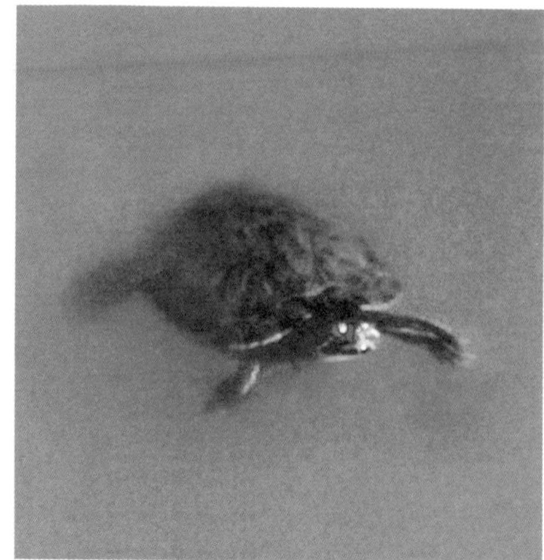

This catalog was published on the occasion of the exhibition "Pages: Mirella Bentivoglio, Selected Works 1966–2012," curated by Frances K. Pohl and presented at the Pomona College Museum of Art, January 20–May 17, 2015.

FIGURE 46——
(left) *Writ in Water*, 2005. Detail of accordion book, 8 × 12 × ½ in. (20.32 × 30.48 × 1.27 cm) closed; 141¼ in. (358.77 cm) in length open.

(right) *Writ in Water*, 2005. Detail of photo-mechanical print on paper, 17⅞ × 13 in. (45.40 × 33.02 cm).

Pomona College Museum of Art
333 North College Way
Claremont, CA 91711
www.pomona.edu/museum
Tel: 909-621-8283

© 2015 Trustees of Pomona College

ISBN: 978-0-9856251-6-0

Available through D.A.P./
Distributed Art Publishers, Inc.
155 Sixth Avenue
New York, NY 10013
www.artbook.com

Design: Kimberly Varella,
Content Object, Los Angeles
Photography:
Pietro Livi (1976), p. 33
Pietro Livi (1982), p. 97–100
Alessandro Alimonti (1985), p. 101
Copy Editing: Elizabeth Pulsinelli
Printing: The Avery Group at Shapco Printing